THE HELSINKI EFFECT

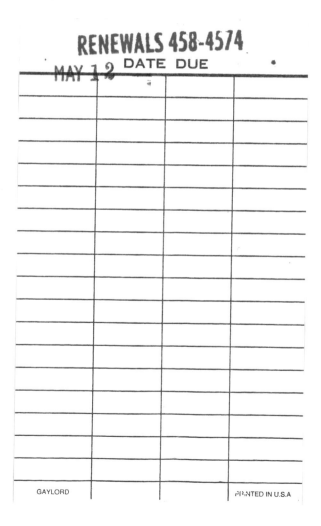

THE HELSINKI EFFECT

INTERNATIONAL NORMS, HUMAN RIGHTS, AND THE DEMISE OF COMMUNISM

Daniel C. Thomas

PRINCETON UNIVERSITY PRESS   PRINCETON AND OXFORD

Library of Congress Cataloging-in-Publication Data
Thomas, Daniel C. (Daniel Charles)
The Helsinki effect : international norms, human rights, and the
demise of communism / Daniel C. Thomas
p. cm.
Includes bibliographical references and index.
ISBN 0-691-04858-4—ISBN 0-691-04859-2
1. Human rights. 2. Europe, Eastern—Politics and government—
1945–1989. 3. Europe, Eastern—Politics and government—1989–
4. Soviet Union—Politics and government—1945–1991. I. Title.
JC571.T455 2001
323'.0947'09045—dc21   2001016375

This book has been composed in Janson

Printed on acid-free paper. ∞

www.pup.princeton.edu

Printed in the United States of America

1   3   5   7   9   10   8   6   4   2

1   3   5   7   9   10   8   6   4   2
(Pbk)

Contents

Conclusions
Appendix

_____ *Acknowledgments* _____

THIS BOOK emerged out of an interest in the relationship between social structures and collective action provoked by studying with Peter Katzenstein and Sidney Tarrow at Cornell University just as a political system (Communism) and an international confrontation (the Cold War), once thought immutable to change, began to crumble. Both scholars nourished my taste for difficult questions and encouraged me to look for answers across subdisciplinary borders. The tension between their approaches to political science lies at the heart of this book. Thomas Risse then urged me to turn an exploratory paper into a dissertation, and Valerie Bunce helped me understand the nature of the Communist party-state, and Yuri Orlov—Soviet human rights campaigner turned Cornell physics professor—reassured me that I was on the right track.

Without the support of numerous other individuals and institutions, though, a research project of this scale would still have been impossible. At Cornell, the Peace Studies Program, East European Studies Program, and the Einaudi Center for International Studies contributed generously to my research across Europe and the United States. The support of Ned Lebow, Judith Reppy, and Lawrence Scheinman, and the resources provided to them by the MacArthur Foundation, were critical. A MacArthur fellowship from Stanford's Center for International Security and Arms Control, as well as insightful comments from Lynn Eden, David Holloway, and Scott Sagan, helped me deepen the empirical research. The writing continued at Harvard University's Center for International Affairs, with support from Robert Keohane and Douglas Bond, followed by Henry Steiner's invitation to join the law school's Human Rights Program. A dissertation grant from the Institute for the Study of World Politics, a Peace Scholar fellowship from the U.S. Institute of Peace, and funding from the College of Arts and Sciences at the University of Illinois at Chicago provided necessary support for further research and writing. Finally, a Jean Monnet Fellowship from the European University Institute's Robert Schuman Centre for Advanced Studies gave me leave from teaching to produce the final manuscript. I cannot thank Yves Mény and Thomas Risse enough for this opportunity.

As any researcher will understand, this book would also not have been possible without the willingness of dozens of human rights activists, diplomats, and government officials in Europe and America to answer endless questions about events from their past (see the Appendix). Librarians and staff at the European Community Historical Archives (Florence), Human Rights Watch (New York), the Institute of Contemporary History (Prague), the International Helsinki Foundation for Human Rights (Vienna), the Polish Helsinki Committee (Warsaw), Radio Free Europe/Radio Liberty (then Munich), and the U.S. Commission on Security and Cooperation in Europe (Washington, D.C.) helped me find critical documents. Only some of these documents are listed in the text, but all helped me piece together a complicated puzzle.

Martha Finnemore, Stephen Krasner, and anonymous reviewers for Princeton University Press read the entire manuscript and made many suggestions that improved the final product considerably. Individual chapters are stronger because of comments from Isaac Balbus, Darren Hawkins, Fiona Ross, Cheryl Shanks, Kathryn Sikkink, Charles Tilly, and Aristide Zolberg. I have also benefited tremendously from the interest and suggestions of Arie Bloed, Eva Busza, Robert Herman, Mary Katzenstein, Elizabeth Kier, Audie Klotz, William Korey, Laszlo Poti, Richard Price, Sylvia Rohde-Liebenau, Erika Schlager, Pavel Seifter, Jan Urban, and Vlad Zubok. Such friends and colleagues more than compensate for the otherwise solitary experience of writing a book.

At Princeton University Press, Malcolm Litchfield's early enthusiasm for the project helped me imagine it as a book. The skills and patience of Alice Calaprice, Margaret Case, Chuck

Myers, Tim Vaughan, and their colleagues at the press then helped me turn that vision into a tangible and readable reality.

I dedicate this book to my parents, Susan and Didier, who continue to inspire, and to Susanne Boesch, who makes it all worthwhile.

Chicago, August 2000

Abbreviations

CPSU	Communist Party of the Soviet Union
CSCE	Conference on Security and Cooperation in Europe
EC	European Community
EPC	European Political Cooperation
EU	European Union
FCO, *The Conference*	Foreign and Commonwealth Office, *The Conference on Security and Cooperation in Europe, 1972–1975*, G. Bennett and K. A. Hamilton, eds., Documents on British Policy Overseas, Series 3, Volume 2 (London: Her Majesty's Stationery Office, 1997)
FRG	Federal Republic of Germany (West Germany)
GDR	German Democratic Republic (East Germany)
ICCPR	International Covenant on Civil and Political Rights
ICESCR	International Covenant on Economic, Social, and Cultural Rights
IPCECS	Inter-Parliamentary Conference on European Co-operation and Security
IPU	Inter-Parliamentary Union
JPRS, *Translations*	Joint Publication Research Service, *Translations on Eastern Europe*
KOR	Workers' Defense Committee (Poland)
MBFR	Mutual and Balanced Force Reductions
MPT	Multilateral Preparatory Talks
NATO	North Atlantic Treaty Organization
NGO	Non-governmental organization(s)
NNA	Neutral and nonaligned

ROPCiO
*Selected
Documents*

Movement for the Defense of Human and Civil Rights (Poland), Secretary of State for Foreign and Commonwealth Affairs, Command Paper 6932, *Selected Documents Relating to Problems of Security and Cooperation in Europe, 1954–1977* (London: Her Majesty's Stationery Office, 1977)

U.S. Helsinki
Commission

U.S. Commission on Security and Cooperation in Europe

VONS

Committee for the Defense of the Unjustly Prosecuted (Czechoslovakia)

THE HELSINKI EFFECT

The International Politics
of Human Rights

ONE of the hallmarks of contemporary diplomacy is the institutionalization of human rights ideas as formal international norms designed to govern the policies and structures of sovereign states. This trend is reflected in global declarations and conventions stretching from the 1948 Universal Declaration of Human Rights to the declarations of the 1993 World Conference on Human Rights and the 2000 Conference of the World's Democracies, as well as regional agreements ranging from the 1950 European Convention on Human Rights and Fundamental Freedoms to the 1981 African Charter on Human and People's Rights, to name just a few. Meanwhile, private human rights groups consistently pressure governments around the world that fail to comply with or promote the ensuing obligations.

Yet if some analysts are correct, these diplomats and activists are wasting their time. According to the skeptics, human rights norms only affect governments already inclined to make reforms. Some critics go even further, arguing that international norms have no significant impact on political outcomes. This apparent contradiction between policy and theory raises two sets of important questions. First, why do repressive states agree to be bound by human rights norms, and how is the content of these norms determined? Second, do human rights norms affect the behavior or institutions of these repressive states? This book argues that repressive states agree to be bound by human rights norms in the belief that they can gain international legitimacy without substantial compliance, and that this "empty" commitment nonetheless promotes local, transnational, and interstate processes that undermine continued repression.

This argument is based on an analysis of the emergence of human rights norms in East-West relations during the Cold War, and their subsequent contribution to political change in Eastern Europe and the Soviet Union. The study focuses in particular on the sources and effects of human rights norms established in 1975 by the Helsinki Final Act, a political agreement among the thirty-five states participating in the Conference on Security and Cooperation in Europe.[1] This document established ten basic principles for relations among the participating states, including "non-intervention in internal affairs" (principle 6) and "respect for human rights and fundamental freedoms, including the freedom of thought, conscience, religion or belief" (principle 7).

Many skeptics doubted that the Helsinki agreement would do anything but reinforce the status quo behind the Iron Curtain, and cited the well-entrenched and repressive nature of Communist rule, the political, ideological, and economic isolation of the Soviet Union and its allies, and the Final Act's explicit reaffirmation of "non-intervention." The *New York Times* editorialized in July 1975 that "nothing signed in Helsinki will in any way save courageous free thinkers in the Soviet empire." And yet, as demonstrated in subsequent chapters, the Helsinki Final Act's formal commitment to respect human rights contributed significantly to the demise of Communism and the end of the Cold War. This "Helsinki effect" surprised the diplomats who negotiated it, the politicians who signed it, and many others who had rushed to criticize it as a concession to dictatorship.

This book's analysis of the "Helsinki effect" draws upon and develops two theories of the international politics of human rights—one based on Liberal and the other on Constructivist approaches to international relations. The present chapter outlines the core logics of Liberalism and Constructivism, and then contrasts their explanations of the sources and the effects of

---

[1] The Helsinki Final Act is also known widely as the Helsinki Accords. The two terms are used interchangeably in this book. The text of the Final Act can be found at http://www.osce.org/docs/english/1990–1999/summits/helfa75e.htm.

international human rights norms. It also explains the methodologies employed in the study and summarizes the contents of the chapters that follow. Before doing so, though, it situates the "Helsinki effect" with respect to conventional explanations for the demise of Communist rule.

REINTERPRETING THE DEMISE OF COMMUNISM

The demise of Communism as a comprehensive system of social engineering and one-party political control is the subject of great controversy among historians and social scientists.[2] Scholarship in this area has long been hampered by the legacy of the "totalitarian model" of Communist rule, which deemphasized social conflict and ignored autonomous societal forces. With the exception of Poland in the 1980s, where Solidarity's power could not be overlooked, most Western scholars viewed the Communist party-state as the only significant locus of political activity in Eastern Europe. Very few paid attention to the widespread dissident and opposition activity that emerged in the mid to late 1970s and persisted through the following decade. As one observer put it, most academic specialists were "too hard-headed, too realistic, and even too dependent on social science models to take [the dissidents'] highly intellectualized discussions seriously."[3] Like the regimes they studied, Western scholars were thus unprepared for the mass mobilizations of 1989, including demands for freedom of travel, roundtable talks, and even free elections. By the end of that year, Communist dictatorships had fallen across the region, and

[2] The democratic election of restructured Communist parties in several East European countries during the 1990s does not constitute a return to the political and social hegemony of the Communist party-state evident from the 1950s through 1980s.

[3] Daniel Chirot, "What Happened in Eastern Europe in 1989?" in Chirot, ed., *The Crisis of Leninism and the Decline of the Left* (Seattle: University of Washington Press, 1991), 22–23. On the media's equal neglect of dissent in the East, see Vladimir Tismaneanu, "Eastern Europe: The Story the Media Missed," *Bulletin of the Atomic Scientists* 46 (March 1990):17–21.

the Cold War that had divided Europe and polarized world politics for over four decades had virtually disappeared.

How then can we explain the ability of mass movements, guided by surprisingly skillful opposition organizations, to overthrow supposedly omnipotent Communist party-states? The conventional wisdom typically explains "the fall" in terms of the Old Guard's inability to control the partial liberalization of the domestic economy and the Warsaw Pact that Mikhail Gorbachev initiated in the hope of reversing economic stagnation in the East and reducing the military challenge from the West. Such arguments have a certain explanatory power—as acknowledged at points throughout this book—but they fail to explain where these mass mobilizations came from, or how they overcame the social divisions that had undermined nascent uprisings in earlier decades.

Unsatisfied social demands and external geopolitical pressures also cannot explain why one-party Communist rule died in the way and when it did. The standard of living in the East was not deteriorating so rapidly that political reform was required in the mid-1980s, or that revolution was inevitable in the late 1980s. "Star Wars" notwithstanding, the Soviet Union remained capable of compensating for the superior quality of Western military technology by maintaining its quantitative edge, just as it had since the 1960s. And as we know from political transitions in many other countries and periods, economic crises and external threats do not necessarily produce the sort of rights-protective states that emerged in Eastern Europe after 1989. In fact, the geopolitical challenge from the West gave conservative Communist party leaders a convenient justification for using force to retain domestic control, as they had in 1956 and 1968, and as China's leaders did in Tiananmen Square. Some other critical factor (or factors) kept the troops in their barracks and thus allowed unarmed crowds to overthrow a political system that had long been maintained by force.

This book attributes the surprising weakness of Communist rule and the emergence of rights-protective states to the transformation of state-society and East-West relations catalyzed by the Communist governments' acceptance of new international norms on human rights in the mid-1970s. In particular, the book traces the weakening of Communist rule not to Gorbachev's reforms but to the unprecedented social movement and opposition activity that emerged across the East bloc in the aftermath of the Helsinki Final Act. It thus argues that the conventional wisdom on Communism's demise must be modified to account for how international norms contributed to fundamental political changes well before the Gorbachev era.

INTERNATIONAL RELATIONS THEORY AND HUMAN RIGHTS NORMS

International norms are standards of appropriate behavior for actors with a given identity in world politics.[4] They are collective in the sense that they are the standards by which actors in international society expect or agree to be judged, but not necessarily in the sense that actors always comply or even that they accept the moral or causal premises upon which the standards are based. Our understanding of international norms should thus not be limited by the reality of inconsistent behavior. As Hedley Bull reminds us, "if there were no possibility that actual behavior would differ from prescribed behavior, there would be no point in having the rule."[5] In this sense, international society is comparable to domestic societies, even those with legitimate courts and reliable police, where a certain level of noncompliance coexists with the legal system. (Remember the cartoon in which a highway patrol officer asks a gas station attendant, "Did you see a car pass here strictly obeying the speed limit?") Recognizing the potential inconsistency between norms and behavior is thus the beginning, not the end, of understanding how norms shape outcomes in world politics.

[4] Peter J. Katzenstein, ed., *The Culture of National Security: Norms and Identity in World Politics* (New York: Columbia University Press, 1996), 5.

[5] Hedley Bull, *The Anarchical Society* (New York: Columbia University Press, 1977), 56.

One of the reasons for inconsistent state behavior is that not all international norms acquire equal salience in world politics. This salience is determined by the prevailing interests or commitment of states, by the presence or absence of contradictory norms, and by the framing or agenda-setting efforts of nonstate actors. The resulting international normative environment is as important a determinant of state action as the content of the norms themselves.

International human rights norms are standards of governance that impose positive and negative obligations on states to ensure the basic security, freedom, and dignity of individuals and groups within their jurisdiction. For example, within the global human rights system established by the United Nations, formal norms are designed to protect individual rights such as the right to life, the right to education, freedom from arbitrary detention or torture, freedom of expression and assembly, freedom from discrimination because of gender, religion and race, and collective rights such as the right to self-determination, freedom from genocide, and the right of indigenous peoples to cultural survival. The right of states, as well as intergovernmental and nongovernmental organizations, to take interest in the human rights records of (other) sovereign states is also increasingly accepted as a correlative norm necessary for the protection of human rights.

International human rights norms are designed to regulate the behavior of state actors toward their societies and toward each other. However, unlike international norms that require coordinated behavior but are potentially neutral on the "equilibrium point," such as those which govern the behavior of ships passing in a narrow channel, human rights norms are not neutral on the acceptability of all forms of governance. For the same reason, the behavioral obligations that they impose on states are not directly contingent on the comparable behavior of others. For example, one state's use of torture does not relieve another state of its duty not to torture. Likewise, one state's refusal to cooperate with the international community's *droit de regard* into its human rights record does not mean that international or nongovernmental organizations are less entitled to monitor human rights conditions elsewhere in the world.

Liberal and Constructivist approaches to international relations theory suggest distinct explanations for why and when states agree formally to be bound by international human rights norms, why and how these norms affect behavioral outcomes, and the conditions under which these effects are most likely. These explanations are introduced below as distinct theories of the politics of international human rights norms. Differences between the two theories are due in large part to their assumptions regarding the fundamental logics of human action: Liberalism incorporates a materialist "logic of expected consequences" according to which interests are formed prior to social interactions, whereas Constructivism incorporates an ideational "logic of appropriateness" in which interests are transformed through social interaction.[6] To place these two theories in context, we first briefly discuss a third theory, Realism, which argues that human rights norms do not affect the behavior of state actors.

Realism

Realist theories of international relations view states as unitary actors seeking to ensure their security against potential competitors within an international system that lacks effective central authority and in which outcomes are determined by the distribution of coercive power.[7] According to Realism's conception of anarchy as the absence of effective authority above states, international human rights norms themselves do not affect the

[6] For more on the logics of appropriateness and expected consequences in international relations theory, see James G. March and Johan P. Olsen, "The Institutional Dynamics of International Political Orders," *International Organization* 52 (Autumn 1998):943–69.

[7] See Kenneth Waltz, *Theory of International Politics* (Reading, Mass.: Addison-Wesley, 1979).

behavior or the identity of states.[8] If a state's policy choices or domestic structure are subject to international influences, Realism would attribute this not to norms but to the uneven distribution of power in the international system.[9] Realism is therefore best treated as the theoretical basis for a null hypothesis, "international human rights norms do not matter," against which Liberal and Constructivist theories can be compared.[10]

Liberalism

According to the explanatory logic of expected consequences that underlies Liberal theories of international relations, actors choose behaviors that appear most likely to satisfy their preexisting interests within an interdependent international environment. The preeminent interests of state actors are to secure their rule and satisfy domestic constituencies.[11] Where state preferences diverge, the design of international institutions is determined primarily by the relative bargaining leverage of states. Once they are established, international institutions affect the behavior (but not the identity or interests) of states by solving coordination problems or by shifting the relative costs and benefits of particular behaviors.[12] Although social movements and comparable nonstate actors have generally not been a central concern, Liberal theory would suggest that they too are instrumental in their quest for power or influence, and thus

[8] See John J. Mearsheimer, "The False Promise of International Institutions," *International Security* 19 (Winter 1994/95):5–49.

[9] See G. John Ikenberry and Charles Kupchan, "Socialization and Hegemonic Power," *International Organization* 44 (1990):283–315.

[10] For further discussion of the limitations of Realist theory with respect to the politics of human rights, see Stephen D. Krasner, "How Little We Know," unpublished memo prepared for the Conference on Human Rights, Northwestern University, May 5–6, 2000.

[11] See Andrew Moravcsik, "Taking Preferences Seriously: A Liberal Theory of International Politics," *International Organization* 51 (Autumn 1997):513–53.

[12] See Robert O. Keohane, "Neo-Liberal Institutionalism," in *International Institutions and State Power* (Boulder, Colo.: Westview Press, 1989), 1–20.

more likely to challenge state actors when the apparent costs of mobilization decline in relation to likely benefits.[13]

On the basis of these premises, Liberal theory explains the formation of states' positions on the creation of international human rights regimes as a calculation by state actors of the trade-off between the norms' prospective impact on their political autonomy and on the security of their rule.[14] By this logic, political elites in weakly institutionalized democracies willingly delegate authority to international regimes in order to insure themselves and their countries' institutions against other domestic forces hostile to democracy. In contrast, politicians in established democratic states will resist the infringements on their domestic autonomy implied by enforceable human rights regimes, but may seek political advantage by supporting unenforceable norms favored by international allies or influential domestic constituencies. Leaders of authoritarian or rights-abusive states will refuse to cooperate in the creation of human rights regimes with effective means of enforcement, but they may accept unenforceable norms if necessary to gain critical resources controlled by other states.

Given such preferences, Liberalism would not expect authoritarian states (or even established democracies) to be interested in creating international human rights regimes. If other states are committed, though, and control access to valued resources, then established democracies and authoritarian states may agree to negotiate with the expectation that they can protect themselves by insisting on vague norms or weak enforcement mechanisms. The resulting bargain should reflect the preferences of the participating states, the intensity of their preferences, their vulnerability to explicit or implicit issue linkage by other states, and their sensitivity to the possibility that the negotiations could fail. In the end, though, the logic of Liberal-

---

[13] See Edward N. Muller and Karl-Dieter Opp, "Rational Choice and Rebellious Collective Action," *American Political Science Review* 80 (June 1986):471–87.

[14] See Andrew Moravcsik, "The Origins of Human Rights Regimes: Democratic Delegation in Postwar Europe," *International Organization* 54 (Spring 2000):217–52.

ism suggests that authoritarian states whose political order could be upset by an effective international human rights regime would rather derail the negotiations than accept the creation of clear norms and strong enforcement mechanisms.

Even if states miscalculate the likely consequences of negotiations on human rights, Liberalism predicts a considerable gap between state rhetoric and subsequent practice. Because the leaders of both established democracies and authoritarian states view international human rights norms as undesirable constraints on their domestic autonomy, they are likely to resist adjusting their policies and state structures. This means that regardless of their rhetorical position, rights-abusive states will seek to avoid implementing the norms at home, whereas established democracies will generally fail to promote the norms abroad. (In comparison, weakly institutionalized democracies will be more willing to adjust their domestic and foreign policies.) For this reason, some Liberals have concluded that international human rights norms will not substantially affect the behavior of rights-abusive states not otherwise inclined toward reform.[15]

According to other strands of Liberal theory, though, international human rights norms can affect states' choices by changing the costs and benefits of repression. Within certain limits, the motivation for authoritarian states to initiate rights-protective reforms should vary with the effectiveness of transborder monitoring, the target state's sensitivity to sanctions and issue linkage, and the intensity of international pressure for compliance.[16] Rights-protective reforms are thus most likely when access to valued goods is linked to compliance with the norms, when other capable actors are committed to enforcing this linkage, and when mechanisms exist to monitor compliance. The resulting concessions will be as minimal as the incen-

---

[15] Andrew Moravcsik, "Explaining International Human Rights Regimes: Liberal Theory and Western Europe," *European Journal of International Relations* 1 (Summer 1995): 157–89.

[16] See Lisa L. Martin, *Coercive Cooperation: Explaining Multilateral Economic Sanctions* (Princeton: Princeton University Press, 1992).

tive structure allows, but they may reduce the popular fear of repression enough to encourage social movements to challenge the state. In the end, though, the Liberal argument that state actors seek first to secure their hold on power indicates that authoritarian states will violate international human rights norms (even if this risks international sanctions) rather than pursue rights-protective reforms that would enable them to be overthrown by domestic challengers.

Constructivism

According to the explanatory logic of appropriateness that underlies Constructivist theories of international relations, actors seek to behave in accordance with norms relevant to their identities.[17] Identities are definitions of self in relation to others that provide guidance for how one should behave in a given context. Although some Constructivist scholars emphasize relations among states defined as unitary actors, most disaggregate the state to incorporate substate and nonstate actors linked together in complex processes of interest transformation.[18] In either case, international relations involve repeated encounters with others that provoke reflection on what shared practices and values make us "us," what characteristics "we" share (or do not share) with "them," and what we need to do to be true to ourselves or to gain the approval of others "like us."[19]

[17] For general overviews, see Friedrich V. Kratochwil, *Rules, Norms and Decisions: On the Conditions of Practical and Legal Reasoning in International and Domestic Affairs* (Cambridge: Cambridge University Press, 1989); and Alexander Wendt, *Social Theory of International Politics* (New York: Cambridge University Press, 1999).

[18] For examples of the latter, see Margaret Keck and Kathryn Sikkink, *Activists beyond Borders: Advocacy Networks in International Politics* (Ithaca: Cornell University Press, 1998), and Thomas Risse, Stephen C. Ropp, and Kathryn Sikkink, eds., *The Power of Human Rights: International Norms and Domestic Change* (Cambridge: Cambridge University Press, 1999).

[19] See Craig Calhoun, "Social Theory and the Politics of Identity," in Craig Calhoun, ed., *Social Theory and the Politics of Identity* (Oxford: Blackwell, 1994), 11–36.

Constructivism also assumes a mutually constitutive relationship between states and international structures, including norms and institutions. The interests that drive state behavior are thus intrinsically related to ongoing and interactive processes of social differentiation, community building, and the respecification of behavioral roles.[20] One of the most important of these processes is communication among actors regarding what "kind" of actor they are and whether or not they are complying with relevant norms.[21]

Because states are, at least in part, products of international society, the identities and interests that drive state action are inextricably intertwined with international norms.[22] As a result, all states are motivated to behave in a manner consistent with international norms or the expectations of other states. Yet states are not simply "normatively alike"—products of a single international society in which all value the same ends and behave accordingly. For one thing, there is more than one international society, each with its own norms related to its functional or ideational purposes. Although most states identify with more than one of these international societies, none identifies with all of them. In addition, there are vast differences in the internal structures of states and in the domestic societies that they rule.[23] Every state thus has multiple identities, and is beholden to multiple standards of appropriate behavior.

[20] See Alexander Wendt, "Collective Identity Formation and the International State," *American Political Science Review* 88 (1994):384–96, and Emanuel Adler and Michael Barnett, eds., *Security Communities* (Cambridge: Cambridge University Press, 1998).

[21] See Thomas Risse, "Let's Argue! Communicative Action and International Relations," *International Organization* 54 (Winter 2000):1–39.

[22] See Inis L. Claude, "Collective Legitimization as a Political Function of the United Nations," *International Organization* 20 (1966):367–79; Robert H. Jackson, *Quasi-States: Sovereignty, International Relations, and the Third World* (Cambridge: Cambridge University Press, 1990); and Martha Finnemore, *National Interests in International Society* (Ithaca: Cornell University Press, 1996).

[23] On the domestic sources of state identity, see Peter J. Katzenstein, *Cultural Norms and National Security: Police and Military in Postwar Japan* (Ithaca: Cornell University Press, 1996).

When the domains of these identities do not overlap or when their respective norms coincide, state actors should have little difficulty complying with the multiple norms. The challenge to compliance comes when identities overlap and their norms conflict. For example, there is often extensive overlap and profound contradictions between domestic and international-level logics of appropriateness. In such situations, the effectiveness of the international norm may depend upon its own characteristics: Constructivist scholars have suggested that international norms will be more effective when their prescriptions are specific (meaning that they clearly distinguish between compliant and noncompliant behavior), durable (meaning that they have survived challenges to their prescriptions and legitimacy), and concordant (meaning consistent with other relevant norms and diplomatic discourses).[24]

Constructivism's logic also suggests, however, that norm effectiveness depends upon the identity of the state actor in question. Given that norms apply to actors with particular identities, and that all actors have multiple identities, we may conclude that a state actor's sense of duty to comply with a norm will vary with the salience of the identity specified by the norm: the more salient the identity specified by an international norm, the more the actor will seek to fulfill its obligations under that norm. For example, the more that state actors value the "European" identity of their state, the more they will seek to comply with norms incumbent upon "European states." In short, state actors will comply with those norms that are connected to the most salient of their multiple identities, and violate or seek to change norms that are connected to less salient identities.

The salience of particular identities is determined first by the density of communications within particular institutional contexts. Given the Constructivist assumption that states create international institutions that reflect their cultural and functional identities, more frequent communications between state

---

[24] Jeffrey W. Legro, "Which Norms Matter? Revisiting the 'Failure' of Internationalism," *International Organization* 51 (Winter 1997):31–63.

actors within and about those institutions should increase the salience of the identities they embody, and thereby increase the binding quality of whatever norms they establish. New information or persuasive arguments may also give salience to a new (or previously marginal) identity, and thus cause state actors to redefine what behaviors are in the state's interests. Non-state actors are particularly important in this latter process of issue reframing.[25]

Based on these premises, Constructivist theory suggests that states will support or resist the creation of international human rights norms according to the multiple identities that define their interests. As members of international society, all states are responsive to the fact that international legitimacy is increasingly linked to formal acceptance of the idea that all individuals have certain inalienable rights, such as freedom from torture, freedom of expression, and freedom of assembly. On the other hand, domestic structures and ideologies vary widely. States that are organized to protect free expression and independent associations, or whose ideologies agree with the premises of universal human rights, will therefore support the creation of international norms with these same goals. In contrast, states whose domestic structures or ideologies are less protective of human rights will be torn between the interests generated by their domestic and international identities.

When a domestically generated identity inconsistent with human rights is more salient than the same state's membership in international society, state actors are likely to pursue the international legitimacy that they gain by signing new human rights conventions while reassuring key domestic audiences of their commitment to adhere to domestic norms. In other words, except in cases of limited state capacity, gaps between a state's rhetoric on human rights at international forums and its record on the actual protection of human rights at home reflect

---

[25] This phenomenon is called "strategic social construction" by Martha Finnemore and Kathryn Sikkink, "International Norm Dynamics and Political Change," *International Organization* 52 (Autumn 1998):887–917.

state actors' efforts to fulfill their international identity without violating their domestic identity.

Yet even when state interests are dominated by a salient domestic identity that is inconsistent with respect for international human rights, other states and non-state actors committed to human rights may seek to shame the "target" state into compliance by publicizing evidence of a gap between its international rhetoric and domestic practices, criticizing it within international organizations, and downgrading or suspending bilateral relations in other issue areas.[26] In addition, people living under the "target" state may organize social movements focused on the protection of human rights that gradually erode the state's hold on society. Such efforts are most likely to reconfigure state interests in favor of compliance with human rights norms (and least likely to provoke a repressive backlash) when the norms in question are embedded within an institutional structure that ensures ongoing dialogue on compliance and when an influential minority of elites within the target state favors compliance, either because they already value the state's international identity or because they were persuaded by the information and arguments of non-state actors committed to human rights).

METHODOLOGIES FOR THE STUDY OF NORMS

This book's empirical investigation of the Helsinki effect assumes that norms are compatible with the basic logics of social science, and can be treated as potential explanations for observable outcomes. They can be integrated into both causal and constitutive forms of social explanation, using data gathered

[26] See Audie Klotz, *Norms in International Relations: The Struggle against Apartheid* (Ithaca: Cornell University Press, 1995), and Neta Crawford and Audie Klotz, eds., *How Sanctions Work: Lessons from the South African Case* (New York: Macmillan, 1998).

through historical process, tracing normative genealogy and structured comparisons across time and across cases.[27]

Causal forms of social explanation identify both the antecedent conditions for the occurrence of independently existing effects and the mechanism or process that links the antecedent condition(s) to the effect(s). Whether or not there is a necessary relationship between cause and effect—meaning that whenever the antecedent condition is present, the effect will be produced, and when the condition is absent, the effect will not be produced—is best treated as an empirical question. As this book demonstrates, it is possible to hypothesize about the mechanisms that link particular constellations of norms and the shared meanings that actors attribute to them to the occurrence of particular discourses and behaviors that matter politically, and then evaluate those linkages empirically. Doing so often requires that the researcher take seriously (albeit not uncritically) references by actors themselves to the material and normative contexts in which they act, and why they did, or did not, take particular actions. As this suggests, the opportunities for process tracing offered by case studies are ideally suited to identifying the mechanisms by which norms affect outcomes; in some situations, larger-N quantitative techniques can also be used to evaluate the causal effects of norms.

This volume's analysis of the causal effects of norms draws evidence from government and media reports, non-governmental organization (NGO) and diplomatic records, and interviews with dozens of policy makers and societal activists involved in relevant events. It searches first for whether indicators of the effectiveness of human rights norms change as expected. Such changes would include increased diplomatic attention to respect for human rights, increased social mobilization, and reduced repression. Beyond simple correlations, it also seeks to

---

[27] See Stephen Van Evera, *Guide to Methods for Students of Political Science* (Ithaca: Cornell University Press, 1997), and Audie Klotz and Cecelia Lynch, *Constructing Global Politics* (Ithaca: Cornell University Press, forthcoming). For further discussion of the causal-constitutive distinction, see Wendt, *Social Theory of International Politics*, 77–91.

determine whether references to norms were part of the relevant decision-making processes. Finally, at each stage of the empirical story, it considers the power of alternative explanations (other factors that may explain the outcome in question) and counterfactual hypotheses (the possibility that the outcome in question would have happened anyway).

Constitutive forms of social explanation are accounts of the construction and reconstruction of the social identities and other convergent meanings that constitute actors and structure relations among them. Like other social structures, norms may be treated as the subject or the object of constitutive explanation. In other words, norms may shape actors' identities and other convergent meanings, or they may be shaped by these factors. More complicated research designs might even permit the analyst to explain the feedback processes by which norms shape meanings and meanings shape norms without disaggregating the two. The historical process tracing of normative genealogy and case study methods are most likely to elicit the evidence necessary for constitutive forms of social explanation.

This volume's constitutive analysis of changes in international norms and attendant meanings seeks to reconstruct how relevant actors understood the normative structures around them at various points in time, and the arguments they offered to reinforce or change those structures. In order to reconstruct the historical meaning of particular normative structures, and to determine what factors made certain arguments effective and others not, the study draws on data from diplomatic histories, documents, and statements from national governments and international organizations, as well as interviews and correspondence with policy makers and diplomats who participated in the events concerned.

As discussed earlier, the study focuses empirically on political change in the member states of the Warsaw Pact: Bulgaria, Czechoslovakia, East Germany, Hungary, Poland, Romania, and the Soviet Union. Where possible, the universality of the Helsinki effect is judged by comparing its salience in each of the seven states, and asking whether observable differences can be explained by variations in the structure of state-society relations in each country. However, the political, ideological, economic, and military nature of the Warsaw Pact means that the seven countries are generally best understood as interdependent parts of a integrated system, rather than as autonomous units subject to systematic cross-case comparison.

OVERVIEW OF THE STUDY

The empirical chapters of the book are arranged to highlight the evolution, framing, and effects of human rights norms in the Helsinki Final Act. Chapters 1 and 2 concern the emergence human rights as a formal norm governing East-West and trans-European relations, with special attention to preparations for the Conference on Security and Cooperation in Europe (CSCE) and negotiation of the Final Act. Chapters 3 and 4 concern the efforts of various political actors to determine the meaning that the new Helsinki norms would acquire in domestic and international contexts. Chapters 5 through 7 concern the subsequent effects of Helsinki norms on the rhetoric and behavior of state and societal actors in Eastern Europe and the Soviet Union.

Chapter 1 traces the normative content of diplomatic proposals and agreements related to trans-European and East-West relations from the mid-1950s through the early 1970s. In the process, it demonstrates that beyond the limited membership of the Council of Europe, respect for human rights was not considered a legitimate diplomatic issue or standard of conduct by all or even most European states during this period. At the same time, it demonstrates that a human rights norm and related substantive issues were introduced to the diplomatic agenda largely through the initiative of the European Community (EC), whose nine member states had identified themselves collectively at home and abroad with the pursuit of human rights. Chapter 2 traces the actual negotiation of international norms and related issues within the CSCE beginning in 1972, focusing on the political commitments, diplomatic strategies, and external events that shaped agreement on human rights in the Helsinki Final Act in 1975. Although it demonstrates the prevalence of instrumental bargaining among state actors, it shows clearly that diplomatic processes engage issues of collective identity and legitimation that can entrap state actors in negotiated outcomes that they neither anticipate nor value. The inclusion of a relatively robust human rights norm in the Helsinki Final Act cannot be explained without attention to this dynamic, manifest in the EC's insistence that human rights are part of European identity and the Eastern bloc's hunger for international recognition via the CSCE. Consistent evidence of the United States' efforts to downplay the human rights issue disconfirm potential explanations of the norms as a simple reflection of hegemonic power and interests.

Chapters 3 and 4 document the multilevel contestation between those political actors who wanted the Helsinki Final Act to be equated politically with its human rights norms and those who, despite the formal norms, wanted to downplay human rights. In particular, Chapter 3 documents an unprecedented mobilization of societal actors in Eastern Europe and the Soviet Union committed to the implementation of Helsinki's human rights norms, which cannot be explained by other political or socioeconomic factors, as well as the Communist party-state's failed attempt to control perceptions of what had been agreed at Helsinki. Chapter 4 shows how the transnational "Helsinki network" reframed the Final Act within American politics and made Helsinki compliance a priority in a U.S. foreign policy, while explaining why these changes cannot be attributed to the election of Jimmy Carter or other factors. Notwithstanding these early constitutive effects, we thus see that the Helsinki norms became most significant as a force for political change when otherwise weak societal actors succeeded in framing the Final Act at home and abroad as an agreement to promote human rights, rather than as an agreement to accept the status quo.

Chapters 5 through 7 trace the longer-term effects of Helsinki norms on political change in Eastern Europe and the Soviet Union. To start, Chapter 5 explains how Helsinki norms enabled local activists to create unprecedented independent organizations and social movements between 1976 and 1978. The persistence and transnational networking of these independent organizations was a serious challenge to the Communist party-state's control over public space and the flow of information. It also shows that these early effects were most evident where some preexisting societal actors were already sympathetic to the concept of individual human rights and were prepared to engage local and foreign authorities in these terms. We thus see significant Helsinki-related activity in Czechoslovakia, Poland, and the Soviet Union (where intellectuals were comfortable with the discourse of "rights"), somewhat less in East Germany and Hungary (where intellectuals were more focused on "class"), and far less in Bulgaria or Romania (where repression had eliminated any semblance of civil society).

The continued power and real limitations of Helsinki norms are seen clearly in Chapter 6, which explains how the CSCE review meeting in Belgrade from 1977 to 1978 failed to prevent these regimes (with the notable exception of Poland) from instituting repressive measures designed to reassert social control. The selective nature of repression (activists known abroad were somewhat shielded) nonetheless demonstrates that the Helsinki norms continued to shape state action even after the failure of the Belgrade meeting to produce any substantive gains for the East in 1978, and then the death of détente in 1979. Meanwhile, the domestic networking and human rights education efforts of Poland's post-Helsinki organizations were essential to consolidating the nationwide alliance of workers, intellectuals, and the Church that became Solidarity, the region's first free trade union and clearest challenge to Communist hegemony. When Solidarity was driven underground by martial law in 1981, Helsinki monitoring activity reemerged as a defense against excessive repression.

Finally, Chapter 7 reinterprets the political changes of the mid to late 1980s, demonstrating how the Kremlin's decision to embark on increasingly radical reforms was shaped by the repercussions of Solidarity and other post-Helsinki movements, as well as the inescapability of human rights on the East-West agenda after Helsinki. Gorbachev's pursuit of political openness and the "common European home" (rather than a stricter version of the status quo, for example) are thus partly legacies of the domestic and international changes set in motion by the Helsinki Final Act. Likewise, the fact that the unraveling of the Communist party-state enabled by Gorbachev's reforms proceeded in a democratic and largely peaceful direction across Eastern Europe is explained by an international normative environment favorable to human rights and by the continued salience of those activists and independent organizations who had made "Helsinki" a watchword for human rights nearly a decade earlier.

The Conclusion discusses the implication of these findings for theories of international relations, summarizes the contribution of Helsinki norms to the demise of Communism and the end of the Cold War, and then identifies areas for future research on the transnational socialization of states.

THE EVOLUTION OF NORMS

CHAPTER ONE

The Emergence of Human Rights Norms in East-West Relations

> Relations between European states should be based on
> the principles of independence and national sovereignty,
> non-intervention in internal affairs and . . . the peaceful
> co-existence of States with different social systems.
> —*Warsaw Pact, Bucharest Declaration, 1966*

> A united Europe must be founded upon the common
> heritage of respect for the liberty and the rights of men,
> and must assemble democratic States having
> freely elected parliaments.
> —*European Community, Luxembourg Report, 1970*

DIPLOMATIC RELATIONS between the states of Eastern and Western Europe during the 1950s and 1960s were governed by the traditional norm of non-intervention in domestic affairs, meaning that a state's behavior within its borders was not a legitimate concern of other states. Whatever various parties felt about the issue, proposals for a multilateral European security conference coming from both sides of the Cold War divide reflect an understanding that respect for human rights was not a "collective expectation for the proper behavior" of European states during this period. The Communist states of Eastern Europe made no attempt to justify their persistent violations of civil and political rights, whereas Western states showed uneven interest in placing the issue on the trans-European agenda. In fact, some Western leaders repeatedly and explicitly asserted that the "internal affairs" of East-bloc countries were nobody else's business.

As the Conference on Security and Cooperation in Europe (CSCE) drew nearer in the late 1960s and early 1970s, governments in East and West expressed different interests regarding the substantive agenda of such a conference, but all were concerned about the conference's implications for the formal norms of international relations. Human rights were placed on the CSCE agenda through the initiative of the European Community (EC), first as a set of issues amenable to East-West cooperation (family reunification, free movement of information, and so on), and later as a proposed principle of relations among European states. These EC initiatives were repeatedly resisted by the United States and several other Western governments.

As this chapter demonstrates, the Warsaw Pact governments' desire to convene a trans-European security conference was motivated in large part by their quest for legitimation as normal members of international society. Likewise, the EC governments' collective insistence on establishing human rights as a basic norm for relations among European states was driven by their shared understandings of what it meant to be a "European" state. The following chapter traces the detailed and tortuous negotiations that actually established "respect for human rights and fundamental freedoms" as a formal European norm, from the Helsinki Consultations in 1972–1973 through the negotiations of the CSCE from 1973 to 1975 and the signing of the Helsinki Final Act in 1975.

SUPERPOWER DIPLOMACY AND THE NORM OF NON-INTERVENTION

Both the importance of formal international norms and the exclusion of human rights from the trans-European normative agenda are reflected in proposals for a European security conference beginning in the 1950s. The Second World War had ended without a comprehensive peace settlement, and the Soviet Union's de facto control of Eastern Europe lacked any basis in international agreement. When the Soviet government first proposed a multilateral European conference, they were thus seeking to prevent a unified Germany under Western influence, to legitimize the territorial (and if possible, political) status quo in Eastern Europe, including international recognition of East Germany as a sovereign state, and to reduce America's role in European affairs.[1] The Communist states sought formal Western recognition of the status quo in Eastern Europe both because of the intrinsic legitimacy it would confer and as a signal to potential revolutionaries there that they should not expect aid from abroad. Beginning in the mid-1960s, the Soviets and their allies began to conceive of the security conference also as a means to achieve much-needed investment and technical assistance from the West. For most of this period, the members of the Western alliance saw little to be gained from such a conference.

The Soviet Union first introduced the idea of a European security conference as part of its effort to forestall West Germany's integration into the new North Atlantic Treaty Organization and proposed European Defense Community. At the February 1954 Berlin Conference of Foreign Ministers, Vjacheslav Molotov revealed a draft all-European collective security treaty and a plan for the reunification of Germany under a coalition government. Ten months later, the Soviets' East European allies came to Moscow for a Conference of European Countries on Safeguarding European Peace and Security, where Molotov again proposed a treaty to establish a "general system of European security." Whether Molotov's proposals were serious or purely rhetorical, the West was more interested in solidifying NATO and pursuing West European integration than in exploring a set of Soviet initiatives whose real purposes it doubted. When Molotov's initiatives failed to elicit a positive response from the West, the Soviets set about consolidating their presence in Eastern Europe and reinforcing East Germany as an independent state. In May 1955, the Soviet Union and its East European allies established the Warsaw Pact.

[1] Following standard parlance, the German Democratic Republic (GDR) is also referred to in this book as "East Germany," whereas the Federal Republic of Germany (FRG) is also referred to as "West Germany." The GDR ceased to exist when Germany was unified in 1990.

The European security conference idea was taken up again later that year at two summit meetings in Geneva, where Britain, France, the United States, and the Soviet Union discussed proposals for arms limitation, demilitarized zones, and ongoing political consultations on European security. At the July summit of heads of government, the Soviets expressed interest in lowering economic, cultural, and scientific barriers between East and West, whereas Western delegations expressed interest in lowering barriers to communication and travel between the blocs. At a follow-on meeting that fall, France's foreign minister introduced a more detailed proposal to reduce censorship and the jamming of foreign broadcasts; to improve the working conditions for journalists and opportunities for individual tourism; to expand professional, cultural, and scientific exchanges; and to facilitate the freer flow of information.

Although a number of issues divided the Geneva conferences—including the West's insistence that German reunification required free elections, and the East's desire to achieve the withdrawal of American forces from Europe—brief and heated discussions of the French proposal revealed deep disagreements between the Soviets and the West over the role of the state as gatekeeper for transborder contacts. The West's proposals at Geneva thus reflect an early desire to use trans-European diplomacy to advance the freedom of movement and information in the East.

None of the Geneva summit proposals assumed, however, that respect for human rights was a norm for relations among European states, nor did they propose establishing it as such. The absence of convergent expectations or even similar discourse between East and West further confirms that respect for human rights was not part of the normative structure of trans-European relations at this point. This is consistent with the primary international agreement on human rights in effect at the time, the 1948 Universal Declaration of Human Rights, which committed states to respect human rights but did not link the issue to relations between states. In the end, though, neither of the Geneva meetings produced any real progress toward a European security conference. Despite occasional proposals from the East bloc, the security conference idea was largely overshadowed by the rise and fall of the Cold War during the next decade, including the invasion of Hungary in 1956, the erection of the Berlin Wall in 1961, the Cuban missile crisis in 1962, and then the first round of superpower détente in the early 1960s.

These developments caught the East European governments in an awkward position. On the one hand, they identified themselves and were identified by the outside world, both to the East and West, as part of the socialist community of states. This identification reflected not only Soviet military hegemony but also substantial economic integration as well as common official ideologies and socioeconomic systems. On the other hand, many of these regimes also identified historically and culturally with European society, which was undeniably represented in the late twentieth century not by the Warsaw Pact or the Council on Mutual Economic Assistance (to which they belonged), but by the European Community and Council of Europe (to which they did not belong). The commitment to the idea of *mitteleuropa* by many East European intellectuals only exacerbated this split identity.

In the mid-1960s, international organizations not connected to the two military blocs tried to explore the agenda for a prospective European security conference. In December 1965, for example, the UN General Assembly adopted a resolution, sponsored by nine small and/or neutral European states, entitled "Actions on the regional level with a view to improving good neighborly relations among European States having different social and political systems."[2] The resolution advocated increased cooperation and the pluralization of relations based upon the norms of national sovereignty and equal participation; its title reflected the consensus on non-intervention in internal

[2] Following Romania's earlier and unsuccessful efforts to introduce similar resolutions in 1960 and 1963, UNGA Resolution 2129 (XX), December 21, 1965, was cosponsored by an ad hoc Committee of Nine, which included Austria, Belgium, Bulgaria, Denmark, Finland, Hungary, Romania, Sweden, and Yugoslavia. On its demise, see Ljubivoje Acimovic, *Problems of Security and Cooperation* (Alphen a/d Rijn: Sijthoff & Noordhoff, 1981), 82.

affairs. The following spring, after the intervention of more powerful states aborted further discussion of the matter at the United Nations, the General Assembly resolution was endorsed by the Inter-Parliamentary Union (IPU), which had been active since the late 1800s in facilitating international peace conferences. Like the General Assembly, though, the IPU soon found that its ability to advance a European security conference was limited by the lack of progress in standard diplomatic channels and by the Kremlin's resistance to second-channel discussions.[3]

The Warsaw Pact countries then launched a new, more concerted campaign for a European security conference, reflecting both the Soviet Union's desire to exploit divisions between the United States and its West European allies and the distinct interests of Moscow's East European allies in improving relations with Western Europe and escaping the diplomatic straight jacket of bipolar bloc-to-bloc diplomacy.[4] In a December 1964 speech at the United Nations, Polish foreign minister Adam Rapacki proposed a conference, with United States participation, to examine "the problem of European security in its entirety." The outline of Rapacki's proposal was endorsed by a Warsaw Pact communiqué in January 1965 and then by the new Soviet premier Leonid Brezhnev in an April 1965 speech in Poland. In his March 1966 address to the Twenty-Third Congress of the Communist Party of the Soviet Union, Brezhnev introduced economic cooperation as a component of the proposed conference on European security. These initiatives culminated in the Declaration on Strengthening Peace and Security in Europe, issued in Bucharest in July 1966 by the Political Consultative Committee of the Warsaw Pact.

Respect for human rights was not included in the Bucharest Declaration's proposal that relations between European states should be based on the principles of "independence and na-

---

[3] See Jukka Huopaniemi, *Parliaments and European Rapprochement: The Conference of the Inter-Parliamentary Union on European Co-operation and Security (Helsinki, January 1973)* (Leiden: A. W. Sijthoff, 1973).

[4] See Jeanne Kirk-Laux, "Divergence ou coalition: La position des pays de l'Europe de l'Est à l'égard de la Conférence sur la Sécurité et la Cooperation en Europe, 1965–1972," *Études Internationales* 4 (March-June 1973):89–120.

tional sovereignty, non-intervention in internal affairs [and] on the basis of the principles of the peaceful co-existence of States with different social systems." Claiming that "the aims of the U.S. policy in Europe have nothing in common with the vital interests of the European peoples and the tasks of European security," the declaration called for the dissolution of NATO and the Warsaw Pact, the withdrawal of foreign troops from European soil, and for recognition of the permanent division of Germany. At the same time, reflecting the interests of the increasingly assertive East Europeans, the declaration included a commitment to the peaceful settlement of disputes, the expansion of East-West trade, and cooperation in science, technology, and culture.[5]

The governments of NATO member states were nonetheless divided during this period over the wisdom of exploring improved political relations with Eastern Europe and the Soviet Union. To maintain unity within the alliance and deflect Moscow's attempt to exploit any divisions, NATO's December 1967 Harmel Report on the future tasks of the alliance identified "the search for progress towards a more stable relationship" with the East as a necessary complement to military readiness.[6] The following June, instead of the European security conference favored by Moscow, NATO proposed talks on Mutual and Balanced Force Reductions (MBFR) to reduce conventional armed forces in Europe, and called for a diplomatic settlement that would ensure the legitimacy of West Berlin and guarantee Western access to that isolated and divided city. In none of these initiatives, though, did NATO propose that respect for human rights should be considered as a norm of East-West relations.

---

[5] Secretary of State for Foreign and Commonwealth Affairs, Command Paper 6932, *Selected Documents Relating to Problems of Security and Cooperation in Europe, 1954–1977* (London: Her Majesty's Stationery Office, 1977), 38–42 (hereafter cited as *Selected Documents*).

[6] "The Future Tasks of the Alliance ('the Harmel Report'); Approved by the North Atlantic Council at Its Meeting in Brussels on the 13th and 14th of December 1967," in *Selected Documents*, 49–52.

Within the Eastern bloc, the Dubcek government of Czechoslovakia began in early 1968 to expand the freedom of cultural expression, followed several months later by greater freedom of association and moves to end the political monopoly of the Communist Party. In August, fearful of the effect this "Prague Spring" could have throughout the bloc, the Kremlin ordered Warsaw Pact military forces to invade Czechoslovakia and ensure a government takeover by Communist hard-liners, who immediately reversed Dubcek's reforms and purged their supporters from the bureaucracy, media, and educational institutions. On November 13, 1968, Soviet premier Leonid Brezhnev announced the doctrine that came to bear his name: that socialist states had an obligation to intervene and defend other socialist regimes when their rule was threatened by "counter-revolutionary" forces. By the end of the year, the practice and the discourse of East bloc leaders had clearly reconfirmed that respect for human rights was not a prevailing norm for relations among Europe states.

Notwithstanding its willingness to crush the Prague Spring, the Soviet leadership still hoped to use a European security conference to legitimate its role in Eastern Europe and establish its voice in all-European affairs. Over time, it became clear to the Soviets that their earlier, maximalist position had failed to disrupt the West Europeans' commitment to alliance with Washington, or to achieve the Kremlin's long-standing objective of Western recognition of the East European status quo, including the legitimacy of the German Democratic Republic. The achievement of effective nuclear parity with the United States in the late 1960s also gave the Soviet Union a degree of diplomatic security and self-confidence it had not previously enjoyed. Finally, Leonid Brezhnev himself believed that détente suited the ideological purposes of the Soviet Union: "in conditions of relaxed international tensions, the arrow of the political barometer moves to the left."[7] Once the invasion of Czechoslovakia and the consolidation of Soviet hegemony in Eastern Europe was complete, Moscow was ready to offer new

[7] *Selected Documents*, 7.

terms for the European security conference that it had so long desired.[8]

At the same time, other East-bloc leaders were increasingly seeing signs of economic stagnation in the late 1960s, especially in contrast with the technological vitality of the West. With fundamental economic reform ideologically and politically undesirable, East European leaders hoped to save their domestic social contract through greater access to Western trade and investment. The fact that such access could never be achieved without a lessening of political confrontation with the West contributed to the growing pro-détente lobby within the Warsaw Pact. Some of the East European leaders also hoped to use a multilateral security conference to expand ties to the West and thereby reduce their absolute dependence on Moscow.[9] As a result of all these factors, the Soviet Union and its allies adopted a more conciliatory approach to the European security conference.

On March 17, 1969, a Warsaw Pact summit in Budapest called for a European security conference at the earliest possible date, and proposed a preparatory meeting toward that end. The Budapest Declaration stipulated participation by both East and West Germany as equal, sovereign states, and proposed three principle items for discussion: renunciation of the threat or use of force in relations between countries in Europe; expansion of trade, economic, scientific, technological, and cultural relations on the basis of equality and aimed at promoting political cooperation among the European nations; and the formation of a permanent multilateral mechanism for peace and security in Europe. It also called for recognition of the inviolability of frontiers, including those between East Germany and Poland and between East and West Germany; renunciation by the Federal Republic of its claims to represent the entire German people; and recognition of West Berlin's separation from the Federal Republic.

---

[8] Pierre Hassner, "Europe in the Age of Negotiations," *Washington Papers* no. 8 (Beverly Hills, Cal.: Sage Publications, 1973), 67.

[9] Kirk-Laux, "Divergence ou coalition."

The absence of any mention of human rights in the Budapest Declaration, combined with the harsh crackdowns against individual dissidents within the Soviet Union and Czechoslovakia, demonstrated the East bloc's continued rejection of any liberalization of domestic affairs and of any role for human rights within international relations. To the extent that it did not criticize Western policies, suggest abolition of the military blocs, refuse American participation, or insist on prior recognition of the territorial status quo, however, the Budapest Declaration represented a fundamentally new position for the East bloc. The timing of the initiative was also crucial, as the escalation of the Vietnam War had begun to cause domestic unrest in several West European countries and thereby heightened elite interest in ending the Cold War.

Many West European governments were relieved by the moderate tone of the Budapest Declaration and anxious to pursue it further. German Chancellor Willy Brandt saw the proposed conference as a complement to his recent initiatives to build links to the East, especially East Germany, via *ostpolitik*. The French government was attracted by the opportunity to promote détente in a forum less biased toward the superpowers or Germany than traditional bloc-to-bloc talks or Bonn's *ostpolitik*. The strength of Italy's leftist parties led Prime Minister Mariano Rumor to favor a constructive response to the new Soviet overture.[10] Whatever their particular priorities, public and parliamentary support for détente meant that no West European government could afford to be disinterested in an apparently reasonable Soviet initiative to reduce East-West tensions. NATO's public commitment two years earlier to pursue more stable relations with the East and to address underlying political problems between the blocs imposed added pressure.

The United States nonetheless remained skeptical about the Soviet initiative. President Nixon expressed concern that a European security conference might embolden Congressional interest in a withdrawal of U.S. troops from Europe, which he

[10] Henry Kissinger, *The White House Years* (Boston: Little, Brown, 1979), 414.

feared in turn would weaken both the NATO deterrent and America's role as leader of the Western alliance. At the same time, Nixon was dubious about Soviet interest in a conference which, according to some analysts, might tighten the Kremlin's grip on Eastern Europe, the Baltic republics, and other areas forcibly incorporated in the Soviet Union. An imperial state like the Soviet Union could not possibly favor a process that might threaten its hegemonic position, he reasoned.[11] Nixon's national security advisor, Henry Kissinger, called the Budapest Declaration "the maximum Soviet program for Europe, put forward in the name of enhancing European security."[12]

Nixon and Kissinger were also suspicious of the multilateral conference because such forums lacked the predictability and control of bilateral diplomacy. In his diary, Kissinger noted that "a conference would probably find the East European countries closely aligned with a rigid Soviet position, while the western participants would be competing with each other to find ways to 'break the deadlock.' "[13] From the U.S. perspective, this presented a difficult dilemma for Western diplomacy: "Being forthcoming vis-à-vis a propagandistic maneuver is no mean feat; to keep it from turning into a slippery slope is more difficult still," said Kissinger.[14] In comparison, West European politicians and diplomats tended to believe that a multilateral, multi-issue conference could serve Western interests, and reassured U.S. officials that NATO's pluralism was a source of strength, not weakness.[15] Willy Brandt reassured President Nixon that a multilateral conference would actually legitimate the U.S. presence in Europe.[16] Capitalizing on its neutrality, the Finnish government circulated a memorandum among European capitals, offering to host both the conference and the preparatory meeting proposed by the Budapest Declaration.

[11] Ibid., 966.
[12] Ibid., 414.
[13] Ibid., 415.
[14] Ibid., 414.
[15] Leif Mevik, interview by author, Brussels, June 27, 1994.
[16] Kissinger, *White House Years*, 414.

In April 1969, one month after the Budapest Declaration, the NATO foreign ministers expressed their willingness to explore substantive issues for a conference. In so doing, they stipulated the necessity of American and Canadian participation, and emphasized the importance of progress on Berlin. They also stated that true European security must be based upon respect for the principles of territorial integrity, nonintervention, self-determination, and the nonuse of force, but made no mention of human rights per se. Finally they committed themselves to preparing a list of issues for the conference agenda, but gave no indication of what this agenda might include.[17] In response, Warsaw Pact foreign ministers recommended two agenda items—the renunciation of force, and economic, technical, and scientific cooperation—but failed to comment on NATO's preconditions.[18]

West Germany entered bilateral talks with the Soviet Union, Poland, and East Germany in early 1970. But with West Germany refusing to sign any such bilateral agreements until the status of West Berlin was confirmed by four-power treaty, the Soviet Union conditioning a Berlin treaty on progress toward bilateral treaties, and NATO insisting that it would not participate in a multilateral security conference until both Berlin and the bilateral treaties were settled, further progress toward the conference was held hostage to resolution of the "German question."[19] Given Kissinger and Nixon's skepticism about multilateral negotiations, the U.S. government was not unhappy with this slow progress. In the meantime, neither NATO nor the Warsaw Pact was proposing that the eventual conference should consider respect for human rights as a basic norm for relations among European states.

[17] "Extracts from the Communiqué of the Twentieth Anniversary Council meeting in Washington on the 10th and 11th of April 1969," in *Selected Documents*, 59–60.

[18] "Extracts from a Statement Issued by a Conference of Warsaw Pact Foreign Ministers Meeting in Prague on the 30th and 31st of October 1969," in *Selected Documents*, 61–62.

[19] Heinrich Bechtoldt, "Berlin Agreement and the Security Conference," *Aussenpolitik* 23 (1972):26–35.

This fact is related to another critical, but less widely recognized development during the final years of the pre-CSCE period: the divergence of goals articulated by NATO and the smaller European Community. As demonstrated below and in the following chapter, the two organizations consulted with each other but pursued different visions of the normative agenda for the CSCE, notwithstanding the fact that some states belonged to both organizations.

HUMAN RIGHTS AS AN ISSUE FOR EUROPEAN COOPERATION

The political momentum created by the Budapest Declaration coincided with the growing sense among EC elites in the late 1960s that the Six needed to move toward greater cooperation in foreign policy. Proposals for "political union" in Europe dated back to the early 1950s, but had never gotten off the ground. As it became clear in the mid-1960s that France would eventually accept British membership in the EC, many felt that geographic widening should be accompanied by political deepening in foreign policy, among other areas. The impassioned public debate over how Europe should respond to the Greek coup d'état in 1967 had also highlighted the importance of political cooperation and especially the question of what values should be represented in the external relations of the European Community.

Shortly after NATO's positive response to the Budapest Declaration in April 1969, the political director of the Belgian Ministry of Foreign Affairs, Étienne Davignon, called his five EC counterparts to a meeting near Rome to explore possibilities for consultation on foreign policy matters of common concern.[20] The six political directors appointed a joint staff committee for foreign policy cooperation and agreed to meet again on a regular basis. Foremost on the minds of members of the

[20] In European foreign ministries, the office of political director is held by the senior civil servant.

"Davignon committee" (as it was soon known unofficially) was the question of how the EC should approach the European security conference, which now seemed increasingly likely.

Senior EC foreign policy makers were divided on whether a large multilateral conference could have any real impact on East-West relations, but all agreed that its agenda would be significant.[21] As the first experiment in EC foreign policy cooperation, the European security conference would set an important precedent for the Community's future role in Europe and the larger world. And given the heavily ideological nature of the Cold War, and the EC's explicit insistence (in its relations with the military junta in Greece since 1967) on being a community of democracies that respect human rights, domestic public opinion and various parliamentary factions were sure to be interested in how the EC approached negotiations with its totalitarian neighbors to the East. As Davignon recalls, "We wouldn't have proposed such a conference, but once we had it, we wanted to set the agenda. . . . We were not just going to accept the other side's agenda."[22]

Although many of the member states had particular national priorities regarding European security (for example, Italy was particularly concerned about Mediterranean issues), all agreed that the EC should take steps toward political union. The political directors thus resolved that each member state would present its positions within an EC caucus, whose decisions would then be pursued jointly by the Six. In other words, no member state would "go it alone" in the security conference. At the same time, they would work together to achieve international recognition of the EC itself as a legitimate voice in world affairs.[23] In

---

[21] Max van der Stoel, interview by author, The Hague, March 18, 1994.

[22] Étienne Davignon, interview by author, Brussels, January 12, 1996.

[23] General sources on this underreported process include Michael Palmer, "The European Community and a Security Conference," *World Today* 28 (June 1972): 296–303; Von Otto Graf Schwerin, "Die Solidarit des EG-Staaten in der KSZE," *Europa Archiv* 30 (August 1975): 483–92; and Gotz von Groll, "The Nine at the Conference on Security and Cooperation in Europe," in David Allen, Reinhardt Rummel, and Wolfgang Wessels, eds., *European Politi-*

this sense, they approached the security conference focused on how the six member states could coordinate their pursuit of national priorities with maximum effectiveness while simultaneously advancing their joint interest in progress toward a truly common foreign policy.

To an important extent, though, they also perceived the issue as being whether or not the EC would act appropriately in its first appearance on the international stage. In other words, would it satisfy the normative expectations of domestic audiences, and would it act in accordance with the norms embedded in the constitutions of the member states or already accepted by them in other international settings? In particular, how could a community of democracies participate in an all-European conference to promote détente without accepting a Warsaw Pact agenda that violated its members' preexisting normative commitments at the domestic and international level? Insisting that the security conference promote greater human contacts across the East-West divide, the Davignon committee concluded, would help satisfy public opinion in Western Europe while denying the Soviet Union an easy propaganda victory.

As a first step, in the fall of 1969, the Belgian delegation to a meeting of the Inter-Parliamentary Union proposed "the freer movement of people, ideas, and information" as a substantive issue (that is, not an explicit norm) that could be addressed by a European security conference. Even more than France's unsuccessful effort at the 1955 Geneva summit to improve opportunities for tourism and cultural exchange with the East bloc, the new proposal's emphasis on "ideas and information" was a direct challenge to the human and ideological isolation of the East. East-bloc delegations blocked consideration of the Belgian initiative within the IPU, but it remained on the EC agenda.

At their meeting at The Hague in December 1969, the EC foreign ministers formally charged the Davignon committee

---

cal Cooperation: Towards a Foreign Policy for Western Europe (London: Butterworths Scientific, 1982), 60–68.

with drafting a proposal for foreign policy cooperation among the Six. At their meeting in Luxembourg in late October 1970, the foreign ministers endorsed the Davignon committee's plan for European Political Cooperation (EPC), including regular meetings of the EC foreign ministers and more frequent consultations among senior staff, henceforth known as the Political Committee.[24] The ministers also established a clear linkage between the internal norms of the European Community and its role in broader European affairs when they declared that "[A] united Europe must be founded upon the common heritage of respect for the liberty and the rights of men, and must assemble democratic States having freely elected parliaments."[25] The Luxembourg Report thus reinforced the gradual integration of human rights issues into EC foreign policy coordination.

The next meeting of the six foreign ministers, held in Munich on 19 November 1970, was to choose a substantive agenda for European Political Cooperation. All agreed that EPC would focus on issues related to the Middle East conflict, but some suggested that planning for the European security conference be left to NATO, where it was already being addressed. Finally, it was agreed to add the conference to the official EPC agenda with the understanding that "political" issues would be left to NATO. Two weeks later, EC candidate-members Denmark, Great Britain, Ireland, and Norway joined the EPC process.[26]

There is remarkably little evidence that EC policymakers were motivated by a strategic quest for power, rather than an effort to realize their principled beliefs or respond to domestic

[24] For the text of the "Davignon Report," see Philippe de Schoutheete, *La Coopération politique européene* (Brussels: Fernand Nathan/Paris: Editions Labor, 1980), 179–87. See also Jean-Claude Masclet, *L'Union politique de l'Europe* (Paris: Presses Universitaires de France, 1973).

[25] "First Report of the Foreign Ministers to the Heads of State and Government of the Member States of the European Community of 27 October 1970 (Luxembourg Report)," in *European Political Cooperation (EPC)* (Bonn: Press and Information Office of the Federal Government, 1988), 24–30.

[26] These four countries participated unofficially in EPC until 22 January 1972, when all but Norway signed treaties to become full members of the EC. Norway discontinued its participation in EPC on 26 September 1972, after a popular referendum rejected EC membership.

expectations. An August 1972 summary of the British position paper on "Cultural Aspects of the CSCE," intended only for internal use, clearly emphasizes principled beliefs: "In our aim to secure genuine improvements in reducing barriers within Europe and generally to spread the 'contagion of liberty' we should not shrink from asserting western beliefs in the freedom of movement, information, and cultural contacts." After predicting likely Soviet responses to the freer movement agenda, the same British paper identifies three reasons for persisting: practical improvements (whether qualitative or quantitative) are desirable in themselves; the Russians should be made to pay a price for the West agreeing to hold the Conference at all; and "the Ministers will presumably wish to demonstrate to domestic opinion here not only their ability to get the better of the Russians in ideological disputation, but to negotiate practical measures to increase close contacts."[27]

In fact, as indicated above, Max van der Stoel concedes that senior EC policy makers expected very little to result from the CSCE, despite their extensive planning. This recollection is supported by repeated comments in internal communications among British diplomats and policy makers that the conference was unlikely to produce any strategic gain for the West.[28] French foreign minister Maurice Schumann's comment to his British counterpart at an EC meeting that a security conference would enable the Allies to pursue "peaceful roll-back" of the Soviet hold on Eastern Europe is a rare but possible exception.[29] The European Community's position on human rights, beginning with the "freer movement of people, ideas, and information," thus appears to have been motivated by a combination of principled beliefs and domestic social expectations.[30]

[27] Foreign and Commonwealth Office, *The Conference on Security and Cooperation in Europe, 1972–1975*, G. Bennett and K. A. Hamilton, eds., Documents on British Policy Overseas, Series 3, Vol. 2 (London: Her Majesty's Stationery Office, 1997), 51 (hereafter cited as FCO, *The Conference*).

[28] See various documents in FCO, *The Conference*.

[29] Ibid., 41.

[30] One interview source asserts that the "freer movement" formula originated in a Nixon administration attempt, through the U.S. Information

44   CHAPTER ONE

RESISTANCE BY THE SUPERPOWERS

Despite the growing commitment of the European Community, the two superpowers and their respective alliances were not anxious to open the East-West agenda to human rights issues. For one thing, both blocs included regimes whose political stability dictated resisting the internationalization of human rights issues. Besides the Soviet Union and allied Communist regimes in Eastern Europe, whose official ideologies and legal codes were largely inconsistent with individual liberties, two NATO members (Greece and Portugal) and one close ally (Spain) were ruled by military dictatorships with poor human rights records during this period.[31] In addition, in the United States neither President Richard Nixon nor National Security Advisor Henry Kissinger believed at the time that human rights was a legitimate subject for international diplomacy. To understand the resulting political dynamics among the Western states, one must compare EC proposals and statements to what NATO was and was not saying or doing during this period.

Unlike the EC's growing interest in establishing human rights as an international norm, the "freer movement" proposals recently introduced by Belgium did not challenge either the Nixon/Kissinger outlook on diplomacy or the vested interests of southern European dictatorships that already permitted foreign media and were anxious to expand tourism revenue.[32] As a result, NATO's December 1969 Declaration on East-West

---

Agency, to prevent the conference from being held by tabling an issue that the Soviets would probably refuse to discuss, and that the EC states then struggled to make it substantive and diplomatically viable. No other evidence has been found to support the American pedigree of the proposal; another interview source specifically rejects this account. In either case, as explained elsewhere in this and the following chapter, the United States did little to advance the human rights agenda until very late in the CSCE negotiations.

[31] Despite the repressiveness of the Franco dictatorship, Spain was linked to NATO through a 1953 mutual defense pact with the United States.

[32] One noteworthy exception was the Greek junta's reluctance to endorse the freer movement of people, which they feared would require them to open their borders to "communist" immigrants from the East.

Relations incorporated Belgium's proposal to the IPU, suggesting that "mutual benefit and understanding . . . could be achieved by freer movement of people, ideas and information." Finally, it stipulated that the conference could not be held without full participation by the United States and Canada, substantial progress on Germany and particularly Berlin, and the opening of MBFR talks. The declaration also stated that the success of an eventual conference would require consensus on the basic principles of territorial integrity, nonintervention, and the right of self-determination, but made no mention of human rights per se.[33] Human rights were also not mentioned in NATO's communiqués of May or December 1970.[34]

Regardless of the difference between the EC and NATO positions, the West's growing interest in addressing human rights issues at the security conference raised concerns in Moscow and other East-bloc capitals, where détente was viewed primarily as a means to consolidate domestic support for the political status quo. The Soviet leadership "knew that the country was in a difficult position," remembers long-serving Soviet ambassador to the U.S. Anatoly Dobrynin: "The Soviet economy was stagnant. Famous dissidents were emerging. . . . Underground samizdat publications showed that discontent was growing among our educated classes. . . . The party establishment gradually began to realize the need to satisfy the population's basic requirements more fully and to narrow the gap with the West in technology and the economy itself."[35] The improvement of relations with the United States and Western Europe was thus increasingly seen as an indispensable part of

[33] "Declaration of the North Atlantic Council Adopted during the Brussels Council Meeting on the 4th and 5th of December 1969," in Selected Documents, 64–67.

[34] See "Extracts from the Communiqué of the North Atlantic Council Meeting in Rome on the 26th and 27th of May 1970," and "Extracts from the Communiqué of the North Atlantic Council meeting in Brussels on the 3rd and 4th of December 1970," in Selected Documents, 73–76, 86–90.

[35] Anatoly Dobrynin, In Confidence: Moscow's Ambassador to America's Six Cold War Presidents (1962–1986) (New York: Random House, 1995), 217–18.

any solution to these problems of economic productivity and political legitimacy.

This did not involve, however, any fundamental rethinking of the relationship between the party-state and the society it ruled. According to Dobrynin, the Soviet leadership "was not prepared to set about solving the country's domestic problems by offering a measure of political or economic liberalization. Dissidents were considered enemies of the regime, and authors who published their works abroad were subjected to reprisals. Nonconformity was still frowned upon. In short, our dogmatic domestic ideology remained unchanged."[36] Any Western attempt to make détente a mechanism for upsetting the status quo thus directly contradicted Soviet motivations for improved relations.

In a May 1970 speech in Kessel, West German chancellor Willy Brandt nonetheless repeated that improved East-West relations required freer movement of people, ideas, and information. The following month, hoping to move things along before they lost control of the agenda, Warsaw Pact foreign ministers formally accepted U.S. and Canadian participation in the conference, and agreed to discuss conventional force reductions—though at the conference rather than in parallel MBFR talks, as NATO had requested. In an effort to limit the West's "free movement" foray to official cultural exchanges, the Warsaw Pact ministers revived their earlier offer to include "cultural ties" as part of the conference agenda. Finally, they proposed the creation of a permanent multilateral mechanism for European security.[37]

Meanwhile, détente proceeded at the bilateral level, as well. The Soviet Union became more flexible in its bilateral talks with West Germany, and thereby achieved a treaty resolving all major outstanding issues between the two countries, including the non-use of force and the inviolability of present borders.

[36] Ibid., 218.
[37] "Extracts from a Memorandum Approved by the Warsaw Pact Ministerial Meeting at Budapest on the 21st and 22nd of June 1970," in *Selected Documents*, 77.

Poland signed a similar treaty with Germany in December 1970, and Czechoslovakia also initiated talks. In separate negotiations, the Soviets also agreed to maintain the Four Power Rights and Responsibilities arrangement for Berlin. In September and October 1971, Willy Brandt visited the Soviet Union, Leonid Brezhnev visited Paris, and the United States and the Soviet Union signed agreements to reduce the risk of nuclear war and to improve "hot-line" communications between their leaders. By satisfying many of the leading diplomatic objectives of the Soviet Union and its allies, the bilateral treaties reduced the Eastern bloc's vulnerability to whatever new issues, such as human rights, the West might bring to the table.

This flurry of diplomatic activity also increased public pressure on Western governments to participate in a comprehensive security conference. In December 1971, NATO ministers proposed that the conference agenda be divided into four areas of discussion: "(A) Questions of Security, including Principles Governing Relations between States and certain military aspects of security; (B) Freer Movement of People, Information and Ideas, and Cultural Relations; (C) Co-operation in the Fields of Economics, Applied Science and Technology, and Pure Science; and (D) Co-operation to Improve the Human Environment."[38] Although human rights was again not mentioned by NATO as basic principle, the continued insistence on "freer movement" continued to raise concerns in the East.

In response, the Warsaw Pact proposed seven fundamental principles of European security and relations among States in Europe, including "mutually advantageous contacts among States." The body of the proposal aimed to develop contacts "in the economic, scientific, technological and cultural fields, as well as in the fields of tourism and protection of the human environment," but its phrasing expressed a fundamentally statist conception of such contacts. In particular, the opening phrase "In the conditions of peace, various mutually advanta-

[38] "Extracts from the Communiqué of the North Atlantic Council Meeting in Brussels on the 9th and 10th of December 1971," in *Selected Documents*, 104–7.

geous contacts among European States must develop" suggested that such contacts would be orchestrated by states, when they suited the interests of those states, and when they served the overriding goal of peace, presumably as defined by those very states with the right to veto any contacts. In other words, transborder contacts would remain under tight state control.

Nonetheless, the United States government continued to downplay the human rights issue. During Congressional hearings about the prospective security conference, from April through August 1972, State Department officials were silent on the issues of human contacts and human rights, and members of Congress expressed no interest in the subject.[39] At the Moscow summit of May 1972, Richard Nixon and Leonid Brezhnev signed a U.S.–Soviet Basic Principles Agreement that directly contradicted the logic of institutionalizing human rights at the international level. As the first principle of the agreement explained, "Differences in ideology and in the social systems of the USA and the USSR are not obstacles to the bilateral development of normal relations based on the principles of sovereignty, equality, noninterference in internal affairs and mutual advantage." The third principle declared likewise that the two superpowers "will seek to promote conditions in which all countries will live in peace and security and will not be subject to outside interference in their internal affairs."[40] Nixon repeated the noninterference theme in an address televised throughout the Soviet Union during the summit: "The only sound basis for a peaceful and progressive international order is sovereign equality and mutual respect. We believe in the right of each nation to chart its own course, to choose its own system, to go its own way, without interference from other nations."[41]

[39] U.S. House of Representatives, Committee on Foreign Affairs, *Conference on European Security*, Hearings, April 25; May 10; August 10, 17; September 7, 27, 1972 (Washington, D.C.: U.S. Government Printing Office, 1972).

[40] John J. Maresca, *To Helsinki: The Conference on Security and Cooperation in Europe, 1973–1975* (Durham: Duke University Press, 1987), 157.

[41] Ibid., 12.

In keeping with this approach, American diplomats invited by the EC for consultations in Brussels about the security conference were instructed by the State Department to focus on procedural matters rather than on revising the basic principles of East-West relations. This public and private commitment to "non-interference" frustrated America's allies in the EC, who remained committed to adding human rights issues to the agenda.[42]

By mid-1972, the only remaining obstacle to the conference was NATO's continuing insistence that the CSCE and MBFR talks open concurrently. Anxious to get the conference started before new prerequisites were imposed or new items added to the agenda, Moscow relented in September and agreed to a rough timetable whereby both the CSCE and MBFR talks would be held "in some related time frame."[43] With all its key prerequisites (Berlin, inter-German relations, and MBFR) satisfied, NATO finally agreed. All sides then accepted a Finnish offer dating back to May 1969 to host the conference and the preparatory talks.[44]

HUMAN RIGHTS AS A FORMAL EUROPEAN NORM

As the EC's preparations for the security conference intensified, so did its commitment to making human rights not just an area of substantive cooperation but also a fundamental norm of relations among all European states, including the Communist bloc. In March 1971, frustrated by NATO's failure to mention human rights, much less to develop concrete proposals in this area, the EC Political Committee reversed its earlier decision to let the alliance handle "political" aspects of conference plan-

[42] Ibid., 157.
[43] *Selected Documents*, 16.
[44] Luigi Vittorio Ferraris, ed., *Report on a Negotiation: Helsinki, Geneva, Helsinki: 1972–1975*, translated by Marie-Claire Barber (Alphen a/d Rijn: Sijthoff & Noordhoff, 1979), 9.

ning, including the normative agenda, and created an interministerial subcommittee for this purpose.[45] In May, they established an ad hoc working group to handle economic aspects of the CSCE with participation by representatives of the European Commission.[46] The two committees worked intensively through the spring and summer of 1972 to develop a comprehensive EC approach to the conference agenda and to decide how EC decision making would proceed during the negotiations. In the process, a British diplomat observed "a growing political consensus among the members of the enlarged Community, born of a natural feeling of shared interest and coming alive in the workings of the Davignon committee."[47]

As they deliberated, participants in the committee were keenly aware that the national constitutions of the member states were all based on democratic norms of free expression, representative government, and the rule of law. As members of the Council of Europe, all EC states were also bound by the 1950 European Convention for the Protection of Human Rights and Fundamental Freedoms, which guaranteed a broad list of rights reinforced by a European Commission of Human Rights with broad investigative powers and a European Court of Human Rights with binding juridical authority.[48] Since the 1962 Birkelbach Report to the European Parliament, and especially since the 1967 Greek crisis, the EC itself had identified democracy and respect for human rights as prerequisites to membership in the Community.[49] As a result, Greece, Portugal, and Spain had been clearly told that they would not be accepted

[45] Gotz von Groll, correspondence to the author, June 3 and 10, 1999.

[46] Groll, "The Nine at the Conference," 64.

[47] FCO, *The Conference*, 35. Note that the unofficial "Davignon committee" had been officially renamed the Political Committee two years earlier, in 1970.

[48] As no East European or Communist states belonged to the Council of Europe at this time, its human rights norms were not authoritative for relations between Eastern and Western Europe.

[49] For the text of the Birkelbach Report, see European Parliament Working Papers, January 15, 1962, Document 122. On Europe and the Greek military junta, see Van Coufoudakis, "The European Economic Community and the 'Freezing' of the Greek Association, 1967–1974," *Journal of Common Market Studies* 16 (December 1977):114–31.

into the EC as long as they were ruled by authoritarian regimes. Although the prospective security conference was never conceived as an enlarged EC, it could not be separated from this conception of European political identity. Consensus thus developed within the EC Political Committee that if the East Europeans truly wanted normal relations with the West, they would have to accept, at least in principle, those norms which both the European Community and the Council of Europe considered integral to European identity.[50]

Within the EC structure, the CSCE subcommittee and ad hoc group worked intensively through early and mid-1972 preparing joint proposals for the conference. Among these was the proposal that the conference subcommittee on Proposals Guiding Relations between the Participants "shall pay special attention to the principles of . . . respect for human rights, for fundamental freedoms and for equal rights and self-determination of peoples."[51] (This language paralleled the 1950 European convention discussed above, which only applied to members of the Council of Europe.) As a signal of EC intentions, a West German foreign ministry official involved in these consultations published an article predicting that human rights and self-determination would be included among the basic principles of the conference.[52] In mid-November, just days before the start of Multilateral Preparatory Talks near Helsinki, the foreign ministers of the Nine met in The Hague and approved the Political Committee's comprehensive proposal for the security conference, including the principle of human rights. The emphasis on human rights originally expressed by the European Community as a key aspect of its internal identity was thus externalized in the Community's approach to relations with the eastern half of the continent.

The EC's suggestion that the protection of human rights is not only a state's obligation to its subjects but also a legitimate issue in relations among states reached well beyond previous

---

[50] Étienne Davignon, interview by author, Brussels, January 12, 1996.
[51] This text was later submitted officially as CSCE/HC/18.
[52] Gotz von Groll, "East-West Talks," *Aussenpolitik* 23 (1972):376.

Western statements on the security conference agenda, as well as accepted norms of diplomatic practice at the time. As mentioned above, the 1948 Universal Declaration of Human Rights spoke of states' obligations to individuals under their control, but not of obligations to other states. The two International Covenants on Human Rights, opened for signature in 1966, lacked the ratifications necessary to come into force, and even they provided no enforcement mechanism unless the signatory state also accepted an Optional Protocol. Most recently, the United Nations' 1970 Declaration on Principles of Friendly Relations among States had recognized non-intervention without making any mention of human rights. By proposing "respect for human rights and fundamental freedoms" as one of the basic principles of relations among European states, the EC was moving to break down the distinction between norms for how states should treat individuals and norms for relations between states.

At the NATO summit in Brussels in early December, the EC foreign ministers discussed their position with the other members of the alliance.[53] The American, Greek, Portuguese, and Spanish governments remained uncomfortable with the idea of establishing respect for human rights as a basic norm of relations among European states, although NATO's own formal norms made a complete rejection untenable. The resulting compromise was reflected in the NATO council's decision to endorse the EC position in private session while issuing a public communiqué that simply repeated the importance of pursuing the "freer movement of people, ideas and information," and declared their "resolve to bring about closer and more harmonious relationships, collectively and individually, among all peoples."[54] EC representatives then visited the capitals of the neutral and non-aligned states of Europe to explain their new agenda, which won immediate approval. The Soviets, however,

[53] EC member Ireland was neutral, and thus not a member of NATO, so its foreign minister was not involved in these talks.

[54] North Atlantic Council, *Texts of Final Communiques, 1949-1974* (Brussels: NATO Information Service, 1975), 282.

were upset by this EC initiative, both because they disliked the content of the proposal and because they preferred to manage the conference agenda bilaterally with Washington.[55]

Back at the Multilateral Preparatory Talks (or Helsinki Consultations), however, the EC itself could not make proposals. The Community's position was thus presented officially on January 15, 1973, by three EC member states. Belgium, representing the presidency of the EC at the time, offered document CSCE/HC/17, a proposal for the structure of the conference, plus a mandate for cooperation on economics and the environment; Italy offered CSCE/HC/18, a proposal for the basic principles guiding relations among participating states, and for measures aimed at strengthening confidence and stability in Europe; and Denmark offered CSCE/HC/19, a proposal for cooperation in humanitarian issues, including the development of human contacts, wider flow of information, and broadening of cultural and educational exchanges.[56] The course of negotiations within the CSCE that transformed these EC proposals into actual European norms are analyzed in the following chapter.

CONCLUSIONS

This account of the background to the Conference on Security and Cooperation in Europe demonstrates, primarily, the absence of anything resembling a human rights norm in trans-European or East-West relations through the 1960s and early 1970s. The Soviet Union and its Communist allies in Eastern Europe repeatedly rejected human rights as a legitimate issue for international relations, whereas several Western states, including the United States, were reluctant to place the issue on the trans-European agenda. Human rights became part of the trans-European agenda only through the initiative of the Euro-

---

[55] Gotz von Groll, correspondence to author, May 20, 1999.

[56] See also the *Times* (London), January 16, 1973, and January 19, 1973, *Le Monde* (Paris), January 17, 1973.

pean Community, which introduced it first as a topic for substantive East-West cooperation, and later as a basic principle of relations among European states. The EC's reasons for insisting on the human rights agenda, as well as other issues related to the sources of international norms, are discussed at greater length in the final chapter.

CHAPTER TWO

Negotiating Human Rights in the Helsinki Final Act

[The Helsinki Final Act represents] nothing else but an
ambitious attempt to define collectively a "good conduct
code" for the relations of 35 countries with different
social systems.
—*West German diplomat Gotz von Groll, 1974*[1]

They can write it in Swahili for all I care.
—*U.S. Secretary of State Henry Kissinger, 1974*[2]

WHEN formal negotiations for a Conference on Security and
Cooperation in Europe began in November 1972, respect for
human rights was not yet recognized as a trans-European norm.
As described in the previous chapter, the European Community
had proposed in 1969 that such a conference promote the "freer
movement of people, ideas and information," and in late 1972
that it establish respect for human rights as a basic principle for
relations among European states. The latter proposal contradicted prevailing international norms; both contradicted the
rhetoric and practice of many states participating in the CSCE.
In addition to repressive regimes in Eastern Europe and the
Mediterranean, which had an obvious interest in preventing
recognition of human rights as a European norm, the United
States government was reluctant to include the issue on the
East-West agenda.

---

[1] Gotz von Groll, "The Geneva CSCE Negotiations," *Aussenpolitik* 25
(1974): 159–60.

[2] William Burr, ed., *The Kissinger Transcripts: The Top-Secret Talks with Beijing
and Moscow* (New York: New Press, 1998), 326.

The present chapter traces the two-and-a-half-year negotiation leading to the Helsinki Final Act, and focuses on the diplomatic process by which thirty-five states with vastly divergent identities, interests, and practices accepted "Respect for human rights and fundamental freedoms, including the freedom of thought, conscience, religion or belief" as one of ten Principles Guiding Relations Between Participating States, as well as a number of concrete measures to expand humanitarian cooperation under "Basket III" of the CSCE. It demonstrates that both the European Community (with nine member states at this time) and the Communist bloc (the Soviet Union and six Warsaw Pact allies) devoted great care and considerable political capital to crafting these new norms and cooperation mandates in a manner that suited their respective preferences. To legitimate their claims, all sides emphasized some preexisting norms and ignored others. At the same time, institutional rules and the appeal of shared identities exerted significant effects on the outcome of the negotiations.

SETTING THE CSCE'S NORMATIVE AGENDA

The Multilateral Preparatory Talks (MPT) for a Conference on Security and Co-operation, held intermittently in Dipoli, Finland, from November 22, 1972, through June 8, 1973, constituted the first postwar meeting of all the states in Europe (except Albania), the first meeting of the two military alliances together with the neutral and nonaligned states, and the first time that the two Germanies had participated openly and jointly in an international meeting.[3] The EC's proposals on

---

[3] For various perspectives on the MPT, see Luigi Vittorio Ferraris, *Report on a Negotiation: Helsinki, Geneva, Helsinki: 1972–1975*, translated by Marie-Claire Barber (Alphen aan den Rijn: Sijthoff & Noordhoff, 1979), 9–40; Ljubivoje Acimovic, *Problems of Security and Cooperation* (Alphen aan den Rijn: Sijthoff & Noordhoff, 1981) 111–23; FCO, *The Conference*, 1–151; Gotz von Groll, "East-West Talks," *Aussenpolitik* 23 (1972): 513–24; Gotz von Groll, "The Helsinki Consultations," *Aussenpolitik* 24 (1973):123–29; François Carle, "Les

"freer movement" and human rights were thus designed to shape the MPT's agenda or mandate for the full-fledged conference, where actual negotiations on European norms would occur. The scope (but not the intensity) of East-West disagreement on human rights and human contacts was reduced only by a consensus that debate on the definition of the principles (as opposed to the titles) would be postponed until the actual conference.

Since earlier in 1972, when the EC's intention to pursue agreement on human rights and contacts became clear, East-bloc leaders and political commentators had criticized it as an unacceptable intervention in internal affairs that undermined the intended purposes of the multilateral conference.[4] In December, perhaps encouraged by the Basic Principles Agreement that he and President Nixon had recently signed, Leonid Brezhnev emphasized non-interference as the norm that should govern all relations between East and West: "One often hears that the West attaches importance to cooperation in the cultural domain and especially to the exchange of ideas, broader information and contacts between nations. Permit us to declare here in all earnesty: we too are in favour of this if, of course, such cooperation is conducted with due respect for the sovereignty, the laws and the customs of each country.... Briefly, the possibilities here are quite broad if the matter is dealt with in a spirit of mutual respect and non-interference in each other's affairs, and not in a cold-war-spirit."[5] Not surprisingly, this first month of the MPT produced little movement toward an agenda acceptable to all parties.

The stalemate on human rights issues deepened when talks resumed in January 1973, particularly in reaction to Belgium's

---

Pourparlers Exploratoires d'Helsinki," *Études Internationales* 4 (September 1973):297–361, continued *ibid* (December 1973):502–51.

[4] See D. Rovensky, "Europe and Ideological War," *Rude Pravo*, 10 February 1972 (from Radio Free Europe, *Czechoslovak Press Survey* no. 2418); F. Puja, "The European System Hangs in the Balance," *Tarsadalmi Szemle*, September 1972 (from Radio Free Europe, *Hungarian Press Survey* no. 2228).

[5] Cited in Y. Nalin and A. Nikolayev, *The Soviet Union and European Security* (Moscow: Progress Publishers, 1973), 108–9.

presentation of the EC proposal to establish respect for human rights as a basic principle of relations among European states. Following an unscheduled consultation, Warsaw Pact diplomats returned to criticize the West's proposals on human contacts and basic principles. Soviet ambassador Lev Mendelevitch complained that the proposal for freer human contacts and cultural relations had overstepped the limited agenda agreed earlier.[6] Speaking on behalf of the Warsaw Pact, the Polish delegate argued that "all activity in the field of information, of culture and contacts between people must respect the principles of the sovereignty of States, of the non-interference in internal affairs, and the respect for the laws and customs" of individual states. It is the "responsibility of States," he added, to define the "general trends of the activities" in this area.[7] Regarding the basic principles, the Soviet delegation argued that human rights and self-determination were not relevant to relations among European states, and should not be included in a list of basic principles of international conduct.[8]

While the Multilateral Preparatory Talks were taking place in Dipoli, the Inter-Parliamentary Union (IPU) convened a Conference on European Co-operation and Security (IPCECS) in Helsinki from January 26 to 31. Planning for the IPU conference had begun two years earlier, but once convened, it never escaped the shadow of the official talks. According to one observer, "most of the national delegations maintained close contact with their diplomatic counterparts in Dipoli, aware that the tightrope walking in the governmental conference was difficult enough without incursions on the part of the parliamentarians." The head of the Belgian delegation proposed that the IPCECS Final Act should include an explicit reference to the individual rights mentioned in the Universal Declaration of Human

[6] *New York Times*, January 16, 1973, 3; Ferraris, *Report on a Negotiation*, 14–16.

[7] Ferraris, *Report on a Negotiation*, 18.

[8] Ibid., 14–16. The Soviet position on the EC proposal regarding "the equal rights and self-determination of peoples" was that this principle concerned colonial territories, and thus could not be applied to Europe.

Rights, and his Bulgarian counterpart responded that human rights was not a principle of interstate relations.[9]

Back in the MPT, the East bloc recognized that its interests in the conference agenda required more than a purely defensive position. On March 1, the GDR proposed an alternative list of seven basic principles: inviolability of frontiers, territorial integrity, refraining from the use of force, sovereign equality, independence, non-intervention, and the peaceful settlement of disputes. The West immediately refused to accept any formulation that did not include human rights and self-determination.[10] For several months, neither side offered anything approaching a compromise proposal on human rights or human contacts. An East-bloc proposal to subordinate all the principles to the inviolability of frontiers was defeated in favor of an agreement that all principles are equal and should be interpreted in light of each other.[11]

In the end, though, the East bloc was faced with a firm EC commitment that its member states would not agree to participate in a security conference unless they were satisfied with the place of human rights and contacts on the agenda.[12] By this point, the EC position was also supported by the NATO caucus and by four of the neutral states (Austria, Finland, Sweden, and Switzerland). To achieve their long-standing goal of a European security conference, including all the rewards they hoped such a conference would bring, the East bloc would have to allow some space for the West's and neutrals' bottom line. Anxious to convene the conference, and confident that they would be able to compensate for any politically risky commitments, the Soviet Union and its allies slowly moderated their position on various aspects of the conference agenda. This did not mean, however, simply accepting Western proposals.

[9] Jukka Huopaniemi, *Parliaments and European Rapprochement: The Conference of the Inter-Parliamentary Union on European Co-operation and Security* (Helsinki, January 1973) (Leiden: A. W. Sijthoff, 1973), v–vi, 92.
[10] Ferraris, *Report on a Negotiation*, 20.
[11] Groll, "The Helsinki Consultations," 125.
[12] FCO, *The Conference*, 77.

Negotiations on human contacts were very tough, with Moscow determined to prevent the free flow of ideas and information, which they viewed as a threat to Communist hegemony, and the EC determined, as one British diplomat put it, to "squeeze the Russian lemon very hard to demonstrate to public opinion how little juice there is in *détente à la russe*."[13] The ultimate compromise nonetheless reflected a combination of rhetorical maneuvers and substantive concessions by both sides. The gap between the East bloc's preference for improved cultural exchange and the West's preference for freer movement of people, ideas, and information was bridged with the ambiguous phrase "Cooperation in Humanitarian and other Fields," including a mandate for the kinds of cultural and educational exchanges preferred by the East, and for cooperation in other areas valued by the West, such as family reunification, expanded access to print and broadcast media from abroad, and improved working conditions for journalists. The West thus dropped its original insistence on referring to the free movement of ideas, and accepted wording in the remaining areas that was less concrete than they would have liked.

Proposed lists of principles for relations among European states were also subject to heated and detailed negotiation, regarding which principles would be included, in what order, as well as their relative length and their translation in the five equally valid languages of the CSCE. As part of their effort to legitimate the status quo, the Soviets wanted the inviolability of frontiers to be an independent principle. In contrast, the West Germans, Irish, and Spanish originally wanted to link inviolability to the non-use of force, which they believed would protect their commitments, respectively, to East Germany, Northern Ireland, and Gibraltar. The impasse was finally broken by a West German proposal to list the non-use of force before a separate principle on the inviolability of frontiers, and a Soviet agreement to translate "inviolability" not as *rushimost* (meaning

[13] Ibid, 121.

immutability) but as *nenarushimost* (meaning that which may not be violated).[14]

Not surprisingly, the principle of human rights was also subject to detailed and contentious negotiation. In the end, though, "Respect for human rights and fundamental freedoms, including the freedom of thought, conscience, religion, and belief" stood out as the longest and best defined of the ten principles. Uniquely among the ten, it also included an explanatory suffix, the content of which reflected the West's general interest in promoting the freedom of expression and the Vatican's special effort to protect the rights of religious believers.[15] In exchange for this concession, the Soviets succeeded in placing the principle of "non-intervention in internal affairs" ahead of the principle of human rights. Whereas the English text read "non-intervention," which Western negotiators interpreted as permitting human rights monitoring, the Russian-language text drafted by the Soviets used a more restrictive word, generally translated as "non-interference." Given that the East bloc intended to use this principle to protect itself against Western references to the human rights principle, this distinction appeared critical. Above all, though, the Soviet leadership had no reason to believe that the formal norms established by the CSCE would ultimately be any more significant than the Universal Declaration of Human Rights, with which they had already lived for twenty-five years.

The resulting "Final Recommendations of the Helsinki Consultations," agreed on June 8, 1973, contained four chapters (later known as "baskets") and ten basic principles. The four chapters were: I. "Questions Relating to Security in Europe"; II. "Co-operation in the Fields of Economics, of Science and Technology and of the Environment, including Commercial Exchanges, Industrial Co-operation and Projects of Common Interest, Science and Technology, Environment; and Co-operation in Other Areas"; III. "Co-operation in Humanitarian and Other Fields, including Human Contacts, Information, Cul-

---

[14] Ibid, 106–7.
[15] Ferraris, *Report on a Negotiation*, 35.

ture, and Education"; and IV. "Follow-up to the Conference." Within Basket I, the ten basic principles to be negotiated at the conference were: 1. "Sovereign equality, respect for the rights inherent in sovereignty"; 2. "Refraining from the threat or use of force"; 3. "Inviolability of frontiers"; 4. "Territorial integrity of States"; 5. "Peaceful settlement of disputes"; 6. "Non-intervention in internal affairs"; 7. "Respect for human rights and fundamental freedoms, including freedom of thought, conscience, religion or belief"; 8. "Equal rights and self-determination of peoples"; 9. "Co-operation among States"; and 10. "Fulfillment in good faith of obligations under international law."[16]

The Dipoli preparatory talks also determined that the CSCE would occur in three stages: a foreign ministers' meeting in Helsinki to open the process; a working conference in Geneva to draft agreements based on the Final Recommendations; and then another meeting in Helsinki to close the conference. The Soviets had pushed for prior agreement that stage 3 would be a summit of heads of state, but the West held out in the hope that the Kremlin's desire for a high-profile finish would make it more forthcoming in substantive negotiations. It was thus agreed that the level of representation at stage 3 would be decided during stage 2, presumably depending upon what was accomplished there.

A final issue addressed at Dipoli was the question of what ongoing multilateral institution for European security, if any, would follow the CSCE itself. The Soviet Union had favored a trans-European security institution since the early 1950s, when it hoped that such a mechanism might replace NATO and weaken American influence on the continent, and Moscow still hoped that a multilateral security institution might give it a legitimate voice (in diplomatic terms, a *droit de regard*) in West European affairs. For this same reason, the West was suspicious of such proposals. On the other hand, if Moscow had concluded that accepting "respect for human rights" as a CSCE principle

---

[16] For the complete text, see John J. Maresca, *To Helsinki: The Conference on Security and Cooperation in Europe, 1973–1975* (Durham: Duke University Press, 1987), Appendix 1.

was unavoidable, then a permanent and effective CSCE body would have been less attractive. This may explain why Czechoslovakia's proposal (on behalf of the Warsaw Pact) was limited to a consultative committee that would simply convene future conferences and expert meetings. The Western states rejected it anyway, insisting that substantial progress in the regular talks must precede any follow-up commitments.[17] In the end, the conferees agreed to keep the door open to "such measures as may be required to give effect to the decisions of the Conference and to further the process of improving security and developing co-operation in Europe."

Notwithstanding some victories for the East, the official agenda for a conference on European security thus reflected Western preferences, including the original EC proposals on human rights and contacts, far more than the Communist bloc had ever intended. Still unknown, though, was whether or not the resulting agenda would really matter once negotiations began in the actual conference.

FRAMING THE CSCE'S NORMATIVE AGENDA

Officially, the meeting of CSCE foreign ministers at Helsinki on July 3–7, 1973, was a largely formal exercise to adopt the Final Recommendations drafted at Dipoli and call for substantive negotiations in Geneva. In practice, though, the meeting was an intensely political exercise in continued agenda setting through normative framing. All parties had made concessions that needed to be justified. More important, they had agreed to indeterminate normative texts that could advance or undermine their interests, depending upon which interpretation triumphed in the negotiations at Geneva and in the public mind. The speeches of the foreign ministers thus provide insight into

[17] *Selected Documents*, 18; Gotz von Groll, "The Foreign Ministers in Helsinki," *Aussenpolitik* 24 (1973): 270–71.

their goals, concerns, and understanding of the European normative bargain emerging through the CSCE.[18]

Notwithstanding the host's obligation to be neutral, Finnish president Urho Kekkonen's opening remarks at the foreign ministers' meeting took a clear position in this brewing interpretive battle: "Security is not gained by erecting fences," he said, but "by opening gates." The British foreign secretary, Sir Alec Douglas-Home, commented that Kekkonen's remark should be the motto of the conference.[19] Not surprisingly, though, East-bloc representatives were not ready to cede the field. The Soviet foreign minister, Andrei Gromyko, immediately countered that détente was based fundamentally on recognition of the political and territorial status quo. Notwithstanding the Dipoli agreement on the equality of all ten basic principles, he specifically argued that the territorial integrity of states and non-interference in internal affairs must take precedence, even on Basket III issues.

All of the East European foreign ministers echoed Gromyko's remarks, though sometimes in a different tone. Hungarian foreign minister Janos Péter, for example, expressed his government's commitment to "expanding the cultural relations of European countries and the interchange of information and in promoting the freer movement of persons and ideas." His reference to the freer movement of "ideas," which had been rejected in the preparatory talks, was a gesture to the West that reflected Hungary's relatively liberal policy on cultural expression. On the other hand, his warning that "if anywhere we have to join forces against the remnants of the cold war it is just in this area," and his conclusion, "We have to take mutually into account the laws, customs, and regulations of our countries," reflected the limits on change in the East bloc.

Other East European foreign ministers emphasized the CSCE's potential contribution to expanding economic, scientific, and technological ties between East and West. Polish for-

[18] *Conference on Security and Cooperation in Europe: Stage 1—Helsinki, Verbatim Records, July 3–7, 1973,* CSCE/I/PV.1.

[19] Groll, "Foreign Ministers in Helsinki," 267.

eign minister Stepfan Olszowski suggested that the CSCE could "give impetus to all-European economic, technological, and scientific co-operation" in trade, industrial cooperation, raw material projects, power systems, transportation networks, agriculture, and the environment. Czechoslovakia's foreign minister added the "joint solution of problems" relating to fuel, engineering, chemistry, shipping, container transport, and communications to the mounting agenda. For these states, the CSCE obviously held the promise of far more than a ratification of the status quo.

The extreme sensitivity of the CSCE agenda was nonetheless brought home to Western delegations later that summer, when the Kremlin renewed its crackdown on the small dissident and samizdat literature movement in the Soviet Union just as the Geneva talks were about to begin. In late August, two members of a small Moscow human rights group were sentenced to imprisonment and internal exile for anti-Soviet activities. One week later, the Communist Party newspaper *Pravda* published a restatement of the Soviet position on cultural exchanges at the CSCE, combined with a polemical portrait of well-known dissidents Andrei Sakharov and Aleksandr Solzhenitsyn as traitors to the nation.[20] Given the very small number of active dissidents and human rights campaigners in the Soviet Union in this period, the timing of this crackdown against them makes sense only as a deliberate demonstration before domestic and foreign audiences of the Kremlin's determination, also voiced by Gromyko at the foreign ministers' meeting, that it would not be constrained by human rights norms in the CSCE.

Confidential correspondence about these incidents among British diplomats reflects the lack of agreement among West European officials on whether, and if so how, individual violations of human rights should affect the course of détente. The British ambassador in Moscow advised Foreign Secretary

---

[20] Ferraris, *Report on a Negotiation*, 299–300; FCO, *The Conference*, 176–79; Ludmilla Alexeyeva, *Soviet Dissent: Contemporary Movements for National, Religious and Human Rights* (Middletown, Conn.: Wesleyan University Press, 1987), 318–30.

Douglas-Home that a firm response was necessary to maintain credibility in the East: "If the West goes ahead with the CSCE as if nothing had happened and ends up accepting minimal concessions under Basket III in return for letting the Russians have more or less what they want under Basket I, it will appear here and throughout Eastern Europe that we have ignored the challenge and come to terms with the newly revealed 'ugly face' of communism."

In contrast, the head of the British delegation in Geneva, obviously more focused on the progress of the CSCE, advised against inflaming the issue. "It certainly would be a pity if we got involved in fighting a propogandist battle over current events instead of pressing steadily for the sort of long-term improvements in the situation which Dipoli encouraged us to think were desirable and possibly attainable." In turn, the foreign secretary's response emphasized that the success of détente depended upon satisfying domestic expectations in the West: "We may have to make it plain to the Russians that the Western negotiators operate within the framework of public opinion and that any further action against Soviet dissidents might seriously prejudice the atmosphere for the CSCE as a whole."[21] All agreed that human rights belonged on the East-West agenda, but this was not the last time that a crackdown in the East would provoke debate in Western political circles about how to be true to the cause of human rights while maintaining a constructive dialogue with repressive Communist regimes.

NEGOTIATING THE NEW EUROPEAN NORMS

When the second stage of the CSCE opened in Geneva in mid-September 1973, it was immediately apparent that the negotiations would be hotly contested.[22] The titles of the CSCE's basic

---

[21] FCO, *The Conference*, 178–79.

[22] Firsthand accounts of the Geneva talks include Maresca, *To Helsinki*; Ferraris, *Report on a Negotiation*; and Groll, "The Geneva CSCE Negotiations,"

principles and substantive baskets had been agreed at Helsinki, but the text that would define them remained to be negotiated. Swiss ambassador Rudolf Bindschedler warned his colleagues, "Attention, Messieurs, le diable est dans les détails," referring both to the difficulty of achieving agreement and to the adverse consequences of an agreement that did not suit one's goals.[23] And just as he predicted, stalemates were created and broken again and again during the talks by the slightest reformulation of a phrase. As demonstrated below, this was especially true of the "central political compromise" of the CSCE: the trade-off between non-intervention, primarily Principle 6, and human rights, including both Principle 7 and Basket III.[24]

The MPT Final Recommendations stipulated that all CSCE decisions would be taken by consensus, defined as the "absence of any objection expressed by a Representative and submitted as constituting an obstacle to the taking of the decision in question." By denying the possibility of majority rule, the consensus requirement permitted the parties to engage sensitive topics confident in the knowledge that they could block any agreement they found unfavorable. Finally, the Helsinki Recommendations had stipulated that "All States participating in the Conference shall do so as sovereign and independent States and in conditions of full equality. The Conference will take place outside of military alliances." This explicit disavowal of alliance obligations was designed to promote a certain degree of independence for those smaller states that wished to stake out an independent position on particular issues. It appealed as well to the neutral and non-aligned countries, who valued a forum devoted, as they saw it, "to rectifying cold war distor-

---

Aussenpolitik 25 (1974):158–65. All official proposals made at the conference are available in the twenty-three-volume collection, Igor I. Kavass, et al., eds., *Human Rights, European Politics, and the Helsinki Accord: The Documentary Evolution of the Conference on Security and Co-operation in Europe, 1973–1975* (Buffalo, N.Y.: William S. Hein, 1981). For background on EC, NATO, and especially British planning, see FCO, *The Conference*.

[23] Ferraris, *Report on a Negotiation*, 299.

[24] Maresca, *To Helsinki*, 133.

tions, especially bloc divisions and inequities in international relations."[25]

Eastern and Western states nonetheless consulted regularly among themselves throughout the Geneva talks. On the Eastern side, the seven Warsaw Pact states generally acted as a "highly co-ordinated group, with a formal division of labour."[26] So even where Hungary or Poland may have preferred a more liberal line, such as in Basket III, Moscow left them little room to maneuver. Except for Romania, the East European diplomats at Geneva were effectively subordinated to their Soviet counterparts in each working group, clearing official proposals in advance and even introducing some on behalf of the Soviets. Every proposal or response made at the working level was cleared through Moscow, often through multiple centers of power, including the Foreign Ministry, the KGB, and often the Politburo.[27] Some East European diplomats used private or off-the-record contacts to express disagreement with the Warsaw Pact position, but Western diplomats generally viewed such communications as cynical attempts to convince them that the advancement of human rights and human contacts would be best served by a softer negotiating position.

Reflecting the importance that Moscow attached to formal norms of interstate relations, the Soviet Union assumed primary responsibility for proposals on Basket I. Meanwhile, East Germany and Hungary took on economics, science, technology, and the environment (Basket II); Poland and Bulgaria took on humanitarian and cultural affairs (Basket III); and Czechoslovakia handled follow-on procedures, including the East

---

[25] Acimovic, *Problems of Security and Cooperation*, 139.

[26] Kalevi J. Holsti, "Who Got What and How: The CSCE Negotiations in Retrospect," in Robert Spencer, ed., *Canada and the Conference on Security and Cooperation in Europe* (Toronto: Centre for International Studies, 1984), 145.

[27] For general discussion of the Soviet negotiating style in the CSCE, see Maresca, *To Helsinki*, 55–63. According to Stuart Parrott, " 'We Have Started Something . . .': The Origins of the Helsinki Final Act," (OSCE Newsletter 2:8 (July/August 1995), 6–7, Soviet negotiator Anatoly Kovalev confirms in his memoirs that every concession on Basket III was approved in advance by KGB director Yuri Andropov.

bloc's proposal for a permanent pan-European organization. The fact that Poland and Bulgaria were assigned to take the lead on Basket III does not mean, however, that Moscow lost control of those issues. Early in the talks, KGB director Yuri Andropov sent Sergei Kondrachev to Geneva to investigate the status of the negotiations and the range of possible concessions. When Kondrachev returned to Moscow and reported to Andropov, he was promptly assigned as a permanent member of the Soviet delegation to Geneva, with special responsibility for Basket III and instructions to permit only those concessions necessary to achieve Soviet objectives in other areas.[28] The KGB presumably exercised at least as much oversight on Principle 7, as well.

There were two overlapping caucuses on the Western side: one for the nine member states of the European Community, and one for the fifteen members of NATO. Unlike the East bloc, though, the Western camp was not united under the strong leadership of a superpower strongly committed to the CSCE and willing and able to impose its agenda. The nine EC member states were externally united in their commitment to human rights and contacts, and had agreed that none would make a proposal, in any area, to which another member state had objected. Within the EC caucus, though, the Nine sometimes disagreed among themselves over priorities within and among the CSCE baskets. For example, France was particularly interested in cultural contacts and educational exchanges, whereas Britain wanted to emphasize the freer flow of information and better working conditions for journalists. The Dutch were notoriously the most hard-line negotiators on questions of human rights, which led them to clash sometimes with West Germany, which was very interested in promoting human contacts, especially family reunification, but generally tended to prefer a non-confrontational approach.[29]

---

[28] These events were revealed years later by a member of the Soviet delegation to the Geneva talks, according to Edouard Brunner, interview by author, Paris, March 10, 1994.

[29] Canadian Department of External Affairs reports cited in Holsti, "Who Got What and How," 143.

The NATO group included the EC members (minus Ireland), plus Canada, Greece, Portugal, Turkey, and the United States. In official sessions, the NATO and EC groups always presented a united front. In closed caucus meetings, though, the EC-Nine often disagreed with the other NATO members, especially the United States. Under Nixon and Kissinger, the U.S. government was more interested in Vietnam, nuclear arms control, and the Arab-Israeli conflict than in the details of the Geneva negotiations. Its strategy for the CSCE was therefore to maintain allied unity and conclude the talks quickly without disrupting détente or making major concessions. According to a member of the U.S. delegation, Washington's unwritten instructions were clear: support the NATO allies, but do not confront the Soviets.[30] As a result, the U.S. delegation generally followed NATO caucus decisions rather than taking the initiative, even in areas where the United States might naturally have taken a strong interest, such as family reunification.

The neutral and non-aligned states—principally Austria, Finland, Malta, Sweden, Switzerland, and Yugoslavia—often met as well in a separate NNA caucus. Except for Yugoslavia, they tended to side with the West on human rights and contacts. At several critical moments in the talks, though, NNA states introduced proposals that allowed the Warsaw Pact and NATO/EC groups to reach a compromise position.

The first round of negotiations at Geneva lasted from September to December 1973. On behalf of their respective caucuses, France (NATO), the USSR (Warsaw Pact), and Yugoslavia (NNA) proposed texts for each of the ten principles agreed at Helsinki, and other countries submitted additional drafts on principles of particular concern. As foreshadowed by the foreign ministers' summit in July, however, these proposals reflected widely divergent perceptions of what the individual principles meant and how they should relate to each other and to preexisting international norms. "In [the ensuing] discussion, which sometimes turned into acrimonious polemics, such con-

---

[30] Guy Coriden, interview by author, Washington, D.C., March 31, 1994; Maresca, *To Helsinki*, 45; Ferraris, *Report on a Negotiation*, 302.

flicting viewpoints were expressed and the negotiating positions were so wide apart that the differences appeared insurmountable," recalls a Yugoslav diplomat.[31]

The most contentious of these principles at Geneva, as it had been at Helsinki, was Principle 7, "Respect for human rights and fundamental freedoms." From the Soviet perspective, it was an unwelcome addition to a conference originally conceived to address geopolitical, and perhaps economic, affairs. Unlike the other parts of the agenda, where they had their own preferred outcomes, the Soviets and most of their allies would have preferred to drop this issue entirely. The Soviets thus worked consistently to narrow the scope and weaken the authoritativeness of the human rights principle. As forecast by Gromyko's speech at the foreign ministers' meeting, the Soviet delegation's initial proposal at Geneva was to reduce its coverage from the "freedom of thought, conscience, religion and belief" agreed at Helsinki to "freedom of religious belief."

Western delegations, on the other hand, had several reasons for insisting on a broad and determinate definition of the principle. For one thing, given that the EC-Nine's interest in the principle reflected in large part their self-proclaimed identity as a political community committed to human rights, backing away from the MPT text was unimaginable. The August crackdown in the Soviet Union only hardened this resolve. In addition, the West intended to use Principle 7 to resolve disputes in the interpretation and application of humanitarian and cultural agreements under Basket 3. As a West German diplomat explained, "Controversies might occur after the Conference. . . . Should the East then refer to principles which restrict cooperation (sovereignty, non-interference), the West can resist this, as regards file 3 by referring to the principle of human rights; in this respect it has to be very carefully defined."[32] All sides' proposals for Principle 7 were also made in light of prospective formulations for other principles in the decalogue and baskets.

[31] Acimovic, *Problems of Security and Cooperation*, 126.
[32] Groll, "The Geneva CSCE Negotiations," 163.

In contrast with their position on Principle 7, the Soviets were strongly committed to Principle 3, on the inviolability of frontiers, and Principle 6, on non-intervention in internal affairs. If Principle 3 represented the Soviet Union's original goals for the CSCE, Principle 6 represented its reaction to the new parts of the CSCE agenda added by the West. They favored Principle 3 as a means to secure the status of the GDR, prevent German reunification, and perhaps achieve Western recognition of the Soviet Union's annexation of the Baltic states. With Principle 6, the Soviets wanted to achieve a non-intervention formula that would ensure their prerogative over that which they considered to be internal affairs—especially ideology, culture, and human rights—without undermining their self-proclaimed right, under the Brezhnev Doctrine, to prevent the overthrow of allied socialist regimes. At the Helsinki preparatory talks, they had succeeded in establishing the inviolability of frontiers as a principle distinct from the non-use of force, with which it had appeared in the 1970 UN Declaration on Friendly Relations among States. The goal in Geneva was thus to secure their victory with favorable wording.

The West, on the other hand, wanted to formulate the principles so as to make coercive interventions and external subversion illegitimate without weakening the international community's right to monitor and press for compliance with international agreements, including human rights norms.[33] Another key normative debate thus centered on Principle 10, the fulfillment in good faith of international obligations. The Soviets' initial proposal was to limit such obligations to those "undertaken bilaterally or multilaterally, in conformity with the United Nations Charter." By this formula, debates over the obligations imposed by one part of the CSCE could not be resolved through reference to common international law or to non-binding agreements, including other parts of the CSCE. The proposal was thus intended to protect the East bloc from any Western attempt after the conference to use Principle 7 to resolve disputes over the meaning or implementation of Basket III.

[33] Ferraris, *Report on a Negotiation*, 128; Maresca, *To Helsinki*, 131.

Little substantive progress was made during the fall of 1973 on the controversial parts of the decalogue. The Soviet quest to blunt Principle 7 by limiting its suffix to "religious freedom" forced the non-Communist delegations into the ironic position of defending the free profession of atheism and other convictions. At the same time, a number of Western and neutral/non-aligned delegations proposed broader and more determinate texts for Principle 7. Great Britain introduced a new, lengthy draft of Principle 7 that emphasized the freedom of information concerning human rights and the participation of non-governmental bodies and individuals in the promotion of human rights. The Holy See introduced a draft text that recognized the individual's right to enjoy "alone or in community with others" all the substantive rights recognized in the heading of the principle. Switzerland proposed a ban against reprisals that violate human rights, and a ban against arbitrary arrests. Yugoslavia proposed that Principle 7 also recognize the rights of national minority groups.

Recognizing that they would not succeed in replacing the title for Principle 7 established at Helsinki, the Soviets shifted their strategy. Rather than reducing its substantive scope, they sought to weaken its authoritativeness by proposing that it be interpreted "in accordance with the international Pacts of the United Nations on human rights," which contain loosely worded escape clauses relating to the protection of public safety, order, health, or morals.[34] In order to ensure that the principle not pose any challenge to the political hegemony of the party-state, they also rejected all proposals that seemed likely to encourage independent societal initiatives by legitimating the independent exercise of human rights.

Soviet negotiators were just as inflexible on Basket III as they had been on Principle 7, perhaps in response to Foreign Minister Gromyko's reported order to "cut the bottom out of the Third Basket."[35] At first, they attempted to convert Baskets II

[34] States' obligations are limited by the International Covenant on Civil and Political Rights, Art. 18, par. 3, and Art. 19, par. 3; and by the Universal Declaration of Human Rights, Art. 29, par. 1–2.
[35] Stuart Parrott, " 'We Have Started Something,' " 7.

and III into distinct documents that would be signed by lower-ranking officials, rather than by the heads of state who would sign the Declaration of Principles. When the West insisted on a unified document, the Soviets' next position was to work for extensive preambles that would effectively disarm the cooperation baskets by subordinating their implementation to national laws and sovereign prerogative. As part of this strategy, they proposed drafting the preambles before addressing the substantive content of the baskets. Western delegations, on the other hand, wanted to draft the content of the baskets first, and limit the preambles to introductory phrases that would not affect their authoritativeness.[36]

Most of the other East European regimes were concerned, as well, about domestic opposition, and the possibility that concessions on Principle 7 and Basket III would promote such activity. If the East bloc was to accept talks on this unwelcome Western agenda, they would make as few concessions as possible and extract whatever benefit they could in other areas. Here, as elsewhere, they took full advantage of the CSCE's consensus rule, which ensured that no text could be adopted without at least the tacit consent of every participating state. Bulgaria, Czechoslovakia, and the German Democratic Republic thus consistently supported the Soviet Union's hard line. Hungary and Poland sometimes appeared more forthcoming on the freer flow of information, but they too fought hard to limit the official text to information that "strengthens peace and security."[37]

As a result, "Western negotiators became stubborn, and progress was measured in terms of words agreed. Each noun, verb, and adjective was disputed."[38] To increase its leverage, the West obstructed progress on the Declaration on Principles Guiding Relations between Participating States, to which the

[36] J.L.R. Huydecoper, interview by author, The Hague, March 18, 1994.

[37] Ferraris, *Report on a Negotiation*, 301–2; Jeanne Kirk-Laux, "Human Contacts, Information, Culture, and Education," in Spencer, *Canada and the Conference*, 259; Kirk-Laux, "Les Négociations est-ouest: Le rôle des pays d'Europe de l'Est au sein de la Conference sur la Sécurité et la Cooperation en Europe (CSCE)," *Études Internationales* 6 (December 1975):478–500.

[38] Maresca, *To Helsinki*, 124.

East was particularly committed.[39] In a cable to Ottawa, the Canadian ambassador to the CSCE reported: "In almost every substantive field an East-West adversary relationship tends to prevail. There is no increase in mutual confidence. Every proposal is viewed as to how it can be used to bring pressure on the opposing bloc."[40]

In the process, the West Europeans grew frustrated by the low profile of the United States in the talks, which seemed to reflect a lack of high-level commitment to the CSCE. For example, the head of the U.S. delegation never personally participated in the critical Basket III negotiations, where American leverage might have been useful, for fear of confronting the Soviets on issues that Washington considered peripheral. "We were the big hitter on the NATO team, but we couldn't come to the plate," recalls a U.S. diplomat involved in the talks.[41] As a result, another member of the U.S. delegation explains, "The West Europeans saw basic similarities between the views of the United States and the USSR, while they themselves were working hard to introduce as much substance as possible into the documents under negotiation."[42]

The first round of CSCE talks ended in Geneva early December 1973 without any real progress on Principle 7 or Basket III. The nine EC foreign ministers nonetheless reiterated their collective commitment to human rights with a new Document on the European Identity, issued in Copenhagen on December 14, 1973.[43] When talks resumed in Geneva on February 6, 1974, all sides agreed to work simultaneously on the preamble and main text of Basket III. Rapid progress was made on Basket II, and in the Basket III subcommittees dealing with cooperation in education and the arts. The Soviets nonetheless linked concessions in the more sensitive areas of Basket III to favorable progress on Principle 3, the inviolability of frontiers, and Prin-

[39] Acimovic, *Problems of Security and Cooperation*, 126.

[40] Holsti, "Who Got What and How," 144.

[41] Guy Coriden, interview by author, Washington, D.C., March 31, 1994.

[42] Maresca, *To Helsinki*, 68.

[43] See *European Political Cooperation (EPC)*, fifth edition (Bonn: Press and Information Office of the Federal Government, 1988), 48–53.

ciple 6, non-intervention in internal affairs, which they believed could be used to deflect whatever tactical concessions were made on the actual terms of humanitarian cooperation.[44] Talks progressed despite West Germany's earlier indication that it would withhold approval of the frontiers principle until the Soviets accepted a satisfactory formulation of Principle 8, on the equal rights and self-determination of peoples.[45]

Then, just when delegates were beginning to feel more optimistic about the prospects for a successful conference, the mood was disrupted by news that the KGB had arrested Alexander Solzhenitsyn for the recent underground publication of his prison-camp exposé *The Gulag Archipelago*. "The Soviet author's plight was uniquely symbolic for the CSCE, and every diplomat in Geneva understood this," according to a member of the American delegation. For the Soviets, it symbolized the question of how much domestic liberalization the regime would accept in order to gain the benefits of détente. For Western delegations, it symbolized the question of what human rights concessions they could expect from the Soviets as part of détente. "Most delegates at the Conference realized that the trial and imprisonment of a man who for Western public opinion epitomized Soviet dissent would make a mockery of the ideals of human rights, fundamental freedoms, and the freer movement of people and ideas, which the West was seeking to have recognized at the CSCE." While the CSCE "held its collective breath," Soviet authorities weighed the political costs of imprisoning or releasing their well-known prisoner. They compromised on February 13, and expelled Solzhenitsyn from the Soviet Union. Had he been imprisoned, "the Conference might not have concluded for a very long time, if ever."[46]

When Henry Kissinger visited Moscow in late March, Brezhnev and Gromyko indicated that they wanted to conclude the Geneva talks in time for a summit of heads of state that summer. At the same time, they complained vociferously that

[44] Maresca, *To Helsinki*, 93.
[45] Groll, "The Geneva CSCE Negotiations," 158.
[46] Maresca, *To Helsinki*, 89.

the West was seeking, by its position on Basket III, to undermine the Soviet regime. "What kind of proposal is it if they want to arrogate to themselves the right to open theaters in the Soviet Union without any control by the Soviet administration? It's just wrong to have ideas like that," said Brezhnev. In response, Kissinger assured them that the United States would "use its influence not to embarrass the Soviet Union or raise provocative issues."[47]

On April 6, back in Geneva, the Western countries accepted a text on Principle 3, the inviolability of frontiers, in exchange for Soviet promises to be more forthcoming on Basket III. The parties also reached agreement on the principles of sovereign equality and the nonuse of force. Although some Western diplomats and observers considered these concessions premature, the strategy was to use Moscow's desire for a summer summit to leverage concessions on the remaining issues.[48] A German diplomat warned in print: "In principle, nobody would like to see the negotiations fail. But if the results in a third phase are possibly, as the Soviet Union would have it, to be approved by the Heads of State or government, they must be worth all this effort."[49]

It soon became clear to Western delegations, however, that negotiations were not proceeding as they hoped in Basket III, which they viewed as a concrete expression of the abstract human rights principle in the Basket I. In response, they resolved to make the obligations in Principle 7 even more specific and binding.[50] When talks resumed after Easter, Great Britain, Switzerland, and the Holy See released a series of new and revised proposals for Principle 7.

Rather than concede on these sensitive points, the Soviets suddenly changed tactics and dropped the pressure they had been exerting for a rapid conclusion to the talks. Instead, they reinforced their calls for recognition of the discretionary right

[47] Burr, *The Kissinger Transcripts*, 248, 220.

[48] Acimovic, *Problems of Security and Cooperation*, 128.

[49] Groll, "Geneva CSCE Negotiations," 159.

[50] Ferraris, *Report on a Negotiation*, 107; Groll, "The Geneva CSCE Negotiations," 163.

of every state in applying the provisions that would emerge in both Basket III and Principle 7. As a result, little progress was made toward consensus on either text. With both sides delaying in hopes of gaining concessions, and the uncertainty caused by recent changes of government or domestic crises in Britain, France, Germany, and United States, a complete stalemate emerged in Geneva by mid-spring 1974. Talks on the non-intervention principle opened officially on May 30, but went nowhere. The Soviets then circulated a memorandum to all participating governments which indicated that they had made all the concessions they were willing to make on Principle 7 and Basket III, and called again for a speedy conclusion to the conference.[51] Their hope, apparently, was that Paris and Bonn's desire to avoid antagonizing the East, combined with the Washington's desire to conclude the conference, would lead the West to abandon further demands.

The Nixon Administration sympathized with Moscow's impatience, and pressed the EC to compromise. For Henry Kissinger, who had earlier reassured Brezhnev that "a Dutch cabaret in Moscow" was not a threat to Soviet rule, the issues raised in Basket III were a political nuisance that threatened to impede relations between the superpowers.[52] This view was echoed in President Nixon's June 5 speech at Annapolis, where he dismissed "eloquent speeches" and "appeals" for the United States to use its influence on behalf of human rights in other countries, including the Soviet Union. As he put it, "We would not welcome the intervention of other countries in our domestic affairs and we cannot expect them to be cooperative when we seek to intervene directly in theirs."[53] At a NATO meeting in mid-June, Kissinger urged the Europeans to be more flexible, saying that he agreed with promoting Western values in the CSCE, but that the Soviet system had survived for fifty years and "would not be changed if Western newspapers were put on sale in a few kiosks in Moscow."[54]

[51] Kirk-Laux, "Human Contacts," 260.
[52] Burr, *Kissinger Transcripts*, 248.
[53] *New York Times*, June 6, 1974, p. 16.
[54] FCO, *The Conference*, 306 n. 8.

Such remarks were not well received by the EC states, for whom establishing a human rights norm was a high priority. Soon after the NATO meeting in June, the head of the British delegation in Geneva cabled the Foreign Office in London: "It sometimes seems that Dr. Kissinger misunderstands the significance of the CSCE to the West . . . to get it accepted for the first time by the Communist states that relations between peoples—and therefore the attitudes of Governments towards their own citizens—should be the subject of multilateral discussion." Another member of the delegation concurred, "I do not think he understands the genuinely idealistic elements in the European approach but rather, in the manner of his hero Metternich, wants stability and détente (in the Russian sense of the word) for their own sakes."[55]

During the superpowers' Moscow summit later that month, Brezhnev again pleaded with Nixon and Kissinger for more flexibility in the CSCE. Kissinger was thus frustrated by the stalemate in multilateral negotiations that he had never particularly favored, and contemptuous of what he considered "pedantic drafting problems . . . discussed inconclusively at considerable length."[56] Ever more anxious to bring the CSCE to a close, he approved a summit communiqué that infuriated West European foreign ministry officials. One British diplomat noted upon seeing an advance copy, "At first glance, the section on the CSCE reads like a Soviet draft."[57] When Kissinger stopped in Brussels after the summit to propose a thorough review of the Western position, the other NATO foreign ministers expressed their displeasure.[58]

One week after Kissinger left Brussels, the nine EC foreign ministers gathered in Paris to decide how to proceed. As the Soviets had predicted, several governments agreed with Kissinger that enough had been accomplished on human rights,

[55] Ibid., 324, 325 n. 14.
[56] Henry Kissinger, *Years of Upheaval* (Boston: Little, Brown, 1982), 1,165.
[57] FCO, *The Conference*, 305 n. 5.
[58] Ibid., 304–6.

and that it was time to conclude the negotiations. However, the American willingness to compromise a position developed over several years "had had a dispiriting effect on the members of the Nine," according to the British foreign secretary.[59] Several of the foreign ministers argued that stopping at this point would undermine the Community's self-identification with the promotion of human rights in Europe. Dutch foreign minister Max van der Stoel, who had been active on human rights in the Council of Europe since the late 1960s, was particularly outspoken on this point.[60]

In the discussion, van der Stoel drew his colleagues' attention to the EC's recommitment to human rights in the Document on the European Identity, which they had endorsed in Copenhagen only six months earlier. It read, in part: "Sharing as they do the same attitudes to life, based on a determination to build a society which measures up to the needs of the individual, [the EC states] are determined to defend the principles of representative democracy, of the rule of law, of social justice—which is the ultimate goal of economic progress—and of respect for human rights. All of these are fundamental elements of the European Identity."[61] With the issue framed in this manner, the ministers resolved to maintain the EC's strong position on human rights and contacts in the CSCE.

When the NATO heads of delegation met in Geneva to consider the new U.S. interest in more "reasonable" proposals, the reaction was "fairly hostile," according to the British delegate. He had already advised the foreign secretary, just before the European Political Cooperation meeting in Paris, "We should not cause unnecessary delays but nor should we allow ourselves to be bullied by pressure from the Russians . . . or by U.S. concern

[59] Ibid., 311.
[60] Max van der Stoel, interview by author, The Hague, September 14, 1994; FCO, *The Conference*, 311 n. 4.
[61] Ironically, the drafting of the Copenhagen Document was actually inspired in part by Kissinger's 1973 "Year of Europe" speech, which called on the EC to define its role in world affairs. For the full text of the document, see *European Political Co-operation (EPC)*, 48–53.

to bring the Conference to an early end."[62] With Norway also supporting the EC-Nine, the Western position did not change. The stalemate thus continued for several more weeks. On the freer movement of information in Basket III, for example, the Soviets accepted an English-language reference to "access by the public," but then offered a restrictive Russian translation that the West promptly rejected.[63] Notwithstanding the ideological fears that had motivated the East's hard line, however, Leonid Brezhnev was increasingly anxious to claim victory in the CSCE in time for the Twenty-fifth Communist Party Congress, scheduled for February 1976. Romania and Yugoslavia had also indicated for their own reasons that as long as the CSCE was stalemated, they would block the conference of European Communist parties that Brezhnev was hoping to convene later the same year. Finally convinced that the West would concede no further, the Soviets began to show greater flexibility in the mid-summer.[64]

As they had before, the neutral and nonaligned states played an essential role in resolving the stalemate. On July 26, the NNA states presented a package deal that addressed all the sticking points in a manner which pleased neither East nor West, but which all could accept.[65] Instead of the Soviet call for reference to the nonintervention principle in the Basket III preamble, the NNA text referred to the entire decalogue, and thus by implication to the human rights principle, as well. The Soviets won language that recognized each state's right to choose its own "laws and regulations," but it was placed under the principle of sovereign equality, rather than in Basket III, as they would have preferred. The Soviets also accepted an explicit commitment in Principle 10 to implement international obligations, including the Final Act, when exercising sovereign

---

[62] Maresca, *To Helsinki*, 67; Charles Gati, "The Forgotten Region," *Foreign Policy* 19 (Summer 1975), 144.

[63] FCO, *The Conference*, 316.

[64] Ferraris, *Report on a Negotiation*, 401–2.

[65] Acimovic, *Problems of Security and Cooperation*, 251–52.

authority over national laws and regulations.[66] At last, it seemed that the logjam had been broken.

When negotiations resumed in September after the summer break, the Soviets began to compromise again on both Principle 7 and Basket III. In exchange for a "gentleman's agreement" that the Western delegations would include a mention of the international human rights pacts within the final text, the Soviets accepted extensive Western language on individual rights and liberties, their basis in human dignity, and their status as an essential factor for peace and the development of friendly relations among states. However, "profound differences in ideological, political and legal conceptions of the problems concerning human rights" continued to affect the negotiations.[67] Notwithstanding their newfound flexibility in some areas, the Soviets flatly rejected Switzerland's proposals on freedom from arbitrary arrests and reprisals, which would have extended the list of substantive rights enumerated in the text and complicated standard police tactics in the East bloc.

With regard to the heading of Principle 7, the Soviets continued to insist on a Russian word meaning "faith" rather than a direct translation of the broader concept of "belief" contained in the other language texts. The Soviets also continued to push for reference to the international human rights covenants in the text of Principle 7, both because the covenants recognized economic, social, and cultural rights, and because they imposed numerous restrictions on the exercise and enforcement of human rights. Although the West had not intended to refer to any other texts in Principle 7, it responded to the Soviet focus on the covenants by proposing reference to the Universal Declaration of Human Rights, which was philosophically more liberal (though substantively less comprehensive) than the covenants.[68]

After several weeks, the Soviets agreed to language that fell far short of their original demand: "In the field of human rights

[66] Maresca, *To Helsinki*, 129; Ferraris, *Report on a Negotiation*, 131.

[67] Ferraris, *Report on a Negotiation*, 135.

[68] Victor-Yves Ghébali, "L'Acte final de la Conference sur la Securité et la Cooperation en Europe et les Nations Unies," *Annuaire Français de Droit International* 21 (1975), 83.

and fundamental freedoms, the participating States will act in conformity with the purposes and principles of the Charter of the United Nations and with the Universal Declaration of Human Rights. They will also fulfill their obligations as set forth in the international declarations and agreements in this field, including inter alia, the International Covenants on Human Rights, by which they may be bound." Rather than explicitly importing the limitations on states' obligations written into the covenants, as the Soviets had originally intended, this text gave primary emphasis to the UN Charter and Universal Declaration. As for the covenants, it mentioned only the state obligations that they created, not the limitations.[69]

Following a brief interruption in October so the subcommittee could begin work on the principle of self-determination, the Soviets returned to Principle 7 with their newfound flexibility unabated. They accepted almost verbatim the Holy See's revised proposal on the "freedom of the individual to profess or practice, alone or in community with others, his religion or beliefs." After resisting a particular British proposal for fear that it would encourage independent societal activity, the East bloc then accepted a similar Maltese text that confirmed "the right of the individual to know and act upon his rights and duties in this field."[70] West Germany resisted this latter text for several weeks, arguing in the subcommittee that basic human rights should "not be trammeled by corresponding duties," but eventually conceded.[71]

The final obstacle to agreement on Principle 7 concerned the Yugoslav proposal to include text that would guarantee respect for the rights and interests of national minorities. This issue was important to Tito's government, which was seeking to accommodate multiple ethnic identities within a federal state structure. However, as rulers of a multiethnic empire, including republics incorporated by force only a few decades earlier, the Soviets were naturally opposed. In addition, several West Euro-

---

[69] Ferraris, *Report on a Negotiation*, 136–37.

[70] Ibid., 137–38.

[71] FCO, *The Conference*, 347 n. 9.

pean governments (especially the Belgians, French, and Span-
iards) "opposed anything which might imply that national minorities, as distinct from persons belonging to them, enjoyed
rights."[72] In the end, all sides accepted language that recognized
the equality before the law of persons belong to national minorities, ensured their enjoyment of human rights, and committed
states to protect their "legitimate interests within this sphere."

On November 20, 1974, the First Subcommittee registered
the agreed text of Principle 7. Fifty-six negotiating sessions
were required to reach consensus, but both the title and definition were longer than any other in the decalogue of basic principles. The final text nonetheless reflected the Western conception of human rights and fundamental liberties "in a most
satisfactory way, and perhaps beyond any previous expectation," remarked an Italian diplomat.[73] It was comprehensive,
including specific mention of four freedoms plus the rights of
national minorities. It articulated the decidedly non-Marxist
philosophy that human rights "derive from the inherent dignity
of the human person and are essential for his free and full development." It made substantive and detailed provisions on the
duty to respect and promote rights. It imposed a positive obligation on states: not only to respect but also promote and encourage the individual's exercise of their rights. It made respect
for human rights and fundamental freedoms a condition for the
pursuit of peace and friendly relations among states. It asserted
the universal applicability of the principle of human rights. And
finally, its reference to the UN Charter, the Universal Declaration, and the international covenants linked the CSCE to an
evolving system of international human rights law.[74]

All sides reached agreement the following month on Principle 8, regarding the equal rights and self-determination of peoples, but otherwise talks proceeded slowly in late 1974. Negotiators made progress in some areas of Basket III, including the
reunification of families, access to printed information, and cul-

[72] Ibid., 345 n. 3.
[73] Ferraris, *Report on a Negotiation*, 139.
[74] Acimovic, *Problems of Security and Cooperation*, 249–50.

tural and educational exchanges, but the Soviets continued to resist EC proposals that would have required changes in the domestic legislation or legal code of socialist states, or legitimated individual rather than official contacts and exchanges.[75]

During bilateral contacts with Western and neutral leaders during February and March, 1975, Brezhnev again expressed his interest in a rapid conclusion to the CSCE. In early March, he sent a letter to the leaders of the five largest Western states proposing June 30, 1975, as a date for the closing summit.[76] When Basket III talks resumed on April 8, the Eastern delegations made speeches about the importance of concluding the conference, but offered no compromises on remaining issues of human contacts and information. On May 15, NATO presented a "global proposal" that covered outstanding problems on human contacts and information in Basket III. East-bloc reactions were initially skeptical, but Kissinger met with Gromyko in Vienna four days later and described the proposal as the West's absolute precondition for closure. Back in Washington, he advised President Ford that patience would pay off.[77]

Kissinger's newfound firmness, Brezhnev's desire to conclude the conference soon, and the West's refusal to agree to a summit of heads of state (rather than foreign ministers) until the text was agreed, apparently clinched the deal. On May 28, the Soviet delegation in Geneva received instructions from Moscow to make necessary concessions. Given the nature of Soviet decision making on sensitive political topics in the late Brezhnev era, any such instructions would have been cleared, if not initiated, by Andropov's KGB. The following day, speaking on behalf of the entire Warsaw Pact, the Polish delegate accepted virtually the entire NATO text.[78]

At this point, the principal issue still unresolved was the insistence by the EC-Nine that the European Community be al-

[75] Ferraris, *Report on a Negotiation*, 310, 315.
[76] Acimovic, *Problems of Security and Cooperation*, 133.
[77] Henry Kissinger, *Years of Renewal* (New York: Simon & Schuster, 1999), 646–46.
[78] Ferraris, *Report on a Negotiation*, 318–24.

lowed to participate officially in Stage 3, the conclusion of the CSCE. Anxious to proceed, the East bloc accepted a formula by which Aldo Moro would sign the Final Act both as Italy's premier and "in his capacity as President in office of the Council of the European Communities."[79] Though not intended as such, this agreement was fitting tribute to the EC's critical role in placing human rights and contacts high on the CSCE agenda. On France's insistence, the Principality of Monaco was also invited at the last moment to participate in the Helsinki summit and sign the Final Act, bringing the total number of signatories to thirty-five.

The Final Act of the CSCE signed in Helsinki on August 1, 1975, thus embodied more than two and a half years of arduous negotiation. To achieve agreement on the wording of just the ten principles had required 337 official negotiating sessions, thousands of hours of work, innumerable unofficial sessions, consultations and meetings at all levels, as well as considerable exercise of diplomatic skill and muscle.[80] To achieve agreement on Basket III had required 761 negotiating sessions and many more thousands of hours of work behind the scenes.[81] Although its explicit reference to being "not eligible for registration under Article 102 of the Charter of the United Nations" meant that the Final Act was not binding under international law, it did produce significant changes in the formal norms governing relations among participating states. Principle 7 reinforced states' obligations to protect and promote human rights, while establishing unequivocally, for the first time, that respect for human rights, including individuals' rights "to know and act" on their rights, was a legitimate issue in international diplomacy. In Basket III, participating states made new commitments regarding the promotion of human contacts and information, as well as cultural and educational exchanges. In addition, all thirty-five participating states agreed to meet again two years later to pursue the CSCE agenda.

[79] Ibid., 373–84.
[80] Ibid., 164.
[81] Acimovic, *Problems of Security and Cooperation*, 329.

Although the ultimate effects of these new international norms and commitments were hardly apparent at the time, agreement on such a text would have been hard to imagine just five years earlier, when human rights were not on the East-West agenda and proposals to promote "the freer movement of people, information, and ideas" were dismissed as an illegitimate violation of national sovereignty. In fact, the East bloc agreed to such norms and commitments despite demonstrating, both in its bargaining behavior on Principle 7 and Basket III and in its unrelenting denial of fundamental civil rights at home, that it did not accept their underlying moral premises. As a West German diplomat pointed out, "[O]ne has to be aware of the starting positions of the Helsinki consultations to realize what an effort it must have cost the East European countries to concede" as much as they did.[82]

CONCLUSIONS

For the European Community to succeed in placing human rights on the East-West agenda, both as a fundamental norm and as an area for substantive cooperation, it thus had to overcome resistance from one superpower whose foreign policy, at least in recent years, had systematically excluded such considerations, and a second superpower whose official ideology and form of rule were incompatible with respect for individual rights. The fact that the EC nonetheless succeeded in imposing its normative preferences on the relationship between these two superpowers (and thirty-three other states) is thus doubly puzzling. What the negotiation of the Helsinki Final Act conclusively demonstrates is that although power and vulnerability matter, the social and institutional context of international negotiations can entrap governments in bargains that other "interests" would dictate that they avoid. Governments and those

[82] Groll, "Foreign Ministers in Helsinki," 268.

who negotiate on their behalf may seek to achieve outcomes that suit their preferences, but domestic and international constructions of appropriateness inevitably shape their conception of what is desirable, acceptable, and/or feasible. These and other issues related to the sources of international norms are discussed at greater length in the final chapter.

THE FRAMING OF NORMS

CHAPTER THREE

Framing "Helsinki" at Home: Social Movements against the Communist Party-State

Helsinki represents a recognition of what is common to
Europe. . . . It is contrary to the script and spirit of the
Helsinki conference if certain European nations and
states keep alive practices conflicting with the European
civilisation and cultural background. . . . We are not in favor
of external meddling either, we only want the holders of
power to abide by what they themselves have solemnly
promised and signed.
—*Jiri Hajek and Zdenek Mlynar, Czechoslovak dissidents,
September 1975*[1]

We are masters in our own house.
—*Andrei Gromyko, Soviet foreign minister,
summer 1975*[2]

THIS CHAPTER traces the immediate reaction in Eastern Europe
and the Soviet Union to the human rights norms established
by the Helsinki Final Act, from August 1975 through late 1976.
This was a period of political and rhetorical exploration, with
state and societal forces competing to exploit "Helsinki" by imposing an advantageous frame on the formal norms that had
been agreed there. This process was somewhat different in
every country, but compared to the early 1970s, the immediate

[1] Vladimir V. Kusin, "Challenge to Normalcy: Political Opposition in
Czechoslovakia, 1968–77," in Rudolf L. Tokes, ed., *Opposition in Eastern Europe*
(Baltimore: Johns Hopkins University Press, 1979), 47, 49.

[2] Anatoly Dobrynin, *In Confidence: Moscow's Ambassador to America's Six Cold
War Presidents (1962–1986)* (New York: Random House, 1995), 346.

post-Helsinki period is distinguished by an unprecedented blossoming of dissent and independent activity throughout the region. We see how societal forces engaged and reframed the Final Act, and thereby laid the groundwork for more organized challenges to Communist hegemony in the years that followed. The strengths and weaknesses of alternative explanations for these developments are considered in the chapter's conclusion.

By the 1960s, most of the population of Eastern Europe and the Soviet Union was no longer subject to the brutal and often arbitrary terror of the Stalinist era. The inefficacy of "revisionist" and "reformist" strategies for political change had nevertheless already been proven by the crushing of direct challenges to Communist rule in Poland in 1953 and Hungary in 1956, and then by the 1968 Soviet invasion of Czechoslovakia to prevent the Communist Party there from instituting fundamental reforms. Social autonomy was certainly greater in some countries than in others, but the widespread memory of repression, combined with selective imprisonment, frequent harassment, and the denial of education and employment opportunities for dissidents sufficed to limit independent political initiatives throughout the bloc. The only alternative available to potential opposition activists by the mid-1970s was an "evolutionary" bottom-up process by which society would assert increasing autonomy from state control.[3] The question was how societies atomized and immobilized by decades of totalitarian rule could begin to achieve such autonomy. It was not immediately obvious that the Helsinki Final Act would create any such opportunities.

THE STATUS-QUO FRAME: HELSINKI AS "NON-INTERVENTION"

The leadership of the Communist bloc recognized the risk posed by international norms incompatible with the social and political monopoly of the Communist Party. Speaking specifi-

---

[3] Adam Michnik, "The New Evolutionism" (1976) in *Letters from Prison and Other Essays*, translated by Maya Latynski (Berkeley and Los Angeles: University of California Press, 1985), 135–48.

cally about the CSCE, the foreign affairs director of Poland's Central Committee said that the "intellectual and cultural sphere is influenced by international relations as a whole, in all of their aspects, beginning with political activity related to peace, security, and cooperation among nations."[4] The East bloc's negotiating behavior in Geneva (see Chapter 4) had been designed and closely managed to minimize this risk. The crackdown on dissent across the bloc that accompanied the beginning of the talks was thus part of a concerted attempt to frame whatever normative bargain emerged from the security conference as a victory for the Warsaw Pact and its approach to domestic affairs. As the Helsinki summit drew near, the Communist regimes gave no indication that they intended to be less repressive or more liberal at home.

Ideological hard-liners within the Soviet Politburo, as well as Soviet ambassadors abroad, were thus "stunned" when they saw the final draft of the Final Act. Both Principle 7 and Basket III, they feared, had licensed a role for foreign governments in what had once been exclusively internal affairs, such as the control of information and the treatment of dissent. It was not, in other words, an unambiguous endorsement of the status quo version of détente that they had agreed to pursue several years earlier. During the heated debates that ensued, they expressed "grave doubts about assuming international commitments that could open the way to foreign interference in our political life."[5] In response, Foreign Minister Gromyko pointed again to Principle 6, which gave equal priority to a norm of non-intervention in internal affairs, and added that regardless of what international pressures might be felt, "We are masters in our own house."[6] The Kremlin's expectation, in other words, was that as sovereign states, the members of the Warsaw Pact could, if necessary, refuse to comply with Helsinki norms and thereby limit any truly undesirable effects.

---

[4] Interview with Ryszard Frelek, *Tygodnik Kulturalny* (Warsaw), March 4, 1975, from Joint Publication Research Service (JPRS), *Translations on Eastern Europe* 65130 (July 1, 1975):19–24.

[5] Dobrynin, *In Confidence*, 346.

[6] Ibid.

In the short term, though, the surest and cheapest way to guarantee that the normative compromises embodied in the Final Act would not pose political problems was to convince domestic and foreign audiences that the CSCE was a victory for the East. The day after the Helsinki summit, the Soviet Communist daily *Pravda* was devoted to the CSCE, including banner headlines, photos of Leonid Brezhnev at the signing ceremony, and the full text of the Final Act. For months after the summit, East bloc leaders expressed confidence that the Final Act had created a normative environment conducive to the political and material interests of the socialist bloc. The Soviet Politburo announced triumphantly, "The all-European conference is the culmination of everything positive that has been done thus far on our continent to bring about the change-over from the 'cold war' to détente and the genuine implementation of the principles of peaceful coexistence."[7]

Referring to the Soviet Union and its allies as advocates of peace, Hungarian premier Janos Kadar declared, "The international atmosphere after the conference is different from what it was before and those who advocate the cause of peace and security can wage their fight in a new situation and under conditions better than in the period before the conference."[8] Polish foreign minister Stefan Olszowski agreed that the Final Act had created "a new political framework for basing our relations with capitalist countries on the principles of sovereignty, equality, non-intervention and respect for the existing political and territorial realities."[9]

East European leaders were particularly outspoken regarding the economic benefits that they hoped or expected would flow from the CSCE. For example, Czechoslovak premier Gustav Husak celebrated Helsinki's contribution to "the foundations

---

[7] *Current Digest of the Soviet Press* 27:31 (August 27, 1975):14–15.

[8] Cited in Janos Nagy, "One Year after Helsinki," *Tarsadalmi Szemle*, July 1976, from JPRS, *Translations* 67721 (August 9, 1976):7–16.

[9] Stefan Olszowski, "The Foreign Policy of Socialist Poland," *Nowe Drogi* (Warsaw), no. 11, November 1975, from JPRS, *Translations* 66612 (January 19, 1976):15–24.

of new international relations based on the peaceful coexistence of states with different social systems," which would permit expanded economic, scientific, and technological cooperation.[10] Poland's Deputy Foreign Minister Eugeniusz Kulaga explained that "the CSCE results should facilitate the continuing dynamic growth of the economic, industrial, scientific and technical cooperation between East and West, thus also between Poland and capitalist countries."[11] Not all of this was propaganda: bilateral economic and technical agreements between East and West did increase sharply just before and after the Helsinki summit.

The Husak regime in Czechoslovakia was particularly celebratory in its commentary on the CSCE, which it viewed as a means to gain not only expanded economic contacts with the West but also the acceptance as a normal European state, which it had been denied since 1968. Czechoslovak participation in the CSCE and Husak's speech at the Helsinki summit were trumpeted by the official media as evidence of the regime's legitimacy. The party daily *Rude Pravo* provided blanket coverage of the summit, and special postage stamps were issued in honor of the CSCE. On August 8, one week after the summit, the government announced that it would comply with all provisions of the Helsinki Final Act.[12]

Senior officials and commentators in Poland also portrayed the ten Basic Principles of the Final Act as "rules of the game" that are "binding" for international relations.[13] To give the impression that Poland was serious about its Basket III commitments, the media devoted great attention to new agreements such as the Declaration on the Principles and Means of Developing Cultural and Scientific Cooperation, Information and

[10] Gustav Husak, *Speeches and Writings* (Oxford: Pergamon Press, 1986).

[11] *Tiedonantaja* (Helsinki), August 27, 1975, from JPRS, *Translations* 65740 (September 23, 1975):81–83.

[12] Vladimir V. Kusin, *From Dubcek to Charter 77: A Study of "Normalization" in Czechoslovakia* (New York: St. Martin's, 1978), 295.

[13] Jerzy Nowak, "Topic for Today: Peace for Europe," *Trybuna Ludu* (Warsaw), September 10, 1975, from JPRS, *Translations* 65829 (October 2, 1975): 19–23.

Human Relations between Poland and France.[14] Official commentators sometimes even acknowledged the extent of ideological disagreement during the negotiation of the Final Act, including the West's commitment to freedom of expression and the free flow of ideas.[15] Nowhere, though, did they signal that the formal acceptance of Principle 7 would mean greater space for independent social organization or political activity within Poland.

It is thus not surprising that the Final Act was greeted with great caution by the people of the Soviet Union and especially Eastern Europe. To the extent that they followed international affairs at all, most listened to the Communist authorities' celebration of the Final Act, and concluded that the document was nothing more than a Western concession to the Kremlin. Articulating a sentiment widespread across the bloc, an anonymous writer from Prague observed that Helsinki was initially received with the same skepticism reserved for all accomplishments celebrated by the regime: the average citizen, he reported, "at most waves his hand over the matter of European security or possibly gives a deeply skeptical sigh—again another Munich at our expense."[16] According to an unofficial poll of 209 persons conducted by a sociologist in Prague in March 1975, 66 percent believed that the Helsinki conference would produce no benefits for them.[17] Another Czech dissident wrote that "the Helsinki summit has given its blessing to Soviet hegemony in Eastern Europe in exchange for the hope given to the Western heads of state that the USSR will not intervene in the course of events in the West."[18]

---

[14] The text of this June 1975 agreement was published two weeks after the Helsinki summit in *Kultura* (Warsaw), August 17, 1975, from JPRS, *Translations* 65559 (August 27, 1975):52–55.

[15] Mieczyslaw F. Rakowski, "Regarding Basket Three," *Nowe Drogi* (Warsaw), June 1975, from JPRS, *Translations* 65536 (August 25, 1975):11–23.

[16] JPRS, *Translations* 67236 (May 3, 1976):5–9.

[17] A further 15.8 percent hoped for withdrawal of Soviet troops and restoration of sovereignty, whereas 17.7 percent simply gave no answer, according to Kusin, "Challenge to Normalcy," 47–48.

[18] Jiri Pelikan, "Spring in Europe," *Listy* (Rome), from JPRS, *Translations* 65740 (September 23, 1975):29–31.

Observing the Communist regimes' insistence that détente would not mean domestic liberalization, both elite and grassroots voices in the West generally condemned the Helsinki Final Act as a concession to Soviet totalitarianism and regional hegemony. In Europe, West Germany's Christian Democratic Party called on the federal government not to sign the Final Act, while the British weekly the *Economist* editorialized, "The fact that the West is in no position at the moment to argue away the political division of Europe is no reason why it should sign away the possibility of arguing about in the future."[19] Such feelings were even stronger in the United States. One week before the Helsinki summit, a *Wall Street Journal* editorial headline screamed at President Ford, "Jerry, Don't Go."[20] An editorial in the *New York Times* commented likewise, "nothing signed in Helsinki will in any way save courageous free thinkers in the Soviet empire from the prospect of incarceration in forced labor camps, or in insane asylums, or from being subjected to involuntary exile."[21] Even the liberal former Under Secretary of State George Ball described the Final Act as "a defeat for the West."[22] The White House was flooded by letters from irate citizens, many of them East European émigrés, expressing their opposition to the Final Act. Though ideologically anti-Communist, these Western parliamentarians, editorialists, and common citizens had essentially accepted the East bloc's framing of what happened at Helsinki.

THE DYNAMIC FRAME: HELSINKI AS "HUMAN RIGHTS"

The status-quo framing of Helsinki was not accepted, however, by everybody in Eastern Europe and the Soviet Union. As the CSCE negotiations were winding down in Geneva, a Prague

[19] *Economist* (London), August 2, 1975.

[20] *Wall Street Journal* (New York), July 23, 1975.

[21] *New York Times*, August 1, 1975.

[22] *Newsweek*, International Edition, August 11, 1975. For a collection of post-Helsinki editorials, see Judith F. Buncher, ed., *Human Rights and American Diplomacy, 1975–77* (New York: Facts on File, 1977), 9–28.

intellectual wrote to a friend in the West: "Everyone here has his own reaction to this: we, the people from the ghetto, feel a cautious hope; the secret police feel an increased nervousness."[23] Once the postsummit celebrations were over, the Communist regimes tried to protect their status-quo framing of Helsinki by limiting public awareness of the actual content of the Final Act. In Poland, for example, the five hundred copies of the Final Act published by the government along with Gierek's summit speech were removed from circulation at Moscow's orders, and kept in storage except for propaganda use abroad.[24] In Czechoslovakia, thousands of copies of the Helsinki Final Act were published, but never distributed.

As word nonetheless spread about the real content of the Helsinki Final Act (partly through Western radio broadcasts such as the BBC and Radio Free Europe/Radio Liberty), some began to see it not as a ratification of Communist rule but as an opportunity to challenge the repressive regimes under which they lived. Both normative and institutional aspects of the CSCE and the Helsinki Final Act were considered promising. Principle 7 of the Final Act clearly articulated the CSCE states' obligation to respect human rights, reaffirmed the authority of earlier human rights pacts that nearly every government had signed, and linked the human rights obligation to diplomatic progress in other issue areas. Basket III engaged deeply rooted norms of a common European culture and civilization that predated and superseded the ideological and geopolitical divisions of the late twentieth century. As such, no contemporary ideology, not even one like socialism that claimed macrohistorical legitimacy, could escape being judged by its standards. Unlike the earlier UN pacts, though, the CSCE offered an institutional mechanism to hold signatory states publicly accountable for their human rights record: the participating states would re-

---

[23] Anonymous letter, from *Listy* (Rome), December 1974, in JPRS, *Translations* 64128 (February 19, 1975):8–18.

[24] Romuald Spasowski, *The Liberation of One* (New York: Harcourt Brace Jovanovich, 1986), 548–49.

convene to review implementation of past commitments and consider further measures to advance East-West cooperation.[25]

Given that the Communist regimes clearly wanted to legitimate their rule and rebuild their declining economies through improved political and economic relations with the West, it seemed likely that the norms and institutional structure of the CSCE could be a force for political change. For that to happen, though, would require a grassroots challenge to the status-quo interpretation of the Final Act preferred by the Communist authorities and widely accepted in the West. A number of activists in the East thus resolved to reframe the meaning of Helsinki by focusing on its human rights components in "upward" appeals to the Communist authorities and "outward" appeals to Western governments, media, and NGOs. In other words, whatever the Communist governments had intended by signing the Final Act, the dissident activists would invoke the formal commitment to respect human rights and fundamental freedoms *as if* it had been sincere.[26]

The first to attempt this "up-and-out" strategy of issue framing and social mobilization were small groups of veteran dissidents in Moscow and elsewhere in the Soviet Union, who wanted to revive the small human rights movement that had been crushed in its infancy three years earlier, while engaging Western interest in their cause.[27] On June 17, 1975, democratic activists from Estonia and Latvia issued a joint appeal to all governments participating in the forthcoming Conference on Security and Cooperation in Europe to recognize that many rights guaranteed in the Universal Declaration of Human Rights were systematically violated by Soviet authorities in the

[25] Each of these points emerged repeatedly in interviews with dozens of former opposition and human rights activists from Eastern Europe and the Soviet Union conducted by the author from 1990 to 1994.

[26] The phrase *as if* reappears constantly in East European opposition writing of the late 1970s—citizens were encouraged to live *as if* they were free; regimes were rebuked *as if* their normative commitments had been sincere.

[27] Ludmilla Alexeyeva, *Soviet Dissent: Contemporary Movements for National, Religious, and Human Rights* (Middletown, Conn.: Wesleyan University Press, 1985).

Baltic states.[28] Deeper within the Soviet Union, political prisoners in Perm Labor Camp 36 held a one-day hunger strike on July 31, the first day of the Helsinki summit, to call international attention to the violation of human rights in their country.[29] Several weeks after the Helsinki summit, a group of dissidents met with a visiting U.S. congressional delegation to express their hope that the West would hold the Kremlin accountable for its commitments under the Final Act. As discussed in Chapter 4, this meeting and ensuing contacts had a substantial impact on Congressional interest in the CSCE, and thus on U.S. foreign policy. Neither the Baltic appeal nor the prisoners' hunger strike permeated the fanfare of the summit, but they foretold a wave of social mobilization premised on a radically different interpretation of Helsinki norms than that advanced by the Kremlin, its allies in the East, and its critics in the West.

A similar reframing of the Helsinki bargain occurred in Czechoslovakia, where a small segment of the population began to see the Helsinki process as an opportunity for independent activism, and perhaps dialogue with the state, which had not existed since 1968.[30] In an interview on Swedish television in September 1975, two former members of the Dubcek government, Zdenek Mlynar and Jiri Hajek, portrayed the Final Act's principle of nonintervention as a repudiation of the 1968 Soviet invasion, and its human rights components, particularly Principle 7, as the starting point for a reduction in repression.[31] Hajek communicated this message directly in a letter to the prime minister: "The Czechoslovak president's signature under the

[28] Endel Krepp and Konrad Veem, *Testing the Spirit of Helsinki: From Helsinki to Madrid* (Stockholm: National Committee of the Estonian Evangelical Lutheran Church, 1980), 25.

[29] Nina Strokata, "The Ukrainian Helsinki Group," in Allan Wynn et al., eds., *The Fifth International Sakharov Hearing*, Proceedings, April 1985 (London: Andrei Sakharov Campaign/André Deutsch, 1986), 99.

[30] Jiri Hajek, interviews by author, Prague, July 7, 1991 and August 2, 1992. See also Jiri Hajek, *Dix ans après: Prague 1968–1978* (Paris: Éditions du Seuil, 1978), chapter. 7.

[31] *Listy* (Rome) (1975):11–13, as reported in Kusin, "Political Opposition," 47, 49.

Helsinki Final Act and the Czechoslovak government's statement of 8 August 1975 that it would consistently comply with
the undertakings deriving from that document, mean that all
agencies accounting to this government have been obligated to
ensure that no person adhering to these principles and applying
them to the specific situation in Czechoslovakia since 1968 is on
account of such views deprived of employment. . . . [education,
etc.] and especially that no one should be prosecuted and jailed
for views based on such principles."[32]

As a first step to test this logic, Hajek also wrote to the
Czechoslovak Academy of Sciences proposing a discussion of
the implications of Helsinki for analyses of the Prague Spring.
Several weeks later, historian Karel Kaplan sent a similar letter
to the party presidium, the Federal Assembly, and the Federal
Government. Kaplan's letter outlined measures that the government should take in accordance with its signature on the
Final Act, including expanded economic relations with the
West, release and rehabilitation of all political prisoners, protection of freedom of expression and travel, abolition of censorship and state monopolies on information, and more.[33] The regime's only direct response at this point was to expel Hajek
from the Academy of Sciences.[34]

Churches across Europe also began to articulate a dynamic
interpretation of the Helsinki Final Act. From October 27 to
31, 1975, the Conference of European Churches (CEC) held a
large, high-level consultation in East Berlin to assess the significance of the Final Act for the role and teachings of its member churches.[35] With 136 member and affiliated Protestant and
Orthodox churches in all European countries except Albania,
the CEC had a potential audience of hundreds of millions of

[32] *Listy* (Rome) (1976):44–45, as reported in Kusin, *From Dubcek to Charter
77*, 295–96.
[33] *Listy* (Rome) (1976):42–44, as reported ibid., 294–95.
[34] Jiri Hajek, interview by author, Prague, June 7, 1991.
[35] *The Conference on Security and Cooperation in Europe and the Churches*, Report of a Consultation at Buckow, GDR, 27th–31st October 1975, Occasional
Paper No.7 (Geneva: Conference of European Churches, 1976). All subsequent references to this consultation are drawn from this source.

people across the CSCE region.[36] In his opening sermon, Bishop Albrecht Schonherr of the Federation of Evangelical Churches in the GDR criticized the emphasis on status-quo norms such as non-intervention: "Among the ten principles in the first part of the Final Act there are three negations, four affirmations of the status quo and three obligations for a better future. It will depend on us, with others, to see that the emphasis shifts more and more towards the better future." Bishop Werner Krusche, also of the GDR Evangelical Church, continued in the same vein: "When the Church joins others in striving to eliminate man's political distress, this is an entirely proper thing for it to do, because God Himself intends to put an end finally to all human distress. . . . God's Spirit will make us all united in the conviction that everything must be directed to the service of *human beings* in the countries of Europe."[37]

Though necessarily veiled, these comments clearly challenged the Communist regimes' public framing of the Helsinki Final Act. After the CEC meeting in East Berlin in October 1975, Protestant ministers across the GDR began to discuss Helsinki norms with their congregations. The following August, a young Lutheran pastor burned himself to death to protest the Honecker regime's denial of religious rights. The pastor's protest-suicide gained further attention and popular support for the churches' human rights campaign, especially among the young.[38] By the summer of 1976, the Helsinki Final Act was being widely circulated and discussed in churches in the GDR and elsewhere in Eastern Europe.[39]

---

[36] The 1975 consultation, which involved representatives from churches in Belgium, Bohemia, Canada, East Germany, England, Estonia, Finland, France, Hungary, the Netherlands, Norway, Poland, Rumania, Russia, Scotland, Serbia, Silesia, Slovakia, and Switzerland, was only the latest in a series of CEC meetings on the European security negotiations dating back to 1967.

[37] Emphasis in the original.

[38] Werner Volkmer, "East Germany: Dissenting Views during the Last Decade," in Tokes, ed., *Opposition in Eastern Europe*, 123; and Robert F. Goeckel, *The Lutheran Church and the East German State: Political Conflict and Change under Ulbricht and Honecker* (Ithaca: Cornell University Press, 1991).

[39] "Summary of the Member Churches' Replies to the General Secretary's Circular Letter on the Application of the Helsinki Declaration." Unpublished

Recognizing that the Helsinki bargain that they had so recently celebrated was having undesirable domestic effects, Communist authorities tried both rhetoric and repression to bolster their status-quo framing of the Final Act. When addressing Communist Party or international audiences, official commentators criticized the new opposition's "arbitrary reading of the European Conference documents, and attempts to distort their meaning."[40] Leonid Brezhnev told the Seventh Congress of the Polish United Workers' Party in December 1975, for example, "it is highly important to see and understand the significance of this document as a whole, in all its parts, without succumbing to the temptation of pulling out separate pieces which some believe to be more convenient for themselves in tactical terms."[41] At the same time, in an attempt to deter potential petitioners for emigration who might base their requests on the Helsinki Accords, Soviet authorities imprisoned theoretical physicist Mikhail Kazachkov almost immediately upon his application for a visa in late 1975.[42] Societal forces across the region nonetheless began to implement their dynamic Helsinki frame, organizing protests and joint appeals for reform based on its human rights norms.

MOBILIZING AROUND THE DYNAMIC FRAME: EARLY PROTESTS FOR HUMAN RIGHTS

For a variety of historical reasons, the Polish constitution was relatively liberal and protective of human rights, by East European standards. The problem was that many of its key provisions were not implemented in practice, and civil society had no means by which to pressure for reforms. This situation changed after Helsinki, as activists found ways to link Poland's formal

---

paper (in the Harvard Divinity School library) for a World Council of Churches colloquium, July 24–28, 1976.

[40] L. Maximov, "The Helsinki Understandings Must Be Fulfilled," *International Affairs* (Moscow) (1976), no. 6.

[41] Cited ibid.

[42] "The Man in the Window," *Harvard Law Bulletin* 45:1 (Fall 1993):13.

domestic norms to the regime's international commitments.[43] On December 5, 1975, fifty-nine of Poland's most prominent intellectuals, artists, writers, and scientists delivered an open letter to the speaker of the Sejm (the Polish parliament) and the Council of State, demanding that fundamental rights already contained in the constitution be implemented in practice. They framed their manifesto with references to "the conference in Helsinki, during which the Polish government . . . formally asserted the Universal Declaration of Human Rights," and called for protection of the freedoms of conscience and religious practice, work, education, speech, and exchange of information. "Recognition of these freedoms, confirmed at the Helsinki Conference, has today assumed international importance, for where there is no freedom, there can be neither peace nor security," they concluded.[44]

Recognizing that Helsinki-based protest could threaten its grip on power, the Politburo responded by proposing instead to enshrine the country's "unshakable and fraternal bonds with the Soviet Union" within the constitution. When word of the proposed amendment spread across the country in January, leading intellectuals issued another manifesto, calling it a "blatant contradiction" of the principle of sovereign equality "confirmed in the Helsinki Agreements."[45] The Catholic Church joined the protest in March, when the influential Secretariat of the Polish Episcopate declared that any constitutional reforms should be consistent with the principles of the Helsinki Final Act.[46]

The Church's involvement quickly spread beyond the constitutional debate. In Cracow, Cardinal Karol Wojtyla (later Pope

[43] Jan Jozef Lipski, *KOR: A History of the Workers' Defense Committee in Poland, 1976–1981* (Berkeley and Los Angeles: University of California Press, 1985), 24–25.

[44] Association of Polish Students and Graduates in Exile, *Dissent in Poland: Reports and Documents in Translation, December 1975-July 1977* (London, 1979), 12–15.

[45] Ibid., 15–17.

[46] Peter Raina, *Political Opposition in Poland, 1954–1977* (London: Poets and Painters Press, 1978), 224–28.

John Paul II) began to speak of Poland's confrontation with Communism in terms of "its consequences for human dignity, individual rights, human rights and the rights of nations."[47] Such interventions did not require a change in the social doctrine of the Church—the "natural rights" of humanity had long been part of Church teachings—but the new, post-Helsinki salience of "human rights" within public discourse enabled the Church to engage contemporary political issues more directly without appearing to depart from its traditional role.[48] Over the next couple of years, a tacit but crucial Church-opposition alliance solidified in Poland under the human rights banner.

In Czechoslovakia, where repression was far harsher and domestic law provided no basis for protest, activists instead reframed the regime's own initiative to link Helsinki to other international norms. Principle 7 of the Final Act specifically obliged CSCE states to comply with their obligations under the International Covenant on Civil and Political Rights (ICCPR) and the International Covenant on Economic, Social, and Cultural Rights (ICESCR)—a linkage added by the Soviets in the hope that the broad escape clauses within the two covenants would negate the specific obligations agreed in the Final Act.[49] Word spread in early November that the Husak government had instructed the Federal Assembly to ratify the two covenants, which Czechoslovakia had signed in 1968. Here too, though, societal forces refused the status-quo framing of international norms. Confident that legal escape clauses would not matter in their political confrontation with the party-state, three ex-Communist dissidents appealed publicly to the Federal Assembly on November 8 for a positive vote on the Cove-

---

[47] Robert Zuzowski, *Political Dissent and Opposition in Poland: The Workers' Defense Committee "KOR"* (Westport, Conn.: Praeger, 1992), 127.

[48] Branislaw Dembowski, interview by author, Warsaw, June 23, 1992.

[49] For example, the ICCPR, Article 18, paragraph 3, states: "Freedom to manifest one's religion or beliefs may be subject only to such limitations as are prescribed by law and are necessary to protect public safety, order, health, or morals or the fundamental rights and freedoms of others." See Harold Russell, "The Helsinki Declaration: Brobdingnag or Lilliput," *American Journal of International Law* 70 (April 1976):268.

nants. Three days later, as part of its effort to exploit the escape clauses while appearing to be complying with its Helsinki commitments, the Czechoslovak Federal Assembly ratified the ICCPR and ICESCR.[50]

Czechoslovakia's deposit of its instruments of ratification with the UN secretary general on December 23 provided the necessary minimum number of ratifications for the ICCPR to take effect. Before long, Soviet deputy minister of internal affairs Boris Shumilin declared: "Soviet legislation and rules of departure from the Soviet Union are in full accord with the International Covenant on Civil and Political Rights. . . . [R]estrictions that we sometimes impose proceed directly from the clauses of the covenant. The covenant says that a person's right to leave his country . . . can be restricted in cases connected with the protection of state security, public order, health or moral standards of the population, or the rights and freedoms of others."[51]

When the ICCPR came into effect worldwide on March 23, 1976, Czechoslovakia's official media publicized the Husak regime's special role in reaching the ratification threshold. However, the ratification and entry into force of the ICCPR simply strengthened the human rights norms around which East European activists were rapidly mobilizing. The states of the Communist bloc were now not only politically accountable to the Helsinki Final Act, but also legally bound by the ICCPR, which included a broader set of rights and far more specific obligations than the Final Act. Fourteen prominent participants in the Prague Spring reforms promptly issued a joint letter to the Parliament demanding that imprisoned supporters of Dubcek's reforms (former party officials Milan Huebl and Jaroslav Sabata, historian Jan Tesar, student leader Jiri Mueller, and others) be released because their incarceration violated the principles laid down at the Helsinki conference.[52]

---

[50] Kusin, *Dubcek to Charter* 77, 295.

[51] *New York Times*, February 3, 1976. The same justification is offered in L. Maximov, "Fulfillment of the Helsinki Understandings," *International Affairs* (Moscow), no. 10 (1976):29.

[52] CNR/Reuters/AFP/RFE Special newswire item, Vienna, April 6, 1976.

Though less vocal than their East European counterparts since the critical August 1975 meeting with visiting members of the U.S. Congress, Soviet activists were closely following the reinterpretation of the Helsinki bargain and the emergence of Helsinki-oriented protests across the bloc. Yuri Orlov and others concluded that the time was right to establish an independent organization in Moscow to monitor the Kremlin's compliance with the Final Act, particularly the human rights provisions of Principle 7 and Basket III.[53] On May 12, 1976, they announced the formation of the Group to Assist the Implementation of the Helsinki Agreements in the USSR, which soon became known as the Moscow Helsinki Group.[54]

Upon learning about the creation of the Helsinki Group in Moscow, Polish lawyer Zbigniew Romascewski traveled there in late May to speak with its founders. In conversation with Sakharov, Bonner, Sharansky, and others, Romascewski concluded that the Polish opposition should also make an organized attempt to monitor compliance with the Helsinki Final Act, and to use Helsinki norms to press for political reforms. "If they can do it there, in the heart of the empire, we can surely do it here," he told a friend in Warsaw shortly after his return.[55] The first substantial opportunity to act on this conclusion, and on the wider opportunity provided by the Helsinki norms, came that summer, when a few dozen intellectuals responded to the arrest of striking workers by creating an informal human rights organization known as the Workers' Defense Committee (KOR).

Societal appeals for the implementation of Helsinki principles were also heard at the European Youth and Student As-

[53] Yuri Orlov, conversations with author, Ithaca, N.Y., 1990–1992; Orlov, *Dangerous Thoughts: Memoirs of a Russian Life*, translated by Thomas P. Whitney (New York: Morrow, 1991), 188–89; and Paul Goldberg, *The Final Act: The Dramatic, Revealing Story of the Moscow Helsinki Watch Group* (New York: Morrow, 1988), 62.

[54] The declaration is reprinted in the Soviet human rights movement's samizdat journal published in English by Amnesty International, the *Chronicle of Current Events* (London) 40, May 20, 1976 (1979):95–98.

[55] Barbara Rozycka, interview by author, Warsaw, June 22, 1991.

sembly held in Warsaw, June 18–24, 1976. Involving 1,500 delegates from thirty-four countries, this meeting had been hailed
by the East European press as a "mini-Helsinki."[56] Without
warning, however, the British Young Liberal delegation read
aloud a statement from an underground Polish Youth Committee for the Implementation of the Helsinki Agreement, an-
nouncing its "intent in conjunction with similar Committees
set up in Western and Eastern Europe, the U.S.A., and even
in the U.S.S.R. [to] keep a watch on the signatories commitment to carry through the provisions of the Final Act."[57] This
intervention caused a furor among the delegates, and the Polish and Soviet press immediately discontinued coverage of the
conference. The group that claimed to have authored the appeal never reappeared, but the uproar it caused was another
indication that the status-quo framing of Helsinki norms was
slipping.

It slipped still further later that same month, at a meeting in
East Berlin of twenty-nine Communist and Workers' parties,
where the Spanish and Italian delegations succeeded in getting
all the parties to praise the Helsinki Accords and commit to
work for the implementation of the international human rights
covenants. The Communist Party of the Soviet Union could
surely have blocked such a move, but apparently feared that
doing so would only further undermine its legitimacy among
leftist parties across Europe. Like the original Helsinki Final
Act, the Berlin document was published across Eastern Europe
and the Soviet Union.[58] And since no East bloc regime could
claim that the communiqué from a meeting of Communist parties was an instrument of Western imperialism, the Berlin document increased the political utility of Helsinki norms for dissident and opposition forces.

Elsewhere in East Germany, Helsinki-oriented social mobilization began to spread beyond the church. On July 10, 1976, a

---

[56] Association of Polish Students, *Dissent in Poland*, 44.

[57] Raina, *Political Opposition in Poland*, 351–53; and Association of Polish Students, *Dissent in Poland*, 44–49.

[58] Cf. *Neues Deutschland* (East Berlin), June 30, 1976.

doctor from Riesa named Karl-Heinz Nitschke initiated a human rights petition to demand that the East German regime honor its Helsinki commitments, including the freedom of movement. Over a hundred people, many of them workers, signed the petition. When their demand to move to West Germany was rejected, Nitschke smuggled the list of names to the West, and the cases were widely discussed in Western media.[59] For most East Germans who refused the status quo, though, the pervasiveness of Stasi (secret police) surveillance and the quality of life in neighboring West Germany made "exit" a more attractive option than "voice."[60] As people learned from radio or the churches that the Final Act had guaranteed freedom of movement, applications for exit visas skyrocketed: an estimated 100,000 East Germans (roughly 1 percent of the population) applied for visas in the first year after the Helsinki summit. Most cited Helsinki in their applications, despite the authorities' desperate claim that the freedom of movement clause in the Final Act did not apply to emigration to West Germany.[61]

ASCENDENCE OF THE "HUMAN RIGHTS" FRAME

By the first anniversary of the Helsinki Final Act, Communist authorities were coming to terms with the fact that their concessions in the CSCE negotiations had sparked independent political mobilization across the bloc, and even from abroad. In August 1976, for example, Catholic bishops in Western Europe

[59] *Die Welt* (Bonn), August 29, 1977, in JPRS, *Translations* 69892 (September 30, 1977):55–56; and Werner Volkmer, "East Germany: Dissenting Views during the Last Decade," in Tokes, ed., *Opposition in Eastern Europe*, 121–22.

[60] Albert O. Hirschman, "Exit, Voice and the Fate of the German Democratic Republic," *World Politics* 45:2 (January 1993): 173–202. The residual legitimacy of socialist ideology is also emphasized by Christian Joppke, *East German Dissidents and the Revolution of 1989: Social Movements in a Leninist Regime* (New York: New York University Press, 1995).

[61] Gunter Minnerup, "East Germany's Frozen Revolution," *New Left Review* 132 (March-April 1982):12; "Helsinki Accord's Echo in Eastern Europe," *Financial Times* (London), January 12, 1977, p. 4.

called on the Czechoslovak government to adhere to Helsinki principles by releasing political prisoners and protecting the freedom of religion.[62] Meanwhile, as detailed in Chapter 4, a new transnational network was slowly raising the salience of Helsinki compliance in U.S. policy toward Eastern Europe and the Soviet Union. The Communist regimes' response at this stage was to grant somewhat greater leeway to activists identified with Helsinki norms while, for the first time, coupling their insistence on nonintervention with claims that their human rights records actually complied with the Final Act and related agreements.

In fact, East-bloc regimes launched a concerted campaign at home and abroad to portray their treatment of dissidents as consistent with human rights norms contained in international agreements. The evolution of the Honecker regime's rhetoric on human rights in the spring and summer of 1976 illustrates perfectly the increasing defensiveness of the Communist party-state. In April, a regime spokesman asserted that the GDR was fulfilling all its Helsinki commitments.[63] One month later, the party daily *Neues Deutschland* affirmed: "If the draft party program terms the further development and perfection of socialist democracy the main direction in which the socialist state power is developing, this thesis also comprises the idea that the assertion of human rights at an increasingly higher level agrees with the essence of socialism."[64] In the face of escalating critiques of the GDR's human rights record, though, such claims were no longer viable. Recognizing that "old and obsolete bourgeois concepts often still persist, especially regarding the problem of basic rights and duties as met in socialist actuality," the regime charged the GDR Academy of Sciences in August with articulating a more persuasive justification for the treatment of rights within the ruling party program.[65]

---

[62] UPI/Reuter newswire item, Bonn/Linz, August 19, 1976.

[63] See "Two Hundred Days since Helsinki," *Horizont* (East Berlin), from JPRS, *Translations* 67151 (April 16, 1976):1–9.

[64] *Neues Deutschland* (East Berlin), May 18, 1976, from JPRS, *Translations* 67448 (June 14, 1976):19.

[65] "Unfolding of Socialist Democracy as Main Thrust in Development of Political Science and Jurisprudence," *Neue Justiz* (East Berlin), August 1976, from JPRS, *Translations* 67993 (September 29, 1976):3–5.

ALTERNATIVE EXPLANATIONS

This chapter has demonstrated the centrality of the Helsinki Final Act's human rights norms in the emergence of opposition activity in Eastern Europe and the Soviet Union in 1975–1976. This activity contrasts sharply with the weakness (in some cases, absence) of independent activity throughout the region in the early 1970s, including the general despair after the defeat of "socialism with a human face" in 1968. Western leaders had given little indication that they intended to make human rights a central issue in détente once the summit was over, while Leonid Brezhnev and his allies had portrayed the Helsinki Final Act as a confirmation of the political and territorial status quo in Europe and thus overall as a great victory for socialist foreign policy. There is thus strong reason for concluding that the Helsinki Final Act exerted a powerful influence on the emergence of independent opposition voices across Eastern Europe and the Soviet Union.

In addition, other theories of state socialism offer unsatisfying or incomplete explanations for the process described above. The original Western academic theory of state socialism, known as the totalitarian model, was a theory of continuity, not change. Its assumption that political activity independent of the party-state would not be permitted, and thus could not exist, entirely prevents it from explaining the sources or consequences of the social mobilization which did occur. As a result, the model began to lose explanatory power in the 1960s, as the Communist party-states one by one replaced the institutionalized terror of Stalinism with a system whose legitimacy and stability was predicated on economic and social performance. Subsequent scholarship on the developmental accomplishments and crises of state socialism highlight important dynamics in the evolution of the system, but neither focus offers a satisfying explanation for changes in social mobilization and regime tolerance in the mid to late 1970s.

Some have argued that what caused the downfall of Communist rule in the Soviet Union and Eastern Europe was not the creation of new international norms but an underlying process of socioeconomic change whereby wealthier, more educated, and differentiated societies demand political and economic systems responsive to individual rights and escalating material expectations. This argument is based on the theory that all developing societies undergo a process of modernization that challenges the institutions and authority patterns of entrenched, conservative regimes, regardless of their ideological stripe.[66] Only when modernization differentiates social interests and the breakdown of intermediary structures exposes individuals directly to the unregulated power of the state and market do societies become receptive to thinking in terms of "rights," and pressure the state to protect civil and property rights.[67] By this logic, international human rights norms are politically irrelevant until domestic legal systems are committed to protection of individual rights.[68] If this "modernization" theory offers a satisfactory explanation of political change in the Communist bloc, then the "Helsinki hypothesis" would be severely compromised.

The political hegemony of the Communist party-state in Eastern Europe and the Soviet Union *was* threatened in the 1960s by interest groups and a consumerist culture increasingly incompatible with the premodern, totalitarian patterns of Stalinism. The vast labor and material resources devoted to rapid industrialization had succeeded in creating complex, relatively modern economies within a few decades of the end of World War II.[69] Millions of illiterate peasants were transformed into

[66] S. N. Eisenstadt, *Modernization: Protest and Change* (Englewood Cliffs, N.J.: Prentice-Hall, 1966); Cyril A. Black, *The Dynamics of Modernization: A Study in Comparative History* (New York: Harper and Row, 1966); Samuel P. Huntington, *Political Order in Changing Societies* (New Haven: Yale University Press, 1968).

[67] Jack Donnelly, *Universal Human Rights in Theory and Practice* (Ithaca: Cornell University Press, 1989), 68–71.

[68] Andrew Moravscik, "Lessons from the European Human Rights Regime" in *Advancing Democracy and Human Rights in the Americas: An Inter-American Dialogue Conference Report* (Washington, D.C.: Inter-American Dialogue, 1994), 35–58.

[69] Mark G. Field, ed., *The Social Consequences of Modernization in Communist Societies* (Baltimore: Johns Hopkins University Press, 1976); Moshe Lewin, *The*

literate factory workers, creating an industrial working class with expectations of an ever-improving standard of living, while the educated, professional class expanded in size and political appetite.[70] Decision making was increasingly dominated by the interplay of interest groups and bureaucracies within the party-state, often with distinct sectoral interests or policy agendas.[71] As a result, a sort of "corporatism" emerged in the post-Stalin era which incorporated dominant political and economic interests into the policy process while maintaining public support through consumer production.[72] Focusing on the spread and consequences of modernization thus highlights important aspects of change in state socialism. For example, it helps explain why liberal opposition would emerge in much of the Communist bloc in the 1970s rather than the 1950s, and more strongly in the relatively modern societies of Central Europe than in Rumania or Bulgaria.

Because modernization theory identifies only general pressures for change, however, it does not help explain the remarkably similar timing of mobilization, nor the opposition's focus on human rights rather than economic demands. The explanatory weakness of modernization theory is further compounded by its historical indeterminacy. For example, during the breakup of feudalism in Western Europe, the new bourgeoisie pursued property rights before civil or political rights—the reverse of the East European pattern. Likewise, in the early twentieth century, states such as Chile managed to establish liberal democracy even though they were far less developed economi-

Gorbachev Phenomenon: A Historical Interpretation, expanded edition (Berkeley and Los Angeles: University of California Press, 1991).

[70] Gyorgy Konrad and Ivan Szelenyi, *The Intellectuals on the Road to Class Power* (New York: Harcourt, Brace and Jovanovich, 1979).

[71] Chalmers Johnson, ed., *Change in Communist Systems* (Stanford: Stanford University Press, 1970); H. Gordon Skilling and Franklin Griffiths, eds., *Interest Groups in Soviet Politics* (Princeton: Princeton University Press, 1971); Jan Triska and Paul Cocks, eds., *Political Development in Eastern Europe* (New York: Praeger, 1977).

[72] Valerie Bunce and Johns Echols, "Soviet Politics in the Brezhnev Era: Pluralism or Corporatism," in Donald Kelley, ed., *Soviet Politics under Brezhnev* (New York: Praeger, 1980), 1–26.

cally than Taiwan, Singapore, or South Korea were in the 1970s, when economic success often seemed to support authoritarian rule. This indeterminacy fundamentally undermines its contribution to understanding political change, whether in the Soviet bloc or elsewhere.[73]

Other scholars have focused on the developmental crises of state socialism. Through the 1950s and 1960s, the socialist system of central planning successfully promoted growth through the injection of new resources into the economy. Once basic industrialization had been accomplished, though, it proved particularly ill suited to the technological and motivational challenge of promoting growth by increasing factor productivity. Some analysts thus combine the insights of modernization theory with attention to the political economy of this failed transition from extensive to intensive economic growth.[74]

Unfortunately, none of several theories of developmental crisis offers a satisfying explanation for the aforementioned changes in state-society relations in the Communist bloc, either. First, East European economies did not exhaust their potential for extensive growth in a pattern consistent with the sudden and broad-based expansion of social mobilization and regime tolerance in 1975–1977: Czechoslovakia, East Germany, and the Soviet Union reached this transition point some time in the 1960s; Hungary and Poland some time in the early 1970s; and Bulgaria and Romania thereafter, if ever.

Moreover, the mobilization of opposition in the mid to late 1970s cannot be adequately explained as a protest by intellectuals against the state's failure to uphold a general social contract

[73] Andrew C. Janos, "Social Science, Communism, and the Dynamics of Political Change," *World Politics* 44 (October 1991):81–112. The general theory is rigorously tested and found lacking in Adam Przeworski and Fernando Limongi, "Modernization: Theories and Facts," *World Politics* 49 (January 1997):155–83.

[74] Janos Kornai, *The Economics of Shortage* (Amsterdam: North Holland, 1980); and Victor Nee and David Stark, eds., *Remaking the Economic Institutions of Socialism: China and Eastern Europe* (Stanford: Stanford University Press, 1989); Hillel Ticktin, *Origins of the Crisis in the USSR: Essays on the Political Economy of a Disintegrating System* (Armonk, N.Y.: M. E. Sharpe, 1994).

based on material consumption. It is true that when widespread repression and subservience to Moscòw exhausted the Communist authorities' limited reserves of political legitimacy, they had no choice but to promise society an increasing standard of living in exchange for acquiescence to continued party rule. And in the early 1970s, the deteriorating productivity of the centralized economy did begin to hamper the state's ability to fulfill its side of the bargain.[75] But although it does help explain the low level of mass opposition to Communist rule prior to the 1980s, this collapse of the social contract is indeterminate or inaccurate (depending upon the country) with regard to the timing and character of opposition activity that first emerged during the mid-1970s. When Charter 77 emerged in Czechoslovakia, for example, the Husak government had been actually expanding the production of consumer goods for several years.

Another potential explanation for change focuses on the opportunities created by regime fragmentation. We know that regimes are most vulnerable to societal pressure when weakened by internal divisions, especially by elites' loss of self-confidence and/or moves toward reform. Under such conditions, regime opponents rush to take advantage of an unprecedented and perhaps fleeting opportunity to influence political agendas, form new alliances, and thereby shift outcomes in their favor.[76] Some

[75] See Ferenc Feher, "Paternalism as a Mode of Legitimation in Soviet-type Societies," in T. H. Rigby and Ferenc Feher, eds., *Political Legitimation in Communist States* (New York: St. Martin's, 1982); Alex Pravda, "East-West Interdependence and the Social Compact in Eastern Europe," in Morris Bornstein, Zvi Gitelman, and William Zimmerman, eds., *East-West Relations and the Future of Eastern Europe* (Boston: Allen & Unwin, 1981).

[76] On political opportunity structure as a determinant of societal mobilization, see Douglas McAdam, *Political Process and the Development of Black Insurgency 1930–1970* (Chicago: University of Chicago Press, 1982); and Sidney Tarrow, "States and Opportunities: The Political Structuring of Social Movements," in Douglas McAdam, John D. McCarthy, and Mayer N. Zald, eds., *Comparative Perspectives on Social Movements* (New York and Cambridge: Cambridge University Press, 1996), 41–61. For specific application to regime change, see Guillermo O'Donnell and Philippe Schmitter, *Transitions from Authoritarian Rule: Tentative Conclusions* (Baltimore: Johns Hopkins University Press, 1986).

observers of state socialism have argued that an intraparty split recognizable and exploitable by societal forces was created by the struggle between conservatives who wished to maintain the old system and reformers who recognized that the transition from extensive to intensive growth required economic decentralization and other measures favoring the technical intelligentsia.[77]

The question thus becomes whether an intraparty struggle between reformers and conservatives was evident in the mid-1970s, and whether the societal mobilization of this period accords with that split. The answer is that although party elites in several East European countries did debate and experiment with economic reforms, beginning with East Germany's attempt to rationalize central planning and Hungary's moves toward liberalization in the late 1960s, opposition in these countries was less noteworthy than elsewhere in the bloc. In fact, significant societal groups mobilized in both Czechoslovakia and the Soviet Union, which were firmly under the grip of conservative elites who tolerated no talk of reform, and in Poland, where the regime's half-hearted economic reforms of the early 1970s were stalled by the middle of the decade.

As for the possibility that opposition may have mobilized where regimes *failed* to implement the structural reforms necessary for continued economic development, we observe that the opposition critique in the 1970s was primarily directed at abuses of human rights, rather than inefficiency, inflation, or economic shortages, and was thus ill-suited to benefit from whatever intraparty divisions may have existed over economic reform.[78] In fact, given the ideological and geopolitical environment, those who wished to promote economic liberalization knew that challenging the political hegemony of the Commu-

---

[77] Janos Kornai, *The Socialist System: The Political Economy of Communism* (Princeton: Princeton University Press, 1992), chapter 18.

[78] Materially oriented mobilization did occur in Poland, where the economy was weakest, in 1970 and 1976, but was not sustained until after several years of concerted organizing by human rights activists in the late 1970s. On the contribution of Polish human rights groups to the emergence of Solidarity in 1980, see Chapter 6.

nist Party would most likely strengthen the hand of conserva-tives.[79] Moreover, Communist elites in the region did not aban-don their sense of their own "right to rule" before late 1988 or 1989, when the significance of widening opposition in the streets was reinforced by Moscow's new commitment to non-intervention in East European affairs.[80] As such, the actual pat-tern of reformist openings does not provide adequate explana-tion for the timing or the content of opposition mobilization across the region beginning in the mid-1970s.

The interaction of interdependence and pressure for reform by Western states offers yet another perspective on political change in state socialism. The logic of interdependence is that the exchange of goods and ideas across national borders opens societies to influences from abroad, either through cultural contagion, economic restructuring, or deliberate manipulation. (This insight is fully compatible, of course, with both modern-ization theory and the logic of developmental crisis, both of which recognize elite incentives to reduce economic and cul-tural autarchy.) For example, one could argue that mobilization against state socialist regimes, and increased tolerance by those regimes, would be promoted by liberal ideas and information diffused from the West, whether through tourism, cultural and educational exchange, electronic broadcasts, or even historical memories of a presocialist era.[81] If this hypothesis were valid, changes in social mobilization and regime tolerance should fol-low changes in the availability of liberal ideas and information from the West. But although the allure of liberal ideas was sig-nificant in the East, and liberal ideology had a heavy influence on the thinking of the opposition, these ideas did not suddenly become available in the East bloc in the mid-1970s, and thus simply cannot account for the changes in question.

[79] Pavel Bozyk, interview by author, Warsaw, July 8, 1992.

[80] Giuseppe Di Palma, "Legitimation from the Top to Civil Society: Polit-ico-Cultural Change in Eastern Europe," *World Politics* 44 (October 1991):49–80.

[81] For two versions of this argument, see Hedley Bull and Adam Watson, eds., *The Expansion of International Society* (Oxford: Clarendon Press, 1985); and

Alternatively, one could argue that social mobilization responded to the West's policy commitment to liberalism, and its consequent manipulation of the East bloc's economic or strategic dependency.[82] It is undeniable that some political forces in the West were committed to the ideological conversion of the East bloc, and that societal actors in the East sought to benefit from this commitment. Nonetheless, the West's pursuit of ideological conversion in the East was far less aggressive during the détente years of the early-mid 1970s than during the previous three decades, so this was hardly a rational moment to rely on a diffuse ideological commitment. Moreover, the pattern of changes in social mobilization and regime tolerance do not accord with the countries' vulnerability to Western influence. For example, whereas both Poland and Czechoslovakia experienced similar changes in mobilization in 1975–1976, Poland's hard currency debt and trade deficit were roughly ten times greater and climbing far faster than that of Czechoslovakia.[83] Finally, as Chapter 4 makes clear, Western pressure on human rights was largely a result, not a cause, of social mobilization and transnational networking in the East. The West's manipulation of the East's economic dependence thus provides no better explanation for the changes in question than the other hypotheses discussed above.[84]

The point of this review is not to posit another comprehensive account of the decline and fall of Communist rule. The viability of state socialism was clearly challenged by the social strains of modernization, by the institutional difficulty of transition from extensive to intensive growth, and by the political

---

James N. Rosenau, *Turbulence in World Politics: A Theory of Change and Continuity* (Princeton: Princeton University Press, 1990).

[82] On relative vulnerability to interdependence as a source of power, see Robert O. Keohane and Joseph S. Nye, *Power and Interdependence* (Glenview, Ill.: Scott, Foresman, 1978).

[83] United States Congress, Joint Economic Committee, *East European Economies after Helsinki: A Compendium of Papers* (Washington, D.C.: Government Printing Office, 1977), 1,352.

[84] For more on this point, see Bornstein, Gitelman, and Zimmerman, eds., *East-West Relations and the Future of Eastern Europe*.

vulnerability that accompanies international exposure and dependence. As such, the modernization, developmental crisis, and interdependence paradigms (in all their variants) illuminate critical dynamics in East European politics in the 1970s and beyond that any discussion of the region must take into account. The point is simply to demonstrate that none of these theories offers a satisfactory explanation for the nearly simultaneous mobilization of societal opposition and increase in regime tolerance in Eastern Europe and the Soviet Union in the mid to late 1970s. Likewise, none can explain the opposition's tendency to emphasize basic civil rights issues (freedom of expression, freedom of association, and so on) rather than material frustrations. In contrast, the "Helsinki effect" offers persuasive explanation for these developments.

CONCLUSIONS

The individuals in Eastern Europe and the Soviet Union who began to mobilize around Helsinki norms in 1975 were neither riding a preexisting wave of opposition activity nor responding to additional signals from governments at home or abroad that their efforts would be well received. Instead, they were invoking the human rights norms of the Helsinki Final Act to rouse a passive population, engage influence from abroad, and thereby, it was hoped, to reduce the repressiveness of life under Communist party rule. (For geopolitical reasons, overthrowing Communist rule was generally not considered achievable in the near term.) It was not until late 1976 that most of these nascent and disparate oppositionist voices really began to organize as social-political movements, but the petitions of the immediate post-Helsinki period represent the first stages of a sustained challenge to the hegemony of the party-state. This fact is reflected in the unusually broad constituencies that they encompassed, and the development of the themes that dominated organized opposition activity beginning in late 1976: that international norms, including the Helsinki Final Act, obligated the party-state to ensure the individual's freedom of expression, association, and travel, among other rights; and that individuals and independent associations had a right to monitor their implementation.

The latent power of international human rights norms as a basis for independent or opposition activity is nowhere better demonstrated than in the fact that the Communist regimes' reactions to the initial wave of post-Helsinki social mobilization only reinforced the perception that Helsinki had created new opportunities for the opposition. The more the authorities used international human rights norms to justify their own actions while (perhaps begrudgingly) extending the bounds of permitted behavior, the more opposition forces concluded that the Helsinki Final Act actually represented more than a collection of empty promises.

The fact that the party-state had lost control of the transnational process by which the Final Act was framed in public discourse did not eliminate its considerable capacities for repression. It did however transform the emerging confrontation with dissident social movements and their foreign supporters into an "uphill" battle that the Kremlin had not anticipated just a few years earlier. As long as they continued to value the CSCE, the Communist regimes would not be able to dismiss Helsinki's human rights norms as they had ignored the Universal Declaration of Human Rights since 1948. As Soviet ambassador Anatoly Dobrynin later reflected, this development and those which it subsequently enabled were "totally beyond the imagination of the Soviet leadership" that negotiated and approved the norms of the Final Act.[85]

---

[85] Dobrynin, *In Confidence*, 346.

CHAPTER FOUR

Framing "Helsinki" Abroad:
Transnational Networks and U.S. Policy

The Soviet and East European representatives have
always tried to neutralize the humanitarian principles of
the Helsinki accords by emphasizing the principle of
non-interference in the internal affairs of other countries. . . .
Is the West prepared to defend these noble and vitally
important principles? Or, will it, little by little, accept the
interpretation of the principles of Helsinki, and of detente as
a whole, that the leaders of the Soviet Union and of Eastern
Europe are trying to impose?
—*Soviet dissident Andrei Sakharov, 1977*[1]

When the long negotiations ended at the Helsinki summit,
most Western observers thought and said that the Soviets
had gotten the best of the bargain. . . . What happened,
instead, was a remarkable turning of the tables. It was
accomplished not by any brilliant strategic analysts in
Washington or NATO, but by a small band of intrepid Soviet
citizens who began to say out loud. . . . that the Soviet
Union must make good on its laws and its Helsinki
commitments. Their demands made us respond.
—*U.S. congressman Dante Fascell, 1978*[2]

As we have seen, the 1975 Helsinki Final Act provoked a flurry
of opposition petitions and public demands for reform across

---

[1] *International Herald Tribune,* October 6, 1977.

[2] Address before the Chicago Council of Foreign Relations, February 24,
1978, in U.S. Commission on Security and Cooperation in Europe, *The Belgrade Follow-Up Meeting to the Conference on Security and Cooperation in Europe:
A Report and Appraisal* (Washington, D.C.: Government Printing Office, 1978),
Appendix B.

Eastern Europe and the Soviet Union. Over the following two years, this social movement activity coalesced into well-organized human rights and opposition groups, focused on Helsinki norms, whose creation and survival contrasted sharply with the near absence of dissent in the region during the early 1970s. Yet even after Helsinki, the tolerance of the Communist regimes was not unlimited. Had nothing else changed, the brief post-Helsinki opportunity for social mobilization would likely have been slammed shut by conservative Communist elites still inclined to repress all challengers. This reaction was forestalled, however, by the rise of human rights issues, and particularly Helsinki compliance, as a priority in the foreign policy of Western governments. The change was particularly notable in U.S. policy, which (as demonstrated in Chapters 1–2) had previously viewed the CSCE as a concession necessary to maintain détente, and the human rights agenda primarily as a West European concern.

The U.S. policy reversal, however, was itself also an unexpected effect of the Helsinki norms. Otherwise weak and isolated, non-state actors in the East used the Helsinki norms as an ideational frame with which to engage the attention of non-state and substate actors in the West. The members of the resulting transnational "Helsinki network" then used the same frame to engage the interest and influence of Western governments, lobbying and shaming them to adopt a more assertive position on human rights violations in the East bloc. This chapter identifies changes in the discourse of American policy elites, in the behavior of U.S. state actors, and in the underlying sources of U.S. foreign policy, including both the conception of self-interest that drives policy and the institutional forms that shape it. Alternative explanations are considered at the end of the chapter.

TRANSNATIONAL APPEALS TO THE U.S. GOVERNMENT

Following the Helsinki summit, the U.S. State Department continued with its implicit policy, in place since the beginning of negotiations, that the CSCE should be tolerated but not emphasized in East-West relations. Henry Kissinger had become somewhat more active on human rights in the latter stages of the negotiations, and President Ford's speech at the Helsinki summit emphasized "the deep devotion of the American people and their government to human rights and fundamental freedoms." Nonetheless, U.S. policy to downplay the CSCE and the human rights issue remained in place. In fact, when one of the U.S. negotiators at Geneva returned to the State Department after the summit and expressed interest in monitoring compliance with the Helsinki Final Act, he was instructed by senior officials that the CSCE was now completed and no longer required attention.[3]

At the time, there was little reason to expect that the U.S. Congress would take a substantially different position. Most members of Congress viewed the CSCE negotiations in Geneva as, at best, a necessary evil for the maintenance of détente, and at worst, a concession to continued Soviet hegemony. When the House Committee on Foreign Affairs held hearings during the CSCE negotiations, not a single member asked executive branch officials about the CSCE's human rights content, or its probable effects in that area.[4] Moreover, except for the politically powerful issue of emigration and refusniks, which catalyzed the Jackson-Vanik amendment of 1974, the U.S. Congress was not especially engaged with human rights issues in the East bloc during the early to mid 1970s.[5] It was only when dissidents from the East focused on Helsinki compliance that U.S. officials began to take the issue seriously.

The first prominent appeal for a change in U.S. policy came from famous Russian dissident Alexander Solzhenitsyn, who had been expelled from the Soviet Union in February 1974. Invited to address an AFL-CIO meeting in Washington on

---

[3] Guy Coriden, interview by author, Washington, D.C., March 31, 1994.

[4] See U.S. Congress, House of Representatives, Committee on Foreign Affairs, *Hearings before the Subcommittee on Europe*, April 25; May 10; August 10, 17; and September 7, 27, 1972 (Washington, D.C.: Government Printing Office, 1972).

[5] Thomas M. Franck and Edward Weisband, *Foreign Policy by Congress* (New York: Oxford University Press, 1979), 83–97.

June 30, 1975 (just one month before the Helsinki summit), Solzhenitsyn sharply criticized both the Soviet regime and the nonintervention principle in the forthcoming Helsinki Final Act, which he feared would be "the funeral of Eastern Europe." As part of this attempt to shame the Ford administration into action, he called on his influential audience (which also included Secretary of Defense James Schlesinger and U.N. ambassador Daniel Patrick Moynihan) to press for implementation of the Final Act's human rights principles by the East: "Interfere more and more. . . . Interfere as much as you can. We beg you to come and 'interfere.' "[6] The *New York Times* placed its report on Solzhenitsyn's speech alongside a story on the CSCE talks in Geneva that described West European frustrations with Henry Kissinger's willingness to compromise the human rights agenda, and declared in large type, "Security Accord Will Be More Symbolic Than Concrete."[7]

A similar message was articulated by other Soviet activists several weeks after the Helsinki summit, when a Congressional delegation went to the Soviet Union on a routine, multi-issue visit. One member of the delegation, Representative Millicent Fenwick of New Jersey, was particularly struck by the lengths to which Soviet refusniks (those refused emigration visas by the authorities) would go to meet the delegation. "We would meet them at night in hotels in Moscow and Leningrad," she later recalled, "and I would ask, 'How do you dare to come see us here?' " under the eyes of the KGB. "Don't you understand," they replied. "That's our only hope. We've seen you. Now they know you've seen us."[8] This expression of the power of international oversight on behalf of human rights deeply moved the first-term representative.

---

[6] The speech is reprinted in Alexander Solzhenitsyn, *Détente* (New Brunswick, N.J.: Transaction Books, 1980), 19–50; see also Henry Kissinger, *Years of Renewal* (New York: Simon & Schuster, 1999), 649–53.

[7] *New York Times,* July 1, 1975.

[8] Madeleine K. Albright and Alfred Friendly, Jr., "Helsinki and Human Rights," in Edmund Muskie et al., eds., *The President, the Congress and Foreign Policy* (Lanham, Md.: University Press of America, 1986), 291.

An American newspaper correspondent then arranged for Fenwick to meet refusnik Vaniamin Levich and long-time dissident Yuri Orlov at the home of Valentin Turchin, head of the Moscow chapter of Amnesty International. During the discussion, Orlov argued that the recently signed Helsinki Final Act could provide leverage against the Soviet regime, and urged the congresswoman to take advantage of this opportunity.[9] Although Representative Fenwick had no prior experience in foreign policy, and did not represent a district with many East European émigrés, these encounters in Russia had a powerful effect on her. Brezhnev described Fenwick as "obsessive" after she pressed him on several humanitarian cases during a meeting before the delegation's departure.[10] She returned to Washington committed to using the Helsinki Accords and American influence on behalf of those whom she had met.

CREATION OF THE U.S. HELSINKI COMMISSION

Within days of her return, Fenwick introduced a bill proposing that the U.S. Congress establish a Commission on Security and Cooperation in Europe, which would monitor compliance with the Helsinki Final Act, particularly in the human rights field. (Despite the timing of the Congressional visit to the Soviet Union, and the speed with which Fenwick introduced the bill after her return, there is no evidence that she or any other member of the delegation contemplated in advance the creation of such a commission.) As proposed, it would consist of members of both houses of Congress, from both parties, plus representatives from the departments of State, Defense, and Commerce. Twelve days later, Senator Clifford Case, a fellow Republican from New Jersey, introduced a parallel bill in the other chamber.

[9] Interviews with Yuri Orlov, Ithaca, N.Y., 1990–1992; confirmed by the meeting organizer, *New York Times* correspondent Christopher Wren, in telephone interview, August 22, 1995.

[10] William Korey, *The Promises We Keep: Human Rights, The Helsinki Process, and American Foreign Policy* (New York: St. Martin's, 1993), 23.

The executive branch immediately opposed Fenwick's CSCE monitoring initiative. President Ford had been heavily criticized from all sides for his participation in "another Yalta," and with the summit past, his political advisors hoped to let the CSCE issue fade away. Within the State Department, the Final Act was considered "yesterday's news."[11] Senior officials continued to view Eastern Europe as part of the Soviet Union's natural sphere of influence.[12] Henry Kissinger, who was never a CSCE enthusiast or a proponent of human rights in foreign policy, viewed the proposed commission as an intrusion into the prerogative of the executive branch and as an obstacle to the highly personalized method of "shuttle diplomacy" that he preferred.

In fact, the proposed commission did represent a significant congressional foray into foreign affairs, reaching well beyond the Jackson-Vanik Amendment, which had linked most-favored nation status to the emigration policies of Communist states, but did not involve congressional oversight into conditions abroad. The Department of State also argued that the proposed commission would violate the Constitution by subordinating members of the executive branch to legislators in the making of foreign policy. Assistant Secretary of State for Congressional Relations Robert J. McCloskey testified that the commission's "extraordinary composition would not seem to provide an appropriate or effective means for coordinating or guiding our efforts."[13] The White House nonetheless instructed Kissinger to mute his criticisms for fear of further alienating conservatives during an election year.[14]

As the months went by, more and more news reached the West about this new Helsinki-focused wave of human rights

[11] Guy Coriden, interview by author, Washington, D.C., March 31, 1994.

[12] State Department counselor Helmut Sonnenfeldt expressed this view in a private meeting with U.S. ambassadors in Europe in December 1975. See the *New York Times*, April 6, 1976.

[13] U.S. Congress, Senate, Committee on Foreign Relations, *Establishing a Commission on Security and Cooperation in Europe*, Report 94–756 (Washington, D.C., Government Printing Office, April 23, 1976).

[14] Albright and Friendly, "Helsinki and Human Rights," 297.

activity in the East. In addition to Western journalists in the region, human rights and émigré organizations in Washington, New York, and Chicago (as well as Paris, London, Rome, and elsewhere in Western Europe) were flooded with Helsinki-oriented petitions and appeals from Eastern Europe and the Soviet Union. On the op-ed page of the *New York Times*, Soviet dissident Andrei Amalrik criticized the U.S. government's tendency to favor good relations with the Kremlin over frank discussion of human rights conditions and compliance with Helsinki norms: "If the U.S. sets itself the objective of establishing friendly relations with the USSR and wants to be assured of their desirability, then it must strive for the transformation of the closed Soviet system into an open one. The awakening of the Soviet people to human rights is a force working in this direction."[15]

Many of the ethnic lobbies in the U.S. that had once opposed or been skeptical about the Helsinki Final Act began to reconsider their position in light of the positive response that it had evoked in the "home country." Influential Polish, Hungarian, and Czechoslovak émigré organizations endorsed the Case-Fenwick bills, as did the Baltic-American Committee, which had only recently criticized the Final Act for legitimating Soviet rule in Latvia, Lithuania, and Estonia.[16] The National Conference on Soviet Jewry (NCSJ) also supported the bills in the hope that concerted attention to compliance with Helsinki principles would cause Moscow to expand Jewish emigration. The NCSJ was encouraged in this hope by a behind-the-scenes deal at the Helsinki summit, in which Polish and West German officials agreed to "trade" the emigration of ethnic Germans living in Poland for an increase in loans to Warsaw. If the CSCE could facilitate the emigration of ethnic Germans, the NCSJ reasoned, then maybe it could do the same for Soviet Jews.[17] At a February 1976 meeting in Brussels on the problem of Jewish emigration from the Soviet Union, several members of Con-

---

[15] *New York Times*, October 22, 1975.
[16] Korey, *Promises*, 27.
[17] Ibid., 25.

gress heard delegates from around the world call on the United States to monitor implementation of the Helsinki Final Act.[18]

At first, Congressman Dante Fascell, chair of the Foreign Affairs Committee, explained that he was "skeptical about the wisdom of setting up yet another governmental entity for such a specific purpose." In the end, though, he and a majority of the Congress were persuaded by the argument that the U.S. government should expect and monitor compliance with a major international agreement, and by the political might of ethnic lobbies working in favor of the commission: "After our hearings, conversations with many of the 100 cosponsors in the House, and numerous discussions and other contacts with representatives of such diverse groups as the Veterans of Foreign Wars, the National Conference on Soviet Jewry, the Federation of American Scientists, the Polish-American Congress and the Joint Baltic-American Committee, I am now convinced that such an entity would . . . play a vital role in the promotion of human rights and in making certain that détente will be a two-way street."[19] After Fascell reworked the Fenwick-Case legislation to favor the majority party in the House and Senate, bills to create the U.S. Commission on Security and Cooperation in Europe passed both houses of Congress in late May, and became law on June 3, 1976.

Still unresigned to the existence of the commission, President Ford then threatened to "pocket veto" the necessary financing legislation. By this point, though, the network of Helsinki activists in the West was functioning quite well. On the first anniversary of the Helsinki Final Act, the network delivered to Capitol Hill a translation of the Moscow Helsinki Group's recent evaluation of the influence of the Final Act. This firsthand account of Soviet violations reinforced the congressional argument that strict monitoring was absolutely necessary.[20] Faced with such arguments, and a second round of lob-

---

[18] *Congressional Record*, May 17, 1976, 14,051–52.

[19] Ibid., 14,049.

[20] "An Evaluation of the Influence of the Helsinki Agreements as they Relate to Human Rights in the USSR, 1 August 1975–1 August 1976," unpublished

bying from the ethnic organizations, Ford conceded. The U.S. Helsinki Commission (as it was coming to be known) began full-scale operation in the fall of 1976.

During a trip to Europe in November organized by the commission, several members of Congress heard East-bloc dissidents and sympathetic human rights activists speak of "the need to base detente between East and West on the progress on internal change inside the Soviet Union" and repeat the importance of Helsinki monitoring and issue-linkage in U.S. policy.[21] Congressman Donald Fraser later recalled how the West's view of the Helsinki Accords had been influenced by the arguments and example of Soviet and East European activists: "[F]ew suspected that the Helsinki Accords would become a subject of lively political interest. Most thought the agreements were no more than footnotes to the complex, often contradictory history of détente. . . . Now the verdict has been reversed. . . . The changed perception is not of our making. For the first to recognize—indeed, to exalt—the innovative content of the accords were men and women in the Soviet Union and the other Warsaw Pact states."[22]

REVERSING U.S. POLICY

As indicated above, the initial U.S. policy after the Helsinki summit was to deemphasize the CSCE. Although they were more positively inclined than the Ford administration in Washington, the West European governments intended to pursue a non-confrontational approach to implementation of the human

---

paper in the Belgrade conference files of the U.S. Commission on Security and Cooperation in Europe (hereafter, "U.S. Helsinki Commission").

[21] "Working Meeting of the Commission on Security and Cooperation in Europe, Washington, D.C., January 6, 1977," transcript in U.S. Helsinki Commission files.

[22] Council of Europe, Parliamentary Assembly, *Implementation of the Final Act of the Conference on Security and Cooperation in Europe*, "Debate on the General Policy of the Council of Europe, 27, 28 and 29 April 1977," AS/Inf (77) 9 (Strasbourg, 1977), 168.

rights norms that they had insisted on including in the Final Act. This combination of policies within the NATO alliance produced a December 1975 North Atlantic Council communiqué whose tone was remarkably similar to East-bloc commentaries on the Final Act: "In the political sphere, détente requires tolerance and mutual understanding, and accordingly demands that the natural contest of political and social ideas should not be conducted in a manner incompatible with the letter and spirit of the Final Act of Helsinki."[23] As for implementation, the communiqué stated only that the allies expected progress in relations between states, in confidence-building measures, in economic cooperation, and in "lowering barriers between peoples"—an early NATO formula that fell far short of the more determinate norms already established by the Final Act.

By mid-1976, though, U.S. and West European foreign ministries were flooded with massive documentation of human rights violations submitted by nongovernmental organizations in the new "Helsinki network."[24] As a result of this pressure, American and NATO policy on the CSCE began to reflect the priority on human rights favored by dissidents in the East and their supporters in the West. Pressured from all sides, the White House and State Department began to take Helsinki implementation seriously. The North Atlantic Council's May 1976 communiqué struck an entirely new tone: "Ministers . . . emphasised the importance they attach to full implementation of all parts of the Helsinki Final Act by all signatories, so that its benefits may be felt not only in relations between states but also in the lives of individuals."[25] The communiqué continued, acknowledging some progress in the area of human contacts and working conditions for journalists, but pointing out "the importance of what still remains to be done," and expressing the hope for rapid progress on implementation of the basic principles, including human rights.

[23] North Atlantic Council, *Texts of Final Communiqués*, Volume 2 (Brussels: NATO Information Service, 1980), 38–39.

[24] Interviews with former American and West European diplomats, 1993–1995.

[25] North Atlantic Council, *Texts of Final Communiqués*, Volume 2, 45.

By the end of 1976, reports from East European activists and from sympathetic organizations in the West had convinced Western governments that Helsinki norms were not being respected. Though still diplomatic in style, the North Atlantic Council's December communiqué expressed continued frustration: "[m]uch remains to be done before the benefits of the Final Act become significantly apparent in tangible improvements, not only in relations between states, but also in the lives of peoples and individuals. Ministers recalled that the Final Act acknowledges that wider human contacts and dissemination of information would contribute to the strengthening of peace and expressed the hope that the Warsaw pact countries would take measures leading to significant progress in the pace of implementation of the Final Act in the months to come."[26]

REACTIONS FROM THE KREMLIN

This shift in Western policy did not go unnoticed in the Kremlin. On February 24, 1976, Brezhnev's report to the 25th Congress of the CPSU acknowledged "certain difficulties in our relations with a number of capitalist European states" during the seven months since the Helsinki summit. In fact, Brezhnev responded to the unexpected salience of human rights (Principle 7) by focusing on non-intervention in internal affairs (Principle 6), as he had done in his speech at the Helsinki summit: "Certain quarters are trying to emasculate and distort the very substance of the Final Act adopted in Helsinki, and to use this document as a screen for interfering in the internal affairs of the socialist countries, for anti-Communist and anti-Soviet demagogy in cold-war style."[27] Yet despite these frustrations, he remained committed to the Helsinki Final Act as the instrument by which the Soviet Union and its allies could achieve greater economic ties with the West: "The main thing now is

[26] Ibid., 61.

[27] Leonid Brezhnev, *Peace, Détente and Soviet-American Relations: A Collection of Public Statements* (New York: Harcourt, Brace, Jovanovich, 1979), 106.

to translate all the principles and understandings reached in Helsinki into practical deeds. This is exactly what the Soviet Union is doing and will continue to do."[28] Communist authorities nonetheless became less and less patient as East European dissidents became more active, the U.S. Congress more assertive, and U.S. policy slowly more confrontational.

Throughout the summer of 1976, the official Soviet media criticized the formation of the U.S. Helsinki Commission as a violation of Soviet internal affairs and as an act aimed not at the promotion of détente but at "fouling up the process."[29] In September, Polish Ministry of Foreign Affairs counselor Jerzy Nowak warned that "For the good of all-European cooperation the capitalist states should cease trying to force the socialist side to accept a different interpretation of some concepts."[30] By the mid-autumn, the postsummit luster had disappeared from Brezhnev's rhetoric on the CSCE.[31] All of this occurred, of course, before the election of Jimmy Carter, who is often credited with introducing human rights as a U.S. foreign policy priority.

THE 1976 PRESIDENTIAL ELECTION

Transnational feedback from the Helsinki process also shaped U.S. policy by contributing to Jimmy Carter's election as president in 1976. It did so by influencing politics within the Republican Party, and thus weakening President Ford's political base, as well as by shaping the terms of debate between Ford and

[28] Ibid.

[29] *Izvestia* (Moscow), June 17, August 7 and 29, 1976.

[30] Jerzy M. Nowak, "Cooperation between East and West on Humanitarian Issues," *Sprawy Miedzynarodowe* no. 9, September 1976, from JPRS, *Translations* 68273 (November 26, 1976), 12.

[31] See Brezhnev's October 25, 1976, address to a plenary meeting of the CPSU Central Committee, in his *Peace, Détente and Soviet-American Relations*, 131–36.

Carter. To start, public debate over the 1975 Helsinki Accords and then the creation of the Helsinki Commission, plus reports of noncompliance by the East bloc, fed directly into the Republican Party's internal debate over the merits of détente. Conservatives led by Ronald Reagan argued that Gerald Ford had violated America's commitment to freedom in Eastern Europe and the Soviet Union, both by his initial participation in the Helsinki process and then by his resistance to a commission that would monitor compliance with its provisions. As step toward healing this division within the party, Ford agreed to a party platform which stated that "Agreements which are negotiated, such as the one signed in Helsinki, must not take from those who do not have freedom the hope of one day gaining it," and praised Soviet dissident Alexander Solzhenitsyn for "his compelling message that we must face the world with no illusions about the nature of tyranny."[32] This dispute nonetheless forced Ford to run for reelection without the strong support of anti-Communists within his party.

Pressure from the Helsinki network and fallout from related debates affected the Democratic campaign as well, helping to move Jimmy Carter away from his initially skeptical attitude toward the Helsinki process and the larger role of human rights in foreign policy. In June 1976, for example, Carter had told the Foreign Policy Association, "Our people have learned the folly of trying to inject our power into the internal affairs of other nations." Moreover, according to Democratic senator Daniel Patrick Moynihan, the human rights issue "was raised in the Democratic platform drafting committee, and at the Democratic Convention, but in each instance the Carter representatives were at best neutral, giving the impression of not having heard very much of the matter before and not having any particular views."[33]

<hr />

[32] Judith F. Buncher, ed., *Human Rights and American Diplomacy, 1975–1977* (New York: Facts on File, 1977), 78.

[33] Jeanne J. Kirkpatrick, *Legitimacy and Force, Volume 1: Political and Moral Dimensions* (New Brunswick, N.J.: Transaction Books, 1988), 141.

On some campaign stops, though, Carter did take advantage of the fact that President Ford had antagonized East European ethnic voters with his trip to Helsinki and then again with his resistance to the Helsinki Commission. Carter's speeches thus often portrayed the Helsinki Final Act as a "tremendous diplomatic victory for Leonid Brezhnev," while declaring, "We cannot look away when a government tortures people, or jails them for their beliefs or denies minorities fair treatment or the right to emigrate. . . . [I]f any nation . . . deprives its people of basic human rights, that fact will help shape our own people's attitudes towards that nation's government."[34] Hearing of this rhetoric, the newly appointed staff director of the U.S. Helsinki Commission contacted the Carter campaign and urged that the governor adopt a more positive view of the Helsinki process.[35]

Four days later, during a televised debate between the two candidates, Ford seemed to suggest that Eastern Europe was not subject to Soviet domination. Carter quickly rebutted that many Americans felt otherwise and, for the first time, criticized Ford's failure to pressure for compliance with the human rights components of the Helsinki Final Act. Pollster George Gallup called this the "most decisive moment in the campaign."[36] The ensuing controversy lasted for several days, further weakening Ford in the final weeks of the campaign. In the end, Carter's narrow margin of victory, especially in some traditionally Republican areas, depended in part on the conservatives and ethnic East European voters whom Ford had alienated by his apparent commitment to détente over human rights or Helsinki compliance.[37]

---

[34] Buncher, *Human Rights*, 77–78.

[35] Albright and Friendly, "Helsinki and Human Rights," 303–4.

[36] William G. Hyland, *Mortal Rivals: Superpower Relations from Nixon to Reagan* (New York: Random House, 1987), 173.

[37] Leo P. Ribuffo, "Is Poland a Soviet Satellite? Gerald Ford, the Sonnenfeldt Doctrine and the Election of 1976," *Diplomatic History* 14 (Summer 1990):385–404.

THE HELSINKI NETWORK AND THE
CARTER ADMINISTRATION

After Carter's election, various parts of the burgeoning Helsinki network worked to shape the foreign policy priorities of the new administration. As Carter's staff prepared for the inauguration, Dante Fascell wrote to Secretary of State-designee Cyrus Vance urging a strong reference to human rights in the inaugural address.[38] Though surely not the only source, Fascell's message was closely reflected in the inaugural's declaration that "Because we are free, we can never be indifferent to the fate of freedom elsewhere." The same is true of a second inaugural statement, broadcast the same day by the U.S. Information Agency, in which Carter promised listeners around the world, "You can depend on the United States to remain steadfast in its commitment to human freedom and liberty."[39] This rhetoric was noticed in Eastern Europe, by regime and opposition forces alike.

The real question, though, was whether the Carter administration would implement this verbal commitment when it appeared to conflict with other priorities. Before his appointment as national security advisor, Zbigniew Brzezinski had written that the human rights issue could help relegitimate U.S. foreign policy at home and abroad.[40] He and other senior officials were nonetheless determined to avoid a human rights confrontation in the CSCE that would upset the administration's broader détente agenda, especially nuclear and conventional arms control with the Soviets. Marshall Shulman, the State Department's new chief Soviet specialist, had long argued that U.S. policy should not become preoccupied with human rights.[41] Re-

[38] Correspondence from Dante Fascell to Cyrus Vance, January 11, 1977, in U.S. Helsinki Commission files.

[39] Buncher, *Human Rights*, 80–81.

[40] Zbigniew Brzezinski, "America in a Hostile World," *Foreign Policy* 23 (Summer 1976):65–96.

[41] *New York Times*, October 31, 1975; Marshall Shulman, "On Learning to Live with Authoritarian Regimes," *Foreign Affairs* 55 (1977):325–38.

flecting this position, the president-elect's first communication with the Kremlin, relayed privately by Averell Harriman to Soviet ambassador Dobrynin on December 1, 1976, focused on arms control without any mention of human rights.[42] This moderate approach was confirmed in President Carter's first official letter to Leonid Brezhnev, written just a week after the inauguration: "A competition in ideals and ideas is inevitable between our societies. Yet this must not interfere with common efforts towards formation of a more peaceful, just and human world."[43]

Before long, though, East European and Soviet dissidents and their "Helsinki network" allies in the U.S. Congress forced the administration to implement a far more confrontational approach to human rights than was initially intended. Almost immediately after the inauguration, reports began to reach the West through media and NGO channels about a crackdown in Czechoslovakia against signatories of the new human rights initiative, Charter 77. On January 26, the State Department harshly criticized the government of Czechoslovakia for violating its commitments in the Helsinki Accords.[44] Although the statement was apparently issued without prior authorization from the White House or the secretary of state, it was seen publicly as a landmark action by the new administration. Editorial pages across the country praised Carter's break from Ford's failure to insist on Helsinki compliance.[45]

Word also reached Washington through NGO channels that Soviet human rights activist Aleksandr Ginzburg had been arrested and charged with currency violations. One week later, on February 2, the State Department protested Ginzburg's ar-

---

[42] "Ambassador A. F. Dobrynin's Conversation with Averell Harriman, December 1, 1976," in "The Path to Disagreement," Cold War International History Project, Woodrow Wilson International Center for Scholars, Smithsonian Institution, http://cwihp.si.edu.

[43] "President Carter's Letter to General Secretary Brezhnev, January 26, 1977," ibid.

[44] New York Times, January 27, 1977.

[45] On the question of authorization, see Hyland, Mortal Rivals, 204. For a broad sample of editorials, see Buncher, Human Rights, 111–15.

rest as a violation of Helsinki norms. At about the same time, Andrei Sakharov wrote to President Carter, praising his commitment to human rights and calling his attention to human rights violations in the Soviet Union. (Sakharov was closely affiliated with the Moscow Helsinki Group, but unlike Ginzburg, not officially a member.) Although Carter felt obligated to respond personally to this appeal from the Soviet Union's most famous scientist and dissident, National Security Advisor Zbigniew Brzezinski and Secretary of State Cyrus Vance did their best to draft the letter in a way that would avoid provoking the Kremlin.[46]

Notwithstanding the new administration's public criticisms of arrests in Czechoslovakia and the Soviet Union, and Carter's personal correspondence with Sakharov, senior officials sought to maintain the possibility of quiet diplomacy for human rights. For example, when the Soviets complained about Washington's contact with Sakharov, Vance responded, "We do not intend to be strident or polemical," and predicted that the human rights dispute would not affect U.S.-Soviet arms negotiations.[47] The mobilization of the Helsinki network on both sides of the Iron Curtain was nonetheless making it increasingly difficult for the Carter administration to avoid a confrontational policy on human rights. In his second letter to Brezhnev, Carter warned that Helsinki compliance could not be kept off the agenda, but again expressed a preference for quiet diplomacy:

> We expect cooperation in the realization of further steps toward the fulfillment of the agreements reached in Helsinki relating to human rights. . . . It is not our intention to interfere in the internal affairs of other countries. We do not wish to create problems with the Soviet Union, but it will be necessary for our Administration from time to time to publicly express the sincere and deep feelings which our people and I feel. Our obligation to help promote human rights will not be expressed in an extreme form or by means not proportional to achieving reasonable results. We

[46] Zbigniew Brzezinski, *Power and Principle: Memoirs of the National Security Advisor, 1977–1981* (New York: Farrar, Straus, Giroux, 1983), 156.

[47] Buncher, *Human Rights*, 116.

would also welcome, of course, personal, confidential exchanges of views on these delicate questions.[48]

Brezhnev responded brusquely, indicating that he would not "allow interference in our internal affairs, whatever pseudo-humanitarian slogans are used to present it," and objecting strenuously to Carter's correspondence with Sakharov, whom he called a "renegade who has proclaimed himself an enemy of the Soviet state."[49]

SETTING THE BELGRADE CONFERENCE AGENDA

By late winter 1977, the evolution of the U.S. position was subsumed within preparations for a CSCE meeting in June, which would set the agenda for the first official CSCE conference since the Helsinki Final Act, scheduled to open three months later in Belgrade. Knowing that the Belgrade meetings would determine the future of the CSCE, including the salience of human rights, the "Helsinki network" increased its pressure on the U.S. government. Meanwhile, during Cyrus Vance's trip to Moscow in March, the Soviets had again insisted on the principle of noninterference in internal affairs, and indicated that the continued pursuit of the human rights issue could derail other aspects of the détente agenda, including arms control. The Carter administration's policy on human rights in the East was thus formulated amid the political, ideological, and strategic debates of this pre-Belgrade environment, and was greatly influenced by pressure from outside the executive branch.

Human rights activists from across Eastern Europe and the Soviet Union submitted detailed reports of human rights violations by East-bloc regimes, and called on the West to press for greater compliance as a prerequisite to progress in the CSCE. According to Congressman Dante Fascell, "the preparations for Belgrade elicited surprising public attention. Western jour-

---

[48] "Carter's Letter to Brezhnev, February 14, 1977," in "The Path to Disagreement," http://cwihp.si.edu.

[49] Brzezinski, *Power and Principle*, 155.

nalists in Moscow, Berlin, Warsaw, Bucharest and Prague began to write about the Helsinki-related demands of workers, writers, religious believers, Jews and Germans seeking to emigrate from the Soviet Union, and of human rights activists. The Communist regimes reacted critically and sometimes violently to these activities, but—by their repressive measures—only aggravated the concerns of private and official groups in the West."[50] In fact, these human rights activists were quite clear about what should be on the CSCE agenda: "Although the Belgrade Conference should discuss all sections of the Helsinki Agreement, it is 'basket three' which is the most urgent and which therefore should form the central part."[51] Well aware of the likely Soviet response, international lawyers in the United States offered legal arguments that human rights violations are not protected by the shield of domestic jurisdiction, regardless of Principle 6.[52]

Strengthened by NGO lobbying and documentation of developments in Eastern Europe, the U.S. Helsinki Commission continued its political battle with the State Department and the White House to ensure that human rights become the focus of U.S. policy on CSCE. In particular, the commission argued that Belgrade conference should be used for a detailed review of compliance with the Final Act, especially on human rights. It issued numerous reports and held hearings on East-bloc violations related to human contacts, religious liberty and minority rights, information flow, and other human rights issues.[53] During the commission's first public hearings in February, former

[50] Dante B. Fascell, "Did Human Rights Survive Belgrade?" *Foreign Policy* 31 (Summer 1978):108.

[51] "Interview with Jiri Pelikan," *Labour Focus on Eastern Europe* 1:2 (May-June 1977):2.

[52] Louis Henkin, "Human Rights and 'Domestic Jurisdiction,'" in Thomas Buergenthal, ed., *Human Rights, International Law and the Helsinki Accord* (Montclair, N.J.: Allanheld, Osmun, 1977).

[53] For example, see "Soviet Helsinki Watch, Reports on Repression," June 3, 1977, "US Policy and the Belgrade Conference," June 6, 1977, in U.S. Commission on Security and Cooperation in Europe, *Basket III: Implementation of the Helsinki Accords*, Hearings (Washington, D.C.: Government Printing Office, 1977).

ambassador Leonard Garment reminded the government: "The existence of a formal, written document, to which the Eastern regimes gave their public consent and their formal stamp of legitimacy, has made a difference. The words matter and are beginning to move human minds. . . . Perhaps we in the West, who pay such frequent tribute to the worth of ideas, should be a little embarrassed that at the time of Helsinki we entertained such a low opinion of their power."[54]

Though the State Department strongly resisted the inclusion of commission members in pre-Belgrade planning meetings, the influence of the Helsinki network began to show.[55] As Cyrus Vance told a University of Georgia audience in April: "Our belief is strengthened by the way the Helsinki principles and the Universal Declaration of Human Rights have found resonance in the hearts of people of many countries."[56] On June 6, just nine days before the preparatory negotiations for Belgrade were to begin, Brzezinski noted in his journal that congressional pressure had forced the White House to issue a report on CSCE compliance that he considered imprudently critical of the East bloc.[57] Patricia Derian, the State Department's coordinator for humanitarian affairs, acknowledged privately that pressure from the commission was responsible for the critical report.[58] As discussed earlier, the commission had been created

[54] Cited in Rep. Dante B. Fascell's February 24, 1978, address to the Chicago Council of Foreign Relations, in U.S. Commission on Security and Cooperation in Europe, *The Belgrade Follow-Up Meeting to the Conference on Security and Cooperation in Europe: A Report and Appraisal* (Washington, D.C.: Government Printing Office, 1978), Appendix B.

[55] Correspondence from Dante Fascell to Cyrus Vance, February 4, 1977, in U.S. Helsinki Commission files.

[56] For the full text of Vance's April 30, 1977 address, see Buncher, *Human Rights*, 181–82.

[57] Brzezinski, *Power and Principle*, 126. The report in question was the (U.S. Department of State) *Second Semiannual Report by the President to the Commission on Security and Cooperation in Europe, December 1, 1976–June 1, 1977* (Washington, D.C.: Government Printing Office, June 1977).

[58] Correspondence from Patricia Derian to Deputy Staff Director Alfred Friendly, July 20, 1977, in U.S. Helsinki Commission files.

in response to appeals by East European and Soviet activists, and depended almost entirely upon them for its information.

The appointment of the U.S. ambassador to the Belgrade conference was also influenced by these battles. Despite the critical White House report, the State Department remained uncomfortable with the many calls for emphasis on human rights as a diplomatic issue. In the early summer, Vance appointed veteran diplomat Albert Sherer as ambassador to the Belgrade conference, and sent him to Europe to consult with the NATO allies. As former head of the U.S. delegation to the CSCE from 1973 to 1975, Sherer could be expected to maintain at Belgrade the same low profile that the United States had held in the Geneva talks. At about the same time, President Carter invited Arthur Goldberg, a former Supreme Court justice, secretary of labor, and UN ambassador, to serve as the White House's special envoy to the Middle East. Brzezinski and Vance quickly objected that Goldberg was ill suited to the position. Aware of the mounting pressure on the White House from NGOs and the Congress to emphasize human rights at Belgrade, a senior official then suggested that Goldberg, well known for his career-long interest in civil rights and labor issues, be offered the CSCE ambassadorship in place of Sherer.[59] Carter agreed, and Goldberg replaced Sherer just as the Belgrade preparatory negotiations were ending in August. Once appointed, in part through pressure from the Helsinki network, Goldberg created new opportunities (discussed below) for members of the network to shape U.S. foreign policy.

In the meantime, the Soviets and their allies were following the gradual turnaround in U.S. policy, and they prepared for a confrontation at Belgrade over human rights.[60] In a September

[59] Zbigniew Brzezinski and Max Kampelman offer similar accounts of this process, though they differ on who recommended Goldberg for the CSCE. See Brzezinski, *Power and Principle*, 300; and Max M. Kampelman, *Entering New Worlds: The Memoirs of a Private Man in Public Life* (New York: Harper Collins, 1991), 221.

[60] See L. Maximov, "Fulfillment of the Helsinki Understandings," *International Affairs* (Moscow) 10 (1976):22–31.

1977 meeting in Washington, Gromyko reminded President Carter of the Soviet Union's position on human rights and non-interference, adding that Belgrade should be "a constructive forum instead of a place of mutual accusations, some kind of box of complaints."[61] Meanwhile, back in Moscow, the ambassador who had faithfully executed Brezhnev's policy in two years of CSCE negotiations in Geneva was denied an expected promotion to the party's Central Committee. His replacement, Yuli Vorontsov, was instructed to block any compromise on human rights at Belgrade.[62]

THE HELSINKI NETWORK AND WESTERN EUROPE

A similar process of transnational pressure and policy reevaluation occurred in Western Europe as well between 1975 and 1977. Journalists in Paris and London reported on the same Helsinki-oriented mobilization as their colleagues in New York or Washington.[63] Non-governmental organizations, including a new Norwegian Helsinki Committee, appealed for an emphasis on human rights at Belgrade.[64] The British Helsinki Review Group, composed of leading private citizens and diplomatic experts, observed: "Public opinion which for a considerable time in the West was largely indifferent to the Final Act has become increasingly focused on the abuses of human rights in Eastern Europe and such opinion must necessarily influence their dele-

---

[61] "Record of Conversation between Soviet Foreign Minister Gromyko and President Carter, 23 September 1977," in "US-Soviet Relations and the Turn toward Confrontation, 1977–1980," Cold War International History Project, Woodrow Wilson International Center for Scholars, Smithsonian Institution, http://cwihp.si.edu.

[62] Arkady N. Shevchenko, *Breaking with Moscow* (New York: Alfred A. Knopf, 1985), 264–67.

[63] "Helsinki Accord's Echo in East Europe," *Financial Times* (London), January 12, 1977, p. 4.

[64] "Forum on Belgrade," *Labour Focus on Eastern Europe* 1:2 (May-June 1977):1–2.

gates."[65] Somewhat later, the same group observed: "Recognition of human rights and fundamental freedoms has, by the activities of those attempting to act on their rights in the countries of Eastern Europe, become an important factor in Eastern European politics. It is also a major factor in East-West relations."[66] Senior diplomats and policy makers in Western Europe were surprised by the Final Act's impact among independent forces in the East, and many raised their estimate of the CSCE's practical importance in human rights.[67]

This new information and pressure coming from the Helsinki network did not, however, have as large an impact in Western Europe as it had in the United States. For one thing, the relative weakness of West European parliaments on foreign policy matters tends to insulate governments from swings in public opinion.[68] There was also less room for policy reversal in this case because EC foreign ministries had always placed more importance on the CSCE than had the U.S. State Department. And since it was the EC-Nine who had pushed for recognition of human rights during negotiations on the Final Act, pressure groups could less easily accuse them of placing realpolitik over real human beings. Moreover, private groups in Western Europe were less united behind a confrontational CSCE strategy than their American counterparts. For example, the British Helsinki Review Group suggested that "Western pressure on human rights issues creates a complex reaction: on the one hand it can restrain Eastern European governments; on the other, by making those governments more sensitive, such pressure can drive them to act more harshly."[69]

[65] Helsinki Review Group, *From Helsinki to Belgrade* (London: David Davies Memorial Institute of International Studies, September 1977), iv.

[66] Helsinki Review Group, *Belgrade and After* (London: David Davies Memorial Institute of International Studies, undated), 18.

[67] Interviews by author with Leif Mevik, Brussels, March 15, 1994; Max van der Stoel and Harm Hazelwinkel, The Hague, March 18, 1994; Jacques Laurent and Henri Segesser, Brussels, September 14, 1994.

[68] Thomas Risse-Kappen, "Public Opinion, Domestic Structure, and Foreign Policy in Liberal Democracies," *World Politics* 43 (July 1991):479–512.

[69] Helsinki Review Group, *Belgrade and After*, 18–19.

Above all, West European decision makers tended to view the CSCE as part of a long-term strategy to overcome the division of the continent, and thus were less willing than the Americans to antagonize the Soviets over individual human rights abuses.[70] "The Belgrade follow-up meeting must be seen essentially as part of a process and as the first checkpoint along a lengthy and weary road," said the head of the British delegation.[71] This EC view of how to promote human rights in the East, first expressed in relation to the Yakir and Kasin trial during the Geneva talks in September 1973, was tested again at Belgrade, where it conflicted with appeals from the Helsinki network and Ambassador Goldberg's growing interest in public diplomacy.

SHAPING DIPLOMACY AT THE
BELGRADE CONFERENCE

Just as they had already reframed the détente agenda in Washington, information and pressure from the Helsinki network had a significant impact on the agenda and outcome of the Belgrade conference. NATO was potentially less constrained now that Greece, Portugal, and Spain were no longer under dictatorial regimes, but neither the U.S. State Department nor the EC-Nine intended to place too much attention on human rights. In advance of the Belgrade conference, the EC had resolved "to conduct a frank and extensive review but to phrase our comments in non-polemical terms in the hope that, at the end of the review of implementation, the way would be clear to negotiate with the Soviet Union and their allies proposals for improving implementation in the future."[72] They also agreed,

---

[70] Brian Fall, "The Helsinki Conference, Belgrade and European Security," *International Security* 2 (Summer 1977):100–5; Karl E. Birnbaum, "Human Rights and East-West Relations," *Foreign Affairs* 55 (July 1977):783–99.

[71] FCO, *The Conference*, 488.

[72] Ibid., 486.

rather than discussing individual violations during official sessions, to introduce a proposal that would reinforce the right of individuals to assist in the implementation of Helsinki norms. When the conference opened on October 4, 1977, NATO's strategy was to address "those points in the record of other States which required criticism and called for improvement, but to avoid heightening the tension by concentrating on individual cases where practical results were unlikely."[73]

In keeping with this strategy, as well as traditional diplomatic taboos against "naming names," all references to East-bloc violations by Western delegations during the first two weeks of talks were indirect—even countries' names were veiled. One French diplomat criticized the human rights record of an East-bloc country by saying "I won't name names because the person in question is sitting right in front of me, but in his country the practice is. . . ." In turn, an East German diplomat criticized a "country whose language is English with a population of over two hundred million which only published seven thousand copies of the Final Act."[74] Before long, though, this well-established taboo was overturned by a combination of impassioned appeals from East European dissidents and political pressure from the U.S. Congress, both framed in terms of Helsinki norms.

On the eve of the Belgrade conference, forty-eight human rights activists in Moscow announced a one-day fast to protest repression against the Moscow Helsinki Group. The protest was covered in the Washington press.[75] At about the same time, Andrei Sakharov sent a personal appeal to the West that emphasized the importance of human rights in détente. On October 6, the day of Ambassador Goldberg's first speech to the Belgrade

[73] Secretary of State for Foreign and Commonwealth Affairs, *The Meeting Held at Belgrade from 4 October 1977 to 9 March 1978 to Follow up the Conference on Security and Cooperation in Europe*, Command Paper 7126 (London: Her Majesty's Stationery Office, March 1978), 7.

[74] Dorothy Goldberg, "Personal Journal of International Negotiations about Human Rights," unpublished and undated memoirs by the wife of U.S. ambassador Arthur Goldberg, 99, 104.

[75] *Washington Star*, October 5, 1977.

conference, Sakharov's letter appeared in the *International Herald Tribune*. It was pointed and powerful:

> The Soviet and East European representatives have always tried to neutralize the humanitarian principles of the Helsinki accords by emphasizing the principle of non-interference in the internal affairs of other countries. . . . Every person serving a term in the hell of present-day Gulag for his beliefs, or open profession of them—every victim of psychological repression for political reasons, every person refused permission to emigrate, to travel abroad—represents a direct violation of the Helsinki accord. . . . We are going through a period of history in which decisive support of the principles of freedom of conscience in an open society, and the rights of man, has become an absolute necessity. . . . Is the West prepared to defend these noble and vitally important principles? Or, will it, little by little, accept the interpretation of the principles of Helsinki, and of detente as a whole, that the leaders of the Soviet Union and of Eastern Europe are trying to impose?[76]

Ambassador Goldberg was impressed by Sakharov's letter (and other appeals sent to the West over the preceding months), and conveyed this impression to allied delegations.[77] In fact, Sakharov's letter was crucial in persuading Goldberg to reject the one argument against emphasizing human rights that he had found plausible—that it might cause greater hardship to those living under Communist rule.[78] The State Department, however, including Albert Sherer, who was now deputy head of the U.S. delegation, remained unconvinced.[79]

This stand-off within the U.S. delegation was broken by congressional intervention on October 17, when Goldberg received a copy of a letter addressed to President Carter from a bipartisan group of 127 representatives and 16 senators calling

---

[76] *International Herald Tribune*, October 6, 1977.
[77] Korey, *Promises*, 79.
[78] Goldberg, "Personal Journal," 86.
[79] Michael Dobbs, "Goldberg and Aides Differ on Tactics at Belgrade Parley," *Washington Post*, October 17, 1977.

for forceful criticism at Belgrade of all violations of Helsinki norms. Entitled "Make Human Rights a Central Issue," the letter highlighted the repression of the Moscow Helsinki Group and argued that "if the Soviets are allowed to blatantly violate the human rights provisions of the Helsinki Agreement, the credibility and effectiveness of the agreement, and any other bilateral negotiations could be undermined."[80] It was almost certainly drafted and circulated by the Helsinki Commission, whose staff were fully aware of the situation in Belgrade.

The following day, Goldberg appeared in place of Sherer at the Basket III working group, and surprised the assembled diplomats by reading an article from the French Communist Party daily *L'Humanité* which reported on how the Czechoslovak authorities had denied Western reporters access to a trial of human rights activists This move simultaneously broke the taboo against naming names, publicized the plight of Helsinki monitors, and criticized Czechoslovakia's violation of its commitment to the free flow of information. Moreover, by his choice of newspaper, Goldberg demonstrated that not even the Moscow-friendly French Communist Party could overlook Helsinki violations in Eastern Europe.

Given their preference for a less confrontational approach, the EC delegations at Belgrade were not altogether supportive of Goldberg's new tactics. A member of one EC delegation complained, "We seem to spend more time negotiating with Goldberg than negotiating with the Russians."[81] American discussion of proposing a CSCE Committee on Human Rights was blocked within the NATO caucus by EC delegations that considered it a diplomatic "nonstarter." But they also were keenly aware of transnational appeals, reinforced by intense media coverage of the conference, for a strong position on human rights. Though they expected that it too would fail, they thus agreed to support another American proposal that any final document from Belgrade should specifically reaffirm the

---

[80] Goldberg, "Personal Journal," 174–75.

[81] Cited in Don Cook, "Making America Look Foolish: The Case of the Bungling Diplomat," *Saturday Review*, May 13, 1978, 10.

principle of respect for human rights and fundamental freedoms. As the British ambassador explained, "it would have been politically quite impossible for the Governments of the Nine ... to refuse to support a human rights proposal of this kind."[82] As the talks wore on, though, the East bloc's refusal to engage in serious discussion about human rights produced a renewed unity of purpose among Western delegations.[83]

When the conference resumed in January 1978, after a Christmas break, Soviet ambassador Vorontsov made it clear that the Kremlin would not accept any new commitments to human rights.[84] Meanwhile, the NATO states rejected various Soviet proposals on disarmament. Reflecting the deadlock in substantive negotiations, the final document agreed by the thirty-five states on March 9, 1978, simply reaffirmed their resolve to implement fully the provisions of the Helsinki Final Act, recorded the dates and formalities of the Belgrade meeting, and stipulated that they would meet again in Madrid in November 1980.

SUSTAINING THE HUMAN RIGHTS AGENDA AFTER BELGRADE

The Belgrade meeting's failure to achieve a frank discussion of human rights by all parties called into question the new salience of the Helsinki process and especially the focus on human rights. European members of NATO expressed their fear that another stalemated meeting would endanger the CSCE and even détente itself.[85] Other West European voices recognized that East European activists had changed the terms of debate

[82] FCO, *The Conference*, 490.

[83] U.S. State Department, "Weekly Summaries of Belgrade meetings," photocopies of unpublished memos, in the Harvard Law School's International Legal Studies Library.

[84] FCO, *The Conference*, 487.

[85] Frans A. M. Alting von Geusau, "The Nine and Détente," in Nils Andrèn and Karl E. Birnbaum, *Belgrade and Beyond: The CSCE Process in Perspective* (Alphen a/d Rijn: Sijthoff & Noordhoff, 1980), 17–25.

within the CSCE and East-West relations, but doubted the efficacy of Goldberg's approach to promoting human rights: "outside the context of the Belgrade meeting there are dangers that stressing individual cases in public too frequently not only distracts attention from the plight of others, but induces confrontation."[86] First privately, then publicly, U.S. diplomat Albert Sherer criticized Goldberg's approach as a threat to NATO unity and called for a less confrontational policy at Madrid.[87] Influential American columnist William Safire urged the United States to renounce the entire Helsinki process and blasted the Helsinki Commission as "a group with a vested interest in meeting and junketing and tut-tutting at the way the Russians ignore the treaty."[88]

This post-Belgrade threat to the salience of human rights in U.S. policy was the occasion for a second crucial development in the Helsinki network: the creation of the U.S. Helsinki Watch Committee. As discussed above, private human rights groups in the United States had begun to monitor compliance with Helsinki norms two years earlier, in response to appeals from activists in the East. Subsequent reports of repression against Helsinki monitors in the East only increased their commitment to raise the priority of human rights in U.S. foreign policy toward Eastern Europe and the Soviet Union. One of these groups, the International Freedom to Publish Committee of the Association of American Publishers (AAP), had announced in December 1977 that it would not sign any trade protocol with the Soviet book-publishing industry until the Kremlin improved its human rights record.[89] During the Belgrade conference's Christmas break, representatives of the AAP and other groups met in New York with Ambassador Goldberg,

---

[86] Helsinki Review Group, *Belgrade and After*, 19.

[87] Albert W. Shirer, Jr., "Goldberg's Variations," *Foreign Policy* 39 (Summer 1980):154–59.

[88] *New York Times*, June 19, 1978.

[89] U.S. Department of State, *Fourth Semiannual Report by the President to the Commission on Security and Cooperation in Europe, December 1, 1977–June 1, 1978* (Washington, D.C.: Government Printing Office, June 1978), 25.

and agreed that only concerted public pressure in the West would keep the CSCE focused on human rights.[90]

In testimony before the Helsinki Commission less than two weeks after the end of Belgrade meeting, Goldberg spoke about the need for pressure from the nongovernmental sector to support human rights: "Private individuals have a lot to do, outside of government. It's a great anomaly to me that while in the Soviet Union, in Czechoslovakia, in Poland, under conditions of repression, private individuals have had the courage to organize private groups but that in our country individuals have not organized a monitoring group. I would hope they would, as an indication that individuals in our country, in addition to government, have a great interest in the implementation of the Final Act."[91] After Goldberg's testimony, members of Congress affirmed his call for a private organization that could supplement the work of the Helsinki Commission.

Meanwhile private and public members of the Helsinki network worked to maintain the salience of human rights in the East. In late April, the Helsinki Commission convinced the Carter administration to convey to the Kremlin its interest in the trials of several members of the Moscow Helsinki Watch Group.[92] In June, the AAP and the International Publishers Association issued a statement reiterating concern for the fate of Yuri Orlov, who had recently been sentenced to seven years' imprisonment.[93] When two leading members of the Moscow group, Aleksandr Ginzburg and Anatoly Scharansky, were nonetheless found guilty of treason several months later, the Carter administration responded by canceling the sale of an advanced computer to the Soviet news agency Tass and by re-

---

[90] Robert Bernstein, interview by author, New York, January 12, 1994.

[91] U.S. Commission on Security and Cooperation in Europe, *The Belgrade CSCE Follow-Up Meeting: A Report and Appraisal*, Hearings, March 21, 1978 (Washington, D.C.: Government Printing Office, 1978), Appendix F, 18–19.

[92] Correspondence between Commission chair Dante Fascell, Secretary of State Cyrus Vance, and Assistant Secretary of State for Congressional Relations Douglas Bennet, in U.S. Helsinki Commission files.

[93] U.S. Department of State, *Fourth Semiannual Report*, 26.

quiring validated licenses for all exports of oil technology to the Soviet Union.[94] All members of the network nonetheless knew that consistent public pressure would be necessary to sustain the U.S. focus on human rights and Helsinki compliance. During a series of discussions in 1978 between members of the AAP committee, other human rights activists, Ambassador Goldberg, and McGeorge Bundy, president of the Ford Foundation, the decision was made to create an independent Helsinki watch group in the United States.[95] The U.S. Helsinki Watch Committee was formally established in February 1979, with a $400,000 Ford grant as "an independent, non-governmental organization composed of a representative group of private US opinion leaders" to monitor domestic and international compliance with the human rights provisions of the Helsinki Final Act and to provide "moral support for the activities of the beleaguered Helsinki monitors in the Soviet bloc."[96] This was, of course, just what Orlov and his fellow activists had called for two years earlier when they established the Moscow Helsinki Group.

The U.S. Helsinki Watch Committee immediately became a major fixture in the transnational network, and gained a prominent voice in U.S. policy making on the CSCE, Eastern Europe, and the Soviet Union. With its reputation for providing reliable information about human rights conditions in the East, and its ability to organize political pressure within the United States, Helsinki Watch played an especially important role in the early 1980s, when the Reagan administration's initial skepticism about détente and multilateral institutions led to talk of withdrawing from the CSCE.

[94] Lisa L. Martin, *Coercive Cooperation: Explaining Multilateral Economic Sanctions* (Princeton: Princeton University Press, 1992), 199. The computers had already been "lobotomized" to prevent military applications, so there was no direct security motive for this policy change.

[95] Robert Bernstein, interview by author, New York, January 12, 1994; McGeorge Bundy, telephone interview by author, January 24, 1994.

[96] U.S. Helsinki Watch Committee, "The First Fifteen Months, A Summary of the Activities of the U.S. Helsinki Watch Committee from Its Founding in February 1979 through April, 1980," unpublished report, 3–4.

ALTERNATIVE EXPLANATIONS

Although Helsinki norms and the transnational network that emerged around them were certainly not the only factors shaping the rise of the human rights agenda in U.S. policy toward Eastern Europe and the Soviet Union in the mid to late 1970s, potential alternative explanations are all less persuasive. For example, one might argue that the salience of human rights in U.S. policy toward the Communist bloc depended upon the status of East-West geopolitics. By this logic, as long as détente was healthy, Washington would downplay the sensitive issue of human rights, but when détente soured, Washington would use the rights issue as an additional stick to beat its adversary. The first problem with this hypothesis is that the change in U.S. policy began in the fall of 1975, before détente had truly deteriorated; if anything, the new U.S. focus on human rights was a cause, not a result of the decline of détente. Moreover, as documented above, the focus on human rights in Eastern Europe entered U.S. policy not through the geostrategic calculations of the executive branch (as the hypothesis leads one to expect), but through political pressure from private groups and the Congress.

Suggestions that the declining influence of Henry Kissinger in this period permitted U.S. foreign policy to return to its "normal" tendency to support freedom and human rights, based on assumptions about American political culture and institutions, are no better at explaining this case.[97] For one thing, they offer no explanation for why Kissingerian realpolitik should have declined while he was still in office. And although the argument that U.S. foreign policy reflects fundamental aspects of American political identity is certainly plausible, it is logically inconsistent with the ability of an individual to impose

---

[97] On Kissinger as an exception to "American exceptionalism," see Samuel Huntington, "American Ideals versus American Institutions." *Political Science Quarterly* 97 (Spring 1982):1–37; and Tony Smith, *America's Mission: The United States and the Worldwide Struggle for Democracy in the Twentieth Century* (Princeton: Princeton University Press, 1994).

a contrary agenda on U.S. policy for half a decade. Above all, numerous examples of U.S. support for repressive and murderous regimes during this period, and the State Department's stubborn resistance to the agenda of the Helsinki network, are entirely inconsistent with the claim that human rights is a "normal" priority in U.S. foreign policy.

A more common explanation for the rise of human rights in U.S. foreign policy during the period is the influence of Jimmy Carter and the "globalist" outlook prevalent in his early administration.[98] Yet notwithstanding Carter's personal commitment to human rights and the related innovations of his administration, the power of this explanation is seriously undermined by three facts described above. First, U.S. policy toward the East began to change before Carter's election and inauguration. Second, the Helsinki-as-human-rights frame contributed to Carter's narrow victory by weakening the political base of Gerald Ford and delegitimating his administration's approach to foreign policy. And third, once Carter was elected, the transnational Helsinki network was a constant source of pressure that undermined bureaucratic and political forces within the executive branch still committed to downplaying the human rights agenda.

Others have suggested that the Congress had its own reasons in the early to mid 1970s, unrelated to Helsinki norms or transnational networking, for asserting its voice in U.S. foreign policy and raising the salience of human rights.[99] Vietnam and Watergate had weakened the executive branch and discredited the

---

[98] Joshua Muravchik, *The Uncertain Crusade: Jimmy Carter and the Dilemmas of Human Rights Policy* (Washington, D.C.: American Enterprise Institute Press, 1991); Jerel A. Rosati, *The Carter Administration's Quest for Global Community: Beliefs and Their Impact on Behavior* (Columbia: University of South Carolina Press, 1991).

[99] Thomas M. Franck and Edward Weisband, *Foreign Policy by Congress* (New York: Oxford University Press, 1979); Kathryn Sikkink, "The Power of Principled Ideas: Human Rights Policies in the United States and Western Europe," in Judith Goldstein and Robert O. Keohane, eds., *Ideas and Foreign Policy: Beliefs, Institutions and Political Change* (Ithaca: Cornell University Press, 1993), 139–72.

principles of realpolitik that long justified overlooking human rights. Moreover, the Voting Rights Act and other domestic civil rights accomplishments of the 1960s had reduced the internal political obstacles to emphasizing human rights in U.S. foreign policy. Ever anxious to expand congressional authority, and more sensitive to public opinion than the executive branch, some members of Congress viewed the human rights issue as a means to assert their independence from the White House while relegitimating U.S. foreign policy at home and abroad. This much is undeniable.

The first problem with this explanation is the uncertain public commitment to emphasizing human rights in foreign policy. On the one hand, according to a 1978 poll conducted by the Chicago Council on Foreign Relations, 67 percent of Americans agreed that the United States should put pressure on countries that systematically violate human rights. When asked about particular cases, though, public opinion tended not to favor pressuring foreign governments for human rights violations. Only 1 percent listed human rights among the top two or three foreign policy problems for the United States, and only 39 percent considered the promotion of human rights a "very important" foreign policy goal.[100] The simple domestic politics explanation also cannot explain why Congress would press for human rights in U.S. policy toward Latin America, but largely ignore Eastern Europe until 1975, despite U.S. financial assistance to both regions. One might hypothesize that the Congress ceded East European policy to the White House because the stakes of East-West relations were higher, but that argument is undermined by the Congress's dramatic about-face after 1975. More persuasive is the argument that congressional interest in human rights conditions in Eastern Europe and the Soviet Union was catalyzed by the Helsinki network after 1975, just as it had been several years earlier by a transnational network focused on the "dirty war" in Argentina, and would be a

---

[100] Cited in David Skidmore, *Reversing Course: Carter's Foreign Policy, Domestic Politics and the Failure of Reform* (Nashville: Vanderbilt University Press, 1996), 92–93.

decade later by a transnational network focused on apartheid in South Africa.[101]

In short, the change in U.S. policy documented in this chapter cannot be simply attributed to other factors, such as geopolitical trends, an enduring "national interest," a change of government, or domestic political pressure unconnected to transnational networking. The fortunes of détente, American liberalism, the election of Jimmy Carter, and the assertiveness of Congress all mattered, but none provides a satisfactory explanation for this historically significant development in U.S. foreign policy and East-West relations.

CONCLUSION

This chapter illustrates another way in which the interaction between international norms and transnational networks can shape world politics. In contrast to the previous chapter, which focused on changes in social mobilization, the change here is in the way a powerful state defined its self-interest—namely, the elevation of human rights in U.S. foreign policy from a low-priority issue that the White House and State Department preferred to ignore, to an inescapable high priority in U.S. relations with the East bloc, including unprecedented rhetorical confrontations and issue-linkage diplomacy. This transformation in the U.S. definition of self-interest was brought about by the interaction of two forces: the new international norms of the Helsinki Final Act, and the persistent shaming and lobbying efforts of a transnational network combining dissidents and human rights activists in the East, sympathetic private groups in the West, and the specialized agency within the U.S. Congress that they helped create. The result, illustrated in following chapters, was a transnational opportunity structure even

---

[101] Kathryn Sikkink, "Human Rights, Principled Issue-Networks, and Sovereignty in Latin America," *International Organization* 47 (Summer 1993):411–41; Audie Klotz, *Norms in International Relations: The Struggle against Apartheid* (Ithaca: Cornell University Press, 1995).

more conducive to opposition activity in Eastern Europe and the Soviet Union than that established by the Helsinki norms alone.

Subsequent events such as martial law in Poland did cause some in the United States to question the value of the Helsinki process, and even to consider withdrawing from the CSCE, but the new U.S. policy was kept in place by continued pressure from human rights groups in Eastern Europe, the Helsinki Commission in the U.S. Congress, and private, U.S.-based groups such as the U.S. Helsinki Watch Committee. By the time that crisis passed, human rights was established as a permanent fixture in U.S. diplomacy toward Eastern Europe and the Soviet Union.

THE EFFECTS OF NORMS

CHAPTER FIVE

Mobilization: The Expansion of Human Rights Movements

By articulating . . . the problems of human rights and the problems of the so-called Basket III in the Final Act of the Helsinki Conference, that conference made possible a gradual development of civil initiative demanding a greater measure of political democracy than the political power is willing to grant. In that sense, Charter 77 is in fact also a true child of the Helsinki Conference of 1975. The government may treat it like a mean step-mother, yet it cannot destroy that child, if it does not want to renounce completely its own obligations which it adopted in the family of other European nations at Helsinki.

—*Zdenek Mlynar, Charter 77 dissident, 1977*[1]

"We're ready to arrest you, but the Foreign Ministry won't let us."
—*Secret police agent to Martin Palous, Charter 77 dissident, 1978*[2]

THIS CHAPTER traces the contribution of Helsinki norms to the expansion and organization of independent society in the years 1976–1977, particularly the emergence of well-connected human rights movements that posed an unprecedented challenge to the political and ideological hegemony of the Communist party-state. Understanding the expansion of organized opposition in the late 1970s is crucial to understanding the emergence of Solidarity in 1980, the grassroots reaction to

[1] *Listy* (Rome), no. 3–4 July 1977: 22–24, from JPRS, *Translations*, 69803 (September 16, 1977):25–30.
[2] Martin Palous, interview by author, Prague, July 31, 1992.

Gorbachev's reforms in the mid to late 1980s, and finally the nature of the political transition across the region in 1989–1990. As becomes clear, though, Helsinki's contribution to the rise of organized opposition in Eastern Europe in the 1970s cannot be fully understood without attention to changes in the political economy of the region during this period, and changes in the international political salience of the Helsinki process.

The chapter thus continues the evaluation of the impact of the Helsinki Final Act on the ability of societal forces in Eastern Europe and the Soviet Union to challenge their Communist rulers. Chapter 3 demonstrated how state and societal actors responded to normative changes in the transnational opportunity structure, emphasizing the competing efforts of Communist authorities and opposition forces to interpret those changes in a manner advantageous to their political goals. In Chapter 4 we saw how opposition and human rights groups in Eastern Europe and the Soviet Union exploited the new, post-Helsinki norms to build alliances with state and societal forces in the West, and thus to leverage even greater political pressure on Communist regimes in the East. But as this chapter demonstrates, the effects of Helsinki norms were not limited to short-term mobilization or the creation of transnational alliances.

THE SOVIET UNION

The same Soviet dissidents who had initiated the wave of transnational appeals to Helsinki norms in 1975 concluded in early 1976 that a more organized movement to press for Helsinki compliance within the Soviet Union was both necessary and possible. Within another year, their activity had spread across the country and resuscitated the Soviet human rights movement from a low point following the harsh crackdown of the early 1970s.

On May 12, 1976, Yuri Orlov and veteran activists Ludmilla Alexeyeva, Elena Bonner, Aleksandr Ginzburg, Vitaly Rubin, and Anatoly Shcharansky, among others, held a news conference in the apartment of Nobel Laureate Andrei Sakharov to announce the formation of a Group to Assist the Implementation of the Helsinki Agreements in the USSR.[3] Orlov declared that the group would gather information on violations of Principle 7 and Basket III, receive citizens' complaints of such violations, and transmit this material to the governments and peoples of countries that had signed the Final Act. Several days later, Andrei Sakharov and Valentin Turchin, chairman of the Moscow branch of Amnesty International, told a second gathering of Western journalists of their support for the group and their hope that its efforts would be well received in the West.[4]

The primary activity of the Moscow Helsinki Group consisted of making public declarations about human rights conditions in the USSR that specified Moscow's obligations under the Helsinki Final Act and the earlier International Covenants on Human Rights that were reaffirmed in the Final Act.[5] Each declaration was signed by members of the group, and mailed openly to Soviet officials, sent abroad via journalists and foreign embassy personnel, and circulated within the Soviet Union through underground networks. In cases where existing Soviet law was adequate but not enforced, the group sought to juxtapose the law with examples of abuses. According to document 75, "Any government claiming for itself the status of a legally established state, demanding that its citizens obey those laws that are in force, must obey its own laws."[6] More often, the documents contrasted international norms with human rights abuses in the Soviet Union and shortcomings in its legal system. The group thus selected and framed its documents for maxi-

---

[3] See complete text in *Chronicle of Current Events* (London) 40, May 20, 1976 (1979):95–98.

[4] Reuter newswire item, Moscow, May 19, 1976.

[5] U.S. Commission on Security and Cooperation in Europe, *A Thematic Survey of the Documents of the Moscow Helsinki Group*, unpublished photocopy (Washington, D.C., May 12, 1981); idem, *Documents of the Helsinki Monitoring Groups in the U.S.S.R. and Lithuania (1976–1986)*, Vol. 1 (Washington, D.C.: Government Printing Office, 1986).

[6] U.S. Commission on Security and Cooperation in Europe, *Documents of the Helsinki Monitoring Groups in the U.S.S.R. and Lithuania (1976–1986)*, Vols. 1, 2 (Washington, D.C.: Government Printing Office, 1986).

mum political effect: "The group did not try to report all the violations it learned of, but instead chose those that best represented the regime's failure to observe the Helsinki Accords."[7] These included the persecution of ethnic activists, restrictions on free emigration, the denial of religious freedom, interference with postal and telephone communications, and the persecution of human rights monitors.

Before long, the activity of the Moscow Helsinki Group was itself contributing to the expansion of individual activism catalyzed by the Helsinki Accords. As knowledge of the Moscow Helsinki Group spread through samizdat channels and Western radio broadcasts, Orlov and his colleagues were besieged with spontaneous reports of human rights abuses: "One visitor, a taxi driver named Vladimir Pavlov, came from Maikop, an industrial city in the North Caucuses. In 1971, he was convicted of 'anti-Soviet slander' on the basis of remarks he made to passengers; he spent three years in a labor camp. A year after his release, in 1975, he read the Helsinki Accords. The regime was promising to respect the exchange of information, so he asked the Supreme Court to be rehabilitated. The court rejected his appeal. Hearing about the Orlov committee on the radio, he decided to carry his complaint to Moscow."[8] This taxi driver, like thousands of other petitioners, eventually made his way to the Moscow Helsinki Group.[9]

The contribution of the Moscow group to expanding the ranks of the Soviet human rights movement extended, however, far beyond those individual petitioners it attracted. Their invocation of Helsinki norms provided "a logic and a framework for cooperation" among groups and movements that previously had little in common.[10] The example of the Moscow Helsinki

---

[7] Joshua Rubenstein, *Soviet Dissidents: Their Struggle for Human Rights* (Boston: Beacon, 1980), 228.

[8] Ibid., 222–23.

[9] On the number and types of such petitioners, see U.S. Commission on Security and Cooperation in Europe, "Shcharansky on Human Rights and the Soviet Union," undated pamphlet based on testimony before the commission, May 14, 1986.

[10] Yuri Orlov, several interviews by author, Ithaca, N.Y., 1990–1992.

Watch Group encouraged religious believers, nationalists in the various republics, and other activists to recognize the relevance of the Helsinki process to their particular concerns, and to organize accordingly. Two other, high-profile dissident organizations were established in this period, both with close ties to the Moscow Helsinki group: the Christian Committee for the Defense of the Rights of Religious Believers, established in December 1976, and the Working Committee for the Investigation of the Political Abuse of Psychiatry, established in January 1977. Helsinki monitoring committees also emerged in four Soviet republics.

After Moscow, the next Helsinki group to emerge in the Soviet Union was the Helsinki Watch Group in Ukraine, established in Kiev on November 9, 1976.[11] Of the nine founding members, six had already served time in prison for underground nationalist activities. Like its predecessor in Moscow, the Ukrainian Helsinki Watch Group was the first open public association in the Ukraine without official approval. Also like the Moscow group, the Ukrainian group's founding document declared as its goal the implementation of the Universal Declaration of Human Rights and the Helsinki Final Act. In practice, though, the group's thirty documents issued by the end of 1980 concentrated exclusively on Ukraine's lack of national self-determination and on official repression of nationalist activity. The Ukrainian Helsinki group thus represented an important step in the organization and assertion of independent society in Ukraine.

The Lithuanian Public Group to Promote the Observance of the Helsinki Accords was established just two weeks later, on

[11] Ludmilla Alexeyeva, *Soviet Dissent: Contemporary Movements for National, Religious and Human Rights* (Middletown, Conn.: Wesleyan University Press, 1987), 48–58; Lesya Verba and Bohdan Yasen, eds., *The Human Rights Movement in Ukraine: Documents of the Ukrainian Helsinki Group, 1976–1980* (Baltimore: Smoloskyp Publishers, 1980); U.S. Commission on Security and Cooperation in Europe, *Implementation of the Helsinki Accords*, Hearings, "Fifth Anniversary of the Formation of the Ukrainian Helsinki Group," November 16, 1981; Jaroslaw Bilocerkowycz, *Soviet Ukrainian Dissent: A Study of Political Alienation* (Boulder, Colo.: Westview Press, 1988).

November 25, 1976.[12] Like their counterparts in Moscow (but not in the Ukraine), the Lithuanian Helsinki Group addressed a broad range of human and civil rights. The influential and politically active Catholic Church in Lithuania sympathized and sometimes collaborated with the Lithuanian Helsinki Group; on November 29, 1977, for example, the two organizations issued a joint appeal to the participants in the Belgrade CSCE meeting.[13] However, unlike the groups in Moscow and Ukraine, the Lithuanian Helsinki Group never became a focus for independent activity, largely because of the high profile and overlapping agenda of the Lithuanian Catholic Church.

In January 1977, a number of activists in the Soviet republic of Georgia who had long collaborated with the Moscow group established a separate Georgian Helsinki Watch Group. Among its founders was Zviad Gamsakhurdia, who played a major role in the nationalist protests of the late 1980s and then in the transition to an independent Georgia in 1991. The Georgian Helsinki Watch group published only one document under its own name in the 1970s, though most of its members continued to provide information on Georgian developments to the Moscow group. Four months later, another Helsinki Watch Group was announced in the neighboring republic of Armenia. The group issued a number of reports on human rights abuses, including an appeal to the Belgrade conference that documented the oppression of Armenian national culture and discrimination against the use of the Armenian language, but it was disbanded after several of its leaders were arrested later the same year.[14]

The creation of such groups in Armenia, Georgia, Lithuania, and Ukraine clearly demonstrates that the appeal of Helsinki principles for opposition activists extended well beyond the

---

[12] Alexeyeva, *Soviet Dissent*, 60–85; Lithuanian Information Center, "The Helsinki Monitoring Movement," unpublished mimeograph (Brooklyn, N.Y., 1986).

[13] *Chronicle of the Catholic Church in Lithuania*, November 29, 1977.

[14] Alexeyeva, *Soviet Dissent*, 112–16, 127–30.

liberal intelligentsia of Moscow. Helsinki norms thus contributed substantially to the rise of independent human rights and opposition organizations across the Soviet Union in 1976–1977 by encouraging activism and by facilitating cooperation among disparate opposition forces. Besides violating the well-known law against independent organizations and challenging the Communist Party's monopoly on political space, this activity threatened to disrupt the sensitive politics of East-West relations.

Notwithstanding such harassment, the Soviet authorities responded to the post-Helsinki increase in dissent and social mobilization with unprecedented tolerance. The mere fact that the aforementioned independent groups were allowed to exist after 1975 contrasts sharply with the intolerance of opposition evident just as few years earlier. The Soviet police also became more tolerant of public demonstrations: the percentage of demonstrators detained at an average demonstration dropped by a third from the period 1968–1974 to the period 1975–1978. The length of time that the police allowed public demonstrations to be held increased significantly, as shown in Figure 1. Consistent with this pattern, the average number of dissidents and refusniks arrested per year fell by half between these same periods.[15] Such reductions in repression, despite an increasing challenge from below, are compelling evidence that Helsinki norms had expanded the space available for social mobilization in the Soviet Union.

The Kremlin's motivation here was largely instrumental. After several years of slow decline, the gross output and efficiency of the Soviet economy fell precipitously in 1975–1976, demonstrating the failure of the 1973 reforms in enterprise management.[16] The Soviet leadership thus hoped that the Hel-

---

[15] Calculations based on data from Peter Reddaway, "Soviet Policies on Dissent and Emigration: The Radical Change of Course since 1979," Occasional Paper No.192, Kennan Institute for Advanced Russian Studies, Woodrow Wilson International Center for Scholars, Washington, D.C., August 28, 1984.

[16] Ed A. Hewitt, *Reforming the Soviet Economy: Equality versus Efficiency* (Washington, D.C.: Brookings Institution, 1988), chapter 2.

Tolerance of Expressive Demonstrations in the Soviet Union

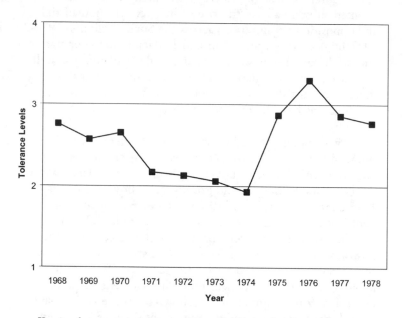

Key: 1 = demonstration dispersed immediately; 2 = demostration held for a short while then dispersed; 3 = demonstration held for duration but harrassed; 4 = demonstration held for duration without harrassment.

Source: David Kowalewski, "Human Rights Protest in USSR: Statistical Trends for 1965–78" *Universal Human Rights* 2:1 (January-March 1980)

sinki process would contribute to the expansion of economic ties and technology exchanges with the West, both of which were integral to the success of the new five-year plan.[17] Brezhnev had also invested considerable personal effort and prestige in the CSCE, and was not anxious to jeopardize the enterprise by violating the norms that defined it.

[17] See Brezhnev's speech to the October 1976 plenary meeting of the CPSU, in Leonid Brezhnev, *Peace, Détente and Soviet-American Relations: A Collection of Public Statements* (New York: Harcourt, Brace, Jovanovich, 1979), 131–44.

POLAND

As discussed in Chapter 4, human rights norms and the Helsinki process contributed substantially to the increased assertiveness of the Polish opposition intelligentsia in late 1975 and early 1976, especially concerning proposed amendments to the constitution. Helsinki norms were also important to the coalition of workers, intellectuals, and the Church whose emergence in 1976–1977 laid the groundwork for Solidarity and the eventual overthrow of Communism in the 1980s.[18]

By early 1976, Premier Edward Gierek was caught between Poland's economic problems and the human rights norms of the Helsinki Accords.[19] On the one hand, high oil prices, low demand for Polish exports, and the growing external debt were rapidly undermining the government's ability to "buy" popular support through price stability, increased wages, and investment, as it had done through the first half of the decade. On the other hand, the Gierek government was keenly aware of the tightening linkage between progress in the Helsinki process and infusions of hard capital from the West. Bilateral economic and technical agreements between Poland and the West had increased sharply just before and after the Helsinki summit.[20] At the Helsinki summit itself, Schmidt and Gierek had signed a side agreement whereby West Germany would provide 2.3 billion Deutsche marks in credits and reparations in exchange for Poland's granting visas to 125,000 ethnic Germans who wished to emigrate.

[18] The organizational and ideological origins of Solidarity are hotly debated. For a critique of those who emphasize the role of intellectuals, see Roman Laba, *The Roots of Solidarity: A Political Sociology of Poland's Working-Class Democratization* (Princeton: Princeton University Press, 1991). For a review of the debate, see David Warszawski, "Rereading Poland's Solidarity Revolution," *Boston Sunday Globe*, May 5, 1991; and the response, *Boston Globe*, July 28, 1991.

[19] *Der Spiegel* (Hamburg), August 25, 1975, from JPRS, *Translations* 65802 (September 30, 1975):14–17.

[20] Henryk Zdanowski, "Interaction of Cause and Effect," *Polityka* (Warsaw), August 7, 1976, from JPRS 67779, *Translations* 67779 (August 18, 1976):1–2.

Full compliance with Helsinki norms was out of the question, though, as it would likely endanger the party-state's hold on power. Reducing economic ties to the West while increasing political repression at home was also rejected as economically short-sighted and politically risky. The only solution, Gierek's advisors concluded, was to restrain consumption while maintaining good relations with the West, in the hope that aid, investment, and technology transfers would somehow rekindle the economy.[21] The trick would be to defuse whatever social unrest emerged without appearing to violate substantially the human rights provisions of the Helsinki Accords, on which East-West relations increasingly depended.

The regime thus sought to demonstrate its positive record on Helsinki compliance to domestic and foreign audiences. One step was to permit greater leeway for discussion of Helsinki among elites. In the semiofficial foreign policy journal *Sprawy Miedzynarodowe,* several commentators argued in the summer and early fall of 1976 that the Final Act was binding on all its signatories, despite the fact that it was not strictly a treaty or legal document.[22] The dean of law at Warsaw University analyzed the drafting and content of Principle 7, linking it to the broader rights guaranteed by the international covenants and speaking positively about the authoritative Optional Protocol, which had not yet come into force, and hinting that Poland would some day join the West European human rights system based on the 1950 European Convention and 1961 Social

---

[21] Kazimierz Poznanski, "Economic Adjustment and Political Forces: Poland since 1970," in Ellen Comisso and Laura D'Andrea Tyson, eds., *Power, Purpose and Collective Choice: Economic Strategy in Socialist States* (Ithaca: Cornell University Press, 1986).

[22] Dr. Alfons Klafkowski, "The CSCE Final Act—Basic Principles in Support of a Legal Interpretation," *Sprawy Miedzynarodowe* no. 7–8, July-August 1976, from JPRS, *Translations* 68135 (October 28, 1976):19–29; and Adam D. Rotfield, "Implementation of the CSCE Final Act and the Development of Detente in Europe," *Sprawy Miedzynarodowe* no. 9, September 1976, from JPRS, *Translations* 68273 (November 26, 1976):1–12.

Charter.[23] Polish authorities even permitted a Warsaw political journal to reprint a review of Poland's Helsinki compliance that an American journalist had recently published in the *International Herald Tribune*.[24]

It was not long, however, before these conflicting incentives collided with opposition from below. From their initial appeals for implementation of the Helsinki Accords in late 1975 through the constitutional reform debates of early 1976, Polish intellectuals were becoming increasingly vocal in their demands for greater freedoms. Then, in June 1976, increases in the price of meat caused industrial workers in Ursus and Radom to organize a protest strike. In the course of the strike, a small group of these strikers sacked and burned the local Communist Party headquarters in Radom. The government responded by labeling all of the strikers as "hooligans" and imprisoning those who had a criminal record, whether or not they had participated in the sacking of the party headquarters.

For those activists frustrated by the disunity of workers and intellectuals since the late 1960s, this series of events offered a new opportunity to establish a broader opposition front in Poland. The challenge for the opposition was thus to identify a platform that could simultaneously support a diverse coalition, express the need for more fundamental reforms than those granted after earlier protests, and frustrate the repressive instincts of the party-state. In the post-Helsinki environment, organizing in defense of internationally recognized human rights was both politically legitimate and institutionally linked to other interests of the Polish regime.

A number of Poland's leading intellectuals, including many from the human rights protests of the preceding winter, got together to provide the imprisoned workers and their families

---

[23] Zbigniew Resich, "Respect for Human Rights in the Declaration of Principles of the CSCE Final Act," *Sprawy Miedzynarodowe* no. 7–8, July–August 1976, from JPRS, *Translations* 68088 (October 19, 1976): 53–60.

[24] *Polityka* (Warsaw), 18 December 1976, from JPRS, *Translations* 68654 (February 18, 1977):1–7.

with free legal assistance and material aid. These efforts continued throughout the summer of 1976. In early September, the group met in a Warsaw apartment to establish a more permanent organization, which they conceived as part of the broader Helsinki human rights movement then emerging across the Communist bloc, including the Soviet Union. As one of the Polish activists put it, referring to the burgeoning Soviet human rights movement, "If they can do it—so can we."[25]

The members of the new group considered calling themselves the Committee in Defense of Human and Civil Rights, believing that this name would "refer simultaneously to the United Nations Charter, the Final Act of Helsinki . . . and to even older tradition: the League for the Defense of Human and Civil Rights that had been active in Poland in the 1930s."[26] Until amnesty was achieved for the imprisoned workers of Ursus and Radom, though, they decided to call themselves the Workers' Defense Committee (KOR). Once the Ursus and Radom workers were freed, the group would adopt the longer name and pursue a broader human rights agenda. The group's strategy and identity were nonetheless linked from the beginning to Helsinki norms; one of its leading members explains: "They issued a challenge to the Communist bureaucracy saying, 'You signed the Helsinki Declaration on Human Rights, and we want to and will make practical use of your signature. Here it is: here is our Workers' Defense Committee."[27]

Besides providing legal aid and material support to the families of the imprisoned and dismissed workers, KOR members worked to organize a broad-based challenge to the state. At KOR's initiative that autumn, large groups of people from different sectors of Polish society sent letters to the government

---

[25] Jan Jozef Lipski, *KOR: A History of the Workers' Defense Committee in Poland, 1976–1981* (Berkeley and Los Angeles: University of California Press, 1985), 98.

[26] Ibid., 50.

[27] Adam Michnik, "The Moral and Spiritual Origins of Solidarity," in William M. Brinton and Alan Rinzler, eds., *Without Force or Lies: Voices from the Revolution of Central Europe in 1989–90* (San Francisco: Mercury House, 1990), 242.

demanding an end to repression and amnesty for all involved in the June strikes. These included a letter to President Gierek from over a thousand industrial workers, and separate letters to the parliament from 34 university professors in Warsaw and Wroclaw, 293 clergymen from the Przemysl diocese southern Poland, 296 intellectuals and artists from Warsaw, 12 workers from the Gdansk shipyards, 5 workers from the Nowa Huta steelworks near Cracow, and approximately 2,000 university students from five cities.[28]

This mounting social pressure at a time when the Gierek government was concerned to maintain its international reputation resulted, on February 3, 1977, in the declaration of a partial amnesty and release of all but five of the imprisoned workers. KOR's ability to achieve such coordination among different sectors of society, and then to force the government to retreat, convinced even more people that the human rights frame was indeed responsive to the interests of both workers and intellectuals, and effective at undermining the government's ability to discredit and then crush organized dissent.[29] "We managed to use the law to protect people," said one activist, remarking how unprecedented this was in a state generally not beholden to its own legal or constitutional commitments.[30]

On March 25, 1977, a different segment of the opposition established the Movement for the Defense of Human and Civil Rights (ROPCiO). The majority of ROPCiO's energies were devoted to Helsinki monitoring functions, including public statements about rights violations and publication of an underground human rights and opposition monthly called *Opinia*. Three weeks after its founding, ROPCiO announced the establishment in Warsaw and Lodz of "Consultation and Information Centres [to] receive Citizens' comments and proposals regarding the implementation of human and civil rights in

---

[28] Robert Zuzowski, *Political Dissent and Opposition in Poland: The Workers' Defense Committee "KOR"* (Westport, Conn.: Praeger, 1992), 89–90.

[29] Henryk Wujec and Antoni Maciarewicz, interviews by author, Warsaw, June 22 and 24, 1991.

[30] Barbara Rozycka, interview by author, Warsaw, June 22, 1991.

Poland."[31] Several KOR members signed the declaration that founded ROPCiO, but the new organization's founders were predominantly nationalist and center-right in philosophy, with close ties to the Church, in contrast to KOR's predominantly lay and social-democratic membership. Within a few months, ROPCiO gained about a thousand members, plus many more sympathizers, mainly among the lower-middle-class technical intelligentsia.

Notwithstanding these social and ideological differences, the overlapping human rights agendas of KOR and ROPCiO helped lay the groundwork for the future Solidarity alliance between labor activists, intellectuals, and the Church. Beginning with the Polish Episcopate's March 1976 intervention into the constitutional debate, the Church was increasingly engaged with the opposition's initiatives related to human rights, including aid for imprisoned workers, hunger strikes to protest repression, and more. The nonviolent, seemingly apolitical nature of human rights norms were well suited to the Church's delicate position as the buffer between state and society. The Helsinki process and the relevance of human rights principles to Church teachings and to social life were discussed openly in Catholic circles, including pulpit sermons, Catholic newspapers, and the influential Clubs of Catholic Intelligentsia. "The growing involvement of the Church with the human rights movement," says one historian, "helped revive the politically dormant sections of the more traditionalistic Catholic public opinion."[32]

In the early summer of 1976, a group of students recently expelled from Krakow's Jagellonian University for establishing an independent discussion group learned about KOR and the Ursus/Radom strikes from Western radio broadcasts. After contacting KOR, they began to circulate its publications among

---

[31] Association of Polish Students and Graduates in Exile, *Dissent in Poland: Reports and Documents in Translation, December 1975–July 1977* (London, 1979), 180–86.

[32] Jacques Rupnik, "Dissent in Poland, 1968–1978," in Rudolf L. Tokes, ed., *Opposition in Eastern Europe* (Baltimore: Johns Hopkins University Press, 1979), 90.

fellow students, and garnered 517 signatures on a petition to free the imprisoned strikers. The question was how to make their appeals effective: "it was evident that we must use the laws which existed, but we had no illusions about the system, about the laws which they break all the time," recalled one of the student organizers. Plus, there was the question of the viability of opposition to a hegemonic state: "For us, the greatest barrier to cross was fear of provocation."[33]

Large numbers of students, including many uninterested in the details of economics or politics, were attracted to discussions of basic human rights, such as freedom of expression and the self-organization of society. Through Western radio broadcasts and contacts with KOR, the students learned about the human rights dialogue spreading across Eastern Europe, and especially about the Helsinki process. Helsinki's human rights principles and Poland's interest in détente were discussed at all of their gatherings. The human rights discourse thus provided the students with a way to articulate their ideals at lesser risk of repression: "It was important for people to know that the state had accepted these principles. This was very important as a tactic for action."

When young activist Stanislaw Pyjas was murdered in Krakow on May 7, 1977, the students responded by establishing the Student Solidarity Committee (SKS). "It was necessary to demonstrate that we were not only students but also citizens with a right to participate in public life," they felt. By October, SKS groups were established by students in Poznan, Wroclaw, Gdansk, and Szczecin (in Warsaw, students tended to join KOR). All of these groups discussed Helsinki principles, and especially the CSCE review conference soon to begin in Belgrade. In the process, hundreds of new people entered the organized opposition and the name "Solidarity" was spread through opposition circles across Poland.

On July 23, 1977, the government signaled its de facto recognition of KOR by inviting a leading member, Edward Lipinski, to the General Prosecutor's Office to inform him that due to a

---

[33] Bronislaw Wildstein, interview by author, Krakow, July 2, 1992.

general amnesty, the remaining five workers would be freed and charges against KOR dropped. As this concession came just a few weeks after the preparatory session for the Helsinki review meeting in Belgrade, at which the United States had signaled its intention to emphasize human rights, Polish activists were further encouraged to pursue the linkage between human rights and the organization of independent society.[34] In September 1977, one year after its founding, KOR adopted a broader human rights and political agenda, and renamed itself the "Committee for Social Self-defense (KOR)," retaining the old initials for the sake of continuity.

Some members of the renamed KSS-KOR believed that the human rights monitoring function should be secondary to a more explicitly political agenda.[35] The resulting Declaration of Democratic Movement, released the following month by 110 persons, including 24 KSS-KOR members, nevertheless listed "the implementation of all those international pacts on human rights which have been ratified by the Council of Ministers" as the "first step" toward realization of its political goals.[36] Among its other functions, KSS-KOR's new *Biuletyn Informacyjny* (Information Bulletin) reported on human rights abuses across Poland, pressed the government to fulfill its Helsinki obligations, and chronicled the activities of KOR and human rights monitoring groups elsewhere in Eastern Europe.

CZECHOSLOVAKIA

As in Poland and the Soviet Union, societal activists in Czechoslovakia had responded almost immediately to the signing of the Helsinki Final Act in August 1975 with a flurry of petitions for domestic reform and appeals for oversight from abroad. Two sets of events in the early fall of 1976 then convinced them that the time was right to attempt a more organized opposition

[34] Zuzowski, *Political Dissent and Opposition in Poland*, 92.
[35] *Labour Focus on Eastern Europe* 1:5 (November-December 1977): 16.
[36] Ibid., 18–19.

movement: a political trial that localized protests failed to block; and mounting evidence that the Husak regime was indeed sensitive to the issue of Helsinki compliance.

In September 1976, the authorities arrested the underground rock band Plastic People of the Universe and charged them with being an illegal organization. Few of Prague's intellectuals were familiar with the band, but a number of them concluded that they ought to protest such a blatant abuse of basic rights. A government that would not tolerate nonconformist music could never be expected to tolerate independent political activity, they reasoned. Vaclav Havel, a poet known for his independent views, and Jiri Nemec, a liberal Catholic theologian, began attending and publicizing the trial. An open letter from ten former lawyers labeled the trial "the latest in a series of administrative interventions limiting and invalidating civil rights and freedoms, especially freedom of artistic creation, scientific research, and freedom of expression."[37]

Although the protests brought together theologians, artists, and ex-Communists in an ad hoc alliance, they failed to gain the release of the imprisoned musicians. How could disparate opposition forces be transformed into a durable and politically viable opposition movement, they wondered. As time went on, and Western leaders began to voice increasing concern about human rights compliance within the CSCE, evidence mounted that the Husak regime was sensitive to criticism about Helsinki violations. In mid-autumn, as part of its effort to portray itself as supportive of Helsinki principles, the regime decided to release to bookstores the international human rights covenants that Czechoslovakia had ratified the previous December.[38]

Very few copies of the UN covenants were actually made available to the public, but activists recognized that the political

---

[37] H. Gordon Skilling, *Charter 77 and Human Rights in Czechoslovakia* (London: Allen & Unwin, 1981), 13.

[38] Ordinance No.120/1976 of the Czechoslovak Foreign Ministry, May 10, 1976, in Vilem Prečan, ed., *Human Rights in Czechoslovakia: A Documentation, September 1981–December 1982* (Paris: International Committee for the Support of Charter 77 in Czechoslovakia, April 1983), 58.

environment was becoming more amenable to an organized opposition movement.[39] As one recalls, "We were near the door of the kitchen when she said it: 'we must do something with this' and she turned on the faucet so that the noise of the water would cover our murmuring voices. . . . It was only the sound of running water, and yet it was the start of a debate on civil and political rights. It was November 11, 1976 that volume 23 of the Collection of Laws of Czechoslovakia went on sale. And in this volume was a decree of the Ministry of Foreign Affairs dated May 10, 1976, numbered 120, with the promising title 'International Covenant on Civil and Political Rights and International Covenant on Economic, Social, and Cultural Rights. . . . The idea was thus born 'to do something.' "[40] Soon thereafter, the early release of political prisoners Huebl, Mueller, Sabata, and Tesar reinforced the activists' growing sense that public appeals for the Czechoslovak government to honor its Helsinki commitments could be effective.[41]

The comprehensive list of human rights established by the covenants and the Helsinki Final Act, and the political salience provided by the Helsinki review process, offered a crucial opportunity to challenge the brutality of the post-1968 "normalization" regime. If random appeals and publicity could bring minor concessions, they reasoned, then an organized independent mechanism to monitor Czechoslovakia's compliance with its human rights obligations might cause the government to improve its behavior substantially. Out of this recognition came a grassroots movement more secure from repression, more open to diverse constituencies, and more politically catalytic over time than any that Czechoslovak society had produced in three decades of Communist rule.

[39] Jiri Dienstbier, interview by author, New Haven, Conn., April 14, 1991; Jiri Hayek, interview by author, Prague, June 7, 1991.

[40] "Un chartiste," "Conscience contre existence: Information à propos de la naissance et de l'évolution de la Charte 77," *Cahiers de l'Est* 9/10 (1977). Running water served to hide conversation from listening devices installed by the secret police in private apartments.

[41] *RFE Research*, Czechoslovak Situation Report/2, 19 January 1977.

The Charter 77 movement was born on January 1, 1977, with the appearance of 242 signatures on a four-page document that chronicled the denial of human rights in Czechoslovakia and appealed for dialogue with state authorities on how those rights could be protected.[42] Though far more than a private petition to the regime, the Charter claimed not to be a formal organization, which would have necessitated either accepting the party line or risking immediate repression. Instead, the Charter presented itself as a "free informal, open community of people of different convictions, different faiths, and different professions." This aspect of the Charter was reflected in a list of signatories whose differences over the means of achieving political and social change, and the type of regime they would prefer, as well as class and religious differences, had previously prevented cooperation. The Charter's initial spokespersons were Professor Jan Patocka, representing the liberal intellectuals; Vaclav Havel, representing the artistic and cultural community; and Jiri Hajek, who had been foreign minister under Dubcek, representing socialists and former party reformers.

Most important, the Charter disavowed any particular ideological or political position beyond protection of those human rights recognized by international agreement. "It does not form the basis for any oppositional activity. . . . It does not aim, then, to set out its own programmes for political or social reforms or changes, but within its own sphere of activity it wishes to conduct a constructive dialogue with the political and state authorities, particularly by drawing attention to various individual cases where human and civil rights are violated, by preparing documentation and suggesting solutions, by submitting other proposals of a more general character aimed at reinforcing such rights and their guarantees, and by acting as a mediator in various conflict situations which may lead to injustice and so forth." The Charter thus presented itself not as an opponent of the Prague regime but as a partner in the implementation of norms already accepted as politically (if not legally) binding.

[42] The text of Charter 77 is reproduced in Skilling, *Charter 77 and Human Rights in Czechoslovakia*, 209–12.

The conception, identity, and strategy of Charter 77 were thus intimately tied to the Helsinki process and international human rights norms. The Charter's opening paragraph reads: "In the Czechoslovak Collection of Laws, no. 120 of 13 October 1976, texts were published of the International Covenant on Civil and Political Rights, and of the International Covenant on Economic, Social and Cultural Rights, which were signed on behalf of our Republic in 1968, were confirmed at Helsinki in 1975 and came into force in our country on 23 March 1976. From that date our citizens have the right, and our state the duty, to abide by them." The body of the text states again that the signatories are: "united by the will to strive, individually and collectively, for the respect of civic and human rights in our own country and throughout the world—rights accorded to all men by the two mentioned international covenants, by the Final Act of the Helsinki conference and by numerous other international documents opposing war, violence and social or spiritual oppression, and which are comprehensively laid down in the United Nations Universal Declaration of Human Rights." The connection to Helsinki norms and détente politics appears a third time in the Charter's concluding paragraph: "By its symbolic name, Charter 77 denotes that it has come into being at the start of a year proclaimed as the Year of Political Prisoners—a year in which a conference in Belgrade is due to review the implementation of the obligations assumed at Helsinki."

Despite these international references, the content of Charter 77 did not seem foreign to citizens of Czechoslovakia. The number of signatories rose rapidly in the weeks following its initial release. Ministers of the Evangelical Church of the Brethren secretly wrote and distributed a letter explaining why support for Charter 77 was consistent with Christian teachings.[43] In fact, Minister of the Interior Jaromir Obzina is reported to have estimated that 90 percent of the public would sympathize with the Charter if it were published openly, and

[43] *Frankfurter Allgemeine* (Frankfurt), 2 April 1977, from JPRS, *Translations* 69008 (April 27, 1977): 22–23.

that two million people would sign it if the state imposed no sanction.[44] Charter 77 thus threatened not only the regime's ability to hide the abuses committed under the guise of "normalization," but also its effort to pacify Czechoslovak society by eliminating all means of self-organization.

The wording of Charter 77 also trapped the regime between its own domestic illegitimacy and its international commitments, both to the West and the East. Exiled Czech activist Jan Kavan explained: "one should not be under any illusion that the government can actually grant these rights. . . . The present structure of government would be unable to defend itself against open discontent and criticism. . . . On the other hand, it cannot declare that the *demands* in the Charter are illegitimate or counter-revolutionary, because that would mean renouncing its signature on the Helsinki agreement and the UN covenants."[45] Zdenek Mlynar, a Charter signatory and former secretary of the Central Committee during the Prague Spring, observed the same dilemma: "Charter 77 is in fact . . . a true child of the Helsinki Conference of 1975. The government may treat it like a mean step-mother, yet it cannot destroy that child, if it does not want to renounce completely its own obligations which it adopted in the family of other European nations at Helsinki."[46]

Looking eastward, the Husak regime was keenly aware of the need to satisfy Moscow's interests as well—namely, securing Communist rule in Czechoslovakia while removing that country as a contentious issue from the politics of détente. "The present leaders regard the washing of Czechoslovakia's dirty linen in public abroad as dangerous not only because it centers world attention on their own precarious position but also because it brings Moscow's wrath down upon them. The Soviet

---

[44] Vladimir V. Kusin, "Challenge to Normalcy: Political Opposition in Czechoslovakia, 1968–77, "in Rudolf L. Tokes, ed., *Opposition in Eastern Europe* (Baltimore: Johns Hopkins University Press, 1979)," 52.

[45] "Czechoslovakia in the Wake of Charter 77," *Labour Focus on Eastern Europe* 1:1 (March-April 1977):5–7.

[46] *Listy* (Rome), no. 3–4, July 1977: 22–24, from JPRS, *Translations* 69803 (September 16, 1977):25–30.

leadership would like nothing better than that the world forget Czechoslovakia. Both Moscow and Prague would like the Czechoslovak case to be less visible, less conspicuous."[47] Only a finely tuned policy could satisfy these potentially conflicting objectives. To complicate matters further, the leadership under Husak was divided between hard-line ideologues led by Vasil Bilak and a more pragmatic faction led by federal prime minister Lubomir Strougal.

Soon after the Charter was established, a Soviet delegation came to Prague to advise the Husak government on how to respond. On the basis of the official actions that followed, the Soviets appear to have counseled a firm response attuned to minimize the international fallout. The regime's first response was an attempt to discredit the Charter and its signatories. The official daily *Rude Pravo* never printed the text of Charter 77, but attacked "Western imperialist countries who organised the Charter" for trying to "impose their own interpretations of human rights on us." Its pages were also filled with accusations that Charter signatories were lazy, reactionary, unpatriotic, and tools of Western imperialism. The regime even resorted to charges of sexual immorality: one signatory was forced to undergo treatment for venereal disease although she was fully healthy, while nude photos of another signatory with his girlfriend were published in a weekly newspaper.[48]

Leading Charter signatories were interrogated by the police and several were arrested; the elderly professor Jan Patocka died of heart failure several hours after returning from police interrogation. Dozens of signatories were fired from their jobs, including many whose professional careers had already been aborted by the purges of the early 1970s. Eventually, all signatories were denied employment except as window washers, furnace stokers, and so on. Other citizens were fired from their jobs merely for refusing to participate in public condemnations of the Charter.[49]

---

[47] Jan Triska, "Messages from Czechoslovakia," *Problems of Communism* 24 (November-December 1975), 36.

[48] *Labour Focus on Eastern Europe* 1:1 (March-April 1977):6.

[49] Ibid.

Where once states would have hidden behind a policy of non-interference on human rights matters, and non-governmental protests would have lacked any punch, international reaction to the harassment of Charter signatories was swift in coming and framed explicitly in terms of Prague's violation of its international commitments. This framing of the issue was enabled by the Helsinki Accords' recognition of human rights as a legitimate subject for diplomacy, and by the Chartists' deliberate decision to identify their campaign with the norms and mechanisms of the Helsinki process.

On January 26, the U.S. State Department strongly condemned Prague's response to the Charter as a violation of its commitments under the Helsinki accords. This was the first time that the State Department had publicly accused another government of failure to live up to the Helsinki accords, and a strong signal that the United States had departed from its traditional policy of non-interference.[50] The governments of Western and neutral/non-aligned states across Europe also issued a string of condemnations and warnings. Swedish Foreign Minister Karin Soder told a Council of Europe meeting in Strasbourg on January 27 that the Prague government's treatment of Charter 77 constituted a threat to détente in Europe and that it could hamper success at the CSCE follow-up meeting to be held in Belgrade in the coming summer.[51] British Foreign Secretary Anthony Crosland, speaking for the EC Council of Ministers, reminded the rulers of Eastern Europe that the EC still expected them to honor the human rights provisions of the Helsinki accords.[52] Austrian Foreign Minister Willibald Pahr told Vienna's *Die Presse* newspaper that the arrest or expulsion of Charter 77 signatories would be "a striking violation of the Final Act" and that such actions would be raised in Belgrade.[53]

Socialist and Communist parties in the West also condemned the Czechoslovak government's response to Charter 77 as a violation of the human rights principles of Helsinki. The British

[50] *New York Times*, January 27, 1977.
[51] UPI newswire item, Stockholm, February 15, 1977.
[52] Special/McGill newswire item, London, January 28, 1977.
[53] Reuter newswire item, Vienna, January 29, 1977.

Labour Party's National Executive Committee passed a unanimous resolution condemning the arrest and harassment of Charter 77 signatories and calling on the Czechoslovak government to abide by its human rights commitments under the Helsinki process.[54] The Italian Communist and Socialist parties expressed their position on the issue by publishing an appeal from Charter 77 signatories in their party newspapers on the eve of the Fifteenth Congress of the Czechoslovak Communist Party.

The Prague regime was publicly criticized by two Communist countries as well, both anxious to defend their independent course. The Yugoslav press carried full coverage of the emergence and repression of Charter 77; on February 7, the Yugoslav Communist Party newspaper *Borba* accused the Prague leadership of violating the spirit of the 1976 Berlin conference of Communist parties, which had explicitly endorsed the Helsinki process and international human rights covenants.[55] Further afield, the Chinese Communist Party's daily newspaper *Renmin Ribao* praised Charter 77 as a document that expressed "resentment against the Soviet occupation and control of the country and determination to fight for political rights," and linked the movement to "growing unrest in Poland, East Germany and the Soviet Union."[56]

The significance of this flurry of condemnations was clear to Gustav Husak and Charter signatories alike: after Helsinki, the Czechoslovak government's treatment of its own citizens would be openly monitored by governments, parties, and independent groups abroad, and its relations with the outside world might be linked to that treatment. The regime's vehement reaction to public and diplomatic charges that it was violating CSCE commitments on human rights betrays its sensitivity to such charges. The regime's failure to eradicate the Charter (which it could easily have done) clearly suggests that the Charter's links to Helsinki converged with the pragmatists' interest in

[54] Special/McGill newswire item, London, January 28, 1977.
[55] *Financial Times* (London), February 8, 1977.
[56] *New York Times*, January 27, 1977. In fact, the issue of Soviet occupation was not mentioned in Charter 77.

détente, and thus outweighed the ideologues' preference for a more thorough campaign against dissent.

In fact, the Foreign Ministry's frequent reports to the Central Committee about the negative impact of domestic repression on relations with the West appear to have directly affected the regime's policy on dissent.[57] One Chartist was actually told by his secret police "tail" that the police were prepared for massive arrests, but were being restrained by order of the Foreign Ministry.[58] Beginning in April, the authorities tried to engage Charter 77 on its own terms. Following a debate within the Federal Assembly on "socialist legality" and a special report by the procurator general on the functioning of the court system, the regime announced that human rights were duly protected in Czechoslovakia: "the social achievements of the Czechoslovak people were in fact their rights and freedoms. Everyone had the right to work, to receive a decent wage, to have paid holidays, to enjoy free medicine and to draw a pension. Through the good offices of social and political organisations of the National Front, the citizens could also put to use freedom of speech and assembly."[59]

The regime's decision to respond to such a serious challenge first with harassment and intimidation and then with reasoned arguments, rather than with the far harsher measures at its disposal, must be attributed, at least in part, to the international legitimacy and profile that Chartists gained through their identification with human rights norms.

HUNGARY

The Helsinki human rights norms that catalyzed an upsurge in activism across Poland, Czechoslovakia, and the Soviet Union after 1975 had far less dramatic effects in Hungary, where re-

---

[57] Ivan Busniak and Zdenek Matejka, interviews by author, Prague, July 27, 1992.

[58] Martin Palous, interview by author, Prague, July 31, 1992.

[59] Vladimir V. Kusin, *From Dubcek to Charter 77: A Study of Normalization in Czechoslovakia, 1968–1978* (New York: St. Martin's Press, 1978), 313–14.

pression was less severe. Any discussion of independent or opposition activity in Hungary must begin, though, with the social compact that emerged out of the failed revolution and Soviet intervention of 1956. In effect, the Hungarian population agreed to forego demands for political liberalization in exchange for greater personal liberty and economic security, including better consumer goods and freedom to operate small-scale private enterprises. In exchange, the Kadar regime operated on the assumption that "If they're not against us, they're with us." As long as they did not explicitly challenge the hegemonic role of the party or Hungary's membership in the Warsaw Pact, intellectuals were permitted considerable autonomy within their research institutes and scholarly reviews to critique the regime's management of the economy.[60]

The authorities in Budapest nonetheless recognized the challenge posed by Helsinki and human rights norms. This concern was partly economic: reports of repression could jeopardize the hard currency loans from the West upon which Hungary increasingly depended. Other evidence reflects a concern that the Helsinki norms could undermine the residual legitimacy of the Communist system itself. Imre Pozsgay warned the Political Academy of the party's Central Committee: "We would be taking a bad road and would be serving the purpose of our enemies if our thinking should be the prisoner of their way of posing the question, if we were to fight from hedgehog positions, following our defensive instincts." The human rights challenge could not be easily dismissed or rebutted, he explained. "I have considerable doubt about the utility and outcome of a debate in which we compare our parliamentary democracy with, for example, English parliamentary democratism [or] with such 'indicators' as freedom of speech and freedom of the press taken in the bourgeois sense. . . . Nor would it be useful to oppose their slanders with an ideal picture of a socialism which does not exist for such an ideal picture—however close it may stand to the possibilities of the society of the future—would contra-

---

[60] George Schopflin, "Opposition and Para-Opposition: Critical Currents in Hungary, 1968–1978," in Tokes, ed., *Opposition in Eastern Europe.*

dict the present reality and everyday experiences and so could not adequately mobilize people to action."[61]

As recommended by Pozsgay, official propaganda began to emphasize socialism's long-term advantage in the satisfaction of human needs alongside its present accomplishments.[62] That same month, Hungary's legal code was revised to guarantee privacy of correspondence and to forbid discrimination on grounds of sex, race, or religion. Meanwhile, the government suspended the sentences of most of the nearly two hundred activists recently sentenced to prison for "incitement to hatred" against the state.[63] Finally, Hungary reached an agreement with the United States that recognized the importance of human rights in American foreign economic policy.[64]

In response to this expansion of official tolerance, Hungarian intellectuals became increasingly bold in their critiques of Hungarian history and society, including the truth about the 1956 revolution and the unavoidable connection between political and economic reform. The quantity of independent or samizdat publishing increased tremendously. In addition to the flourishing of samizdat publishing, independent "Free University" courses proliferated in private apartments. Even at the official Karl Marx University of Economics in Budapest, an independent political club attracted hundreds of students to its discussions of domestic and international issues, including human rights.[65] After the creation of Charter 77 in Czechoslovakia, thirty-four of Hungary's leading intellectuals sent a letter of support to their colleagues in Prague: "We declare our solidarity with the signers of Charter 77, and we condemn the repressive measures used against them. We are convinced that the

[61] Imre Pozsgay, "The Humanism of Our Society," *Elet Es Irodalom* (Budapest) December 10, 1977, from JPRS, *Translations* 70721 (March 2, 1978): 39.

[62] Otto Bihari, "Human Rights—Civic Basic Rights," *Nepszava* (Budapest) July 17, 1977, from JPRS, *Translations* 69599 (August 12 1977):36–39.

[63] Amnesty International, *Amnesty International Report 1978* (London, 1978), 218.

[64] *Guardian* (London), 27 October 1977.

[65] Bill Lomax, "Hungary: The Rise of the Democratic Opposition," *Labour Focus on Eastern Europe* 5:3–4 (Summer 1982):2–7.

defense of human and civil rights is a common concern of all Eastern Europe."[66] The Hungarian police harassed these activists and samizdat authors, but refrained from launching a serious crackdown.

Hungary's system of "Goulash Communism" was thus unique in Eastern Europe, both for the high material quality of life it supported and for the relatively light hand of state repression. Neither intellectuals nor workers were anxious to disturb "the happiest barracks in the Soviet camp." Gyorgy Hajas and several other Budapest activists attempted to establish a Helsinki monitoring group in July 1977, but their initiative never caught on. The Kadar regime's strategy of tolerating cultural and intellectual freedom as long as the resulting activity did not directly challenge the political status quo thus succeeded, at least in the short term, in preempting organized opposition and avoiding the Helsinki spotlight.

BULGARIA, EAST GERMANY, AND ROMANIA

The Helsinki Accords had a limited impact on independent activism or state policy in Bulgaria, East Germany, and Romania in the late 1970s. An anonymous "Declaration 1978" appeared in Sofia, Bulgaria, on March 2, 1978, just as the Belgrade CSCE meeting was ending, but its six demands for the protection of human rights were never answered by the regime or reinforced by additional societal appeals.[67] The Helsinki Accords were widely discussed in East Germany in 1975–1976, including several public appeals for their implementation (see Chapter 3), but after twelve years of Nazism and then decades of Stalinism, eastern Germany had neither the social base for an independent, critical intelligentsia nor an embedded memory of democratic rule. At the same time, the GDR economy was remark-

---

[66] U.S. Commission on Security and Cooperation in Europe, *The Right to Know, the Right to Act: Documents of Helsinki Dissent from the Soviet Union and Eastern Europe* (Washington, D.C., May 1978), 125.
[67] Ibid., 121.

ably productive, guaranteeing a higher and more stable standard of living than anywhere in the bloc except Hungary. Finally, and perhaps above all, the State Security Service (Stasi) had thoroughly infiltrated East German society, guaranteeing that any independent initiative could be discovered and eliminated. Given the risk associated with "voice" against such a repressive state, and the allure of life in neighboring West Germany, most East Germans unhappy with the status quo attempted to "exit" rather than organize a movement for domestic change.[68] For this reason, independent human rights activity in East Germany tended to focus on the freedom of movement guaranteed by the Helsinki Accords.

By the beginning of preparatory talks for the Belgrade CSCE meeting in mid-1977, the number of exit visa applications had swollen to over 200,000 (roughly 2 percent of the GDR's population).[69] By 1978, the number of applications approached 300,000.[70] Virtually every one of these applications referred to the text of the Helsinki Final Act, which *Neues Deutschland* had published in full, but this alone guaranteed neither success nor even the security of the applicant. Dissident Karl-Heinz Nitschke was released from prison in August 1977 when the authorities became convinced that he would use his trial as a public protest against human rights violations on the eve of the CSCE conference in Belgrade. Such cases notwithstanding, the flood of exit applications was seen as a threat by the Honecker regime. Fearful of the numbers that might follow a lenient policy, the regime responded by harassing the applicants, dismissing them from employment, and threatening imprisonment. Only a small percentage of the applications were approved. Helmuth Nitsche, a linguist, was sentenced to five years' im-

---

[68] Albert O. Hirschman, "Exit, Voice and the Fate of the German Democratic Republic," *World Politics* 45: 2 (January 1993): 173–202.

[69] *Die Welt* (Bonn), August 26, 1977, from JPRS, *Translations* 69892 (September 30, 1977):52.

[70] Tufton Beamish and Guy Hadley, *The Kremlin's Dilemma: The Struggle for Human Rights in Eastern Europe* (San Rafael, Cal.: Presidio Press, 1979), 184–85.

prisonment for an eight-minute public demonstration in which he demanded to be allowed to leave East Germany.[71]

The first sign of human rights or opposition activity in Romania was dissident writer Paul Goma's January 26, 1977, letter to Pavel Kohout expressing support for Charter 77.[72] Less than two weeks later, Goma and seven others issued an open letter to the participants in the forthcoming Belgrade CSCE meeting calling upon the other states to pressure the Romanian government to observe the Helsinki Accords and the international covenants on human rights, especially freedom of movement and freedom of expression.[73] As word spread, over two hundred Romanians added their signature to the letter, and many sent individual accounts and documentation of human rights abuses. Six "neo-Protestant" preachers sent a separate letter to Radio Free Europe that spoke of the catalytic impact of the Helsinki Final Act and called on foreign governments to press for its implementation in Romania.[74]

Goma was arrested on April 3, but the protests continued. On May 26, seven people signed another appeal to the participants in the Belgrade conference, again listing specific actions that the outside world should take to promote human rights in Romania. On August 2, ten people who had been denied emigration visas wrote directly to President Ceaucescu to remind him that this action violated the Helsinki Final Act. In August and September, twenty-two Romanian coal miners wrote a series of letters to Radio Free Europe to tell the outside world that 35,000 miners had gone on strike in the Liu Valley,

---

[71] Werner Volkmer, "East Germany: Dissenting Views during the Last Decade," in Tokes, ed., *Opposition in Eastern Europe*, 122. See Nitsche's March 1977 letter to President Carter, in U.S. Commission, *The Right to Know*, 124.

[72] U.S. Commission, *The Right to Know*, 52.

[73] Radio Free Europe/Radio Liberty, "Romanian Situation Report," no. 6 (February 18, 1977):12–15. The full text of the Goma letter appears in U.S. Commission on Security and Cooperation in Europe, *Basket Three: Implementation of the Helsinki Accords*, Vol. 2, Hearings (Washington, DC: Government Printing Office, 1977), 389.

[74] U.S. Commission, *The Right to Know*, 53–54, 62–64.

linking their demands to international human rights norms and to Paul Goma's fledgling human rights committee.[75]

Notwithstanding these appeals to Helsinki norms and diplomacy, Nicolae Ceaucescu was confident that as long as he maintained his distance from the military arm of the Warsaw Pact, the West would overlook his transgressions on human rights. By the end of 1977, Ceaucescu had exiled Goma to Paris, crushed the miners' strikes, and otherwise eliminated this budding human rights movement. No sustained human rights or other opposition movement reappeared in Romania until the late 1980s.

THE CSCE FOLLOW-UP MEETING AT
BELGRADE, 1977–1978

Societal appeals to Helsinki review conferences, as to Helsinki norms in general, reflected a widely recognized irony of Soviet and East European rule: despite its absolute monopoly on domestic political space and its effective military parity with the West, the Kremlin and its allies remained deeply concerned about their image abroad. Soviet and East European dissidents knew, as Marshall Goldman wrote in 1972, that "The Russians frequently respond more readily to international public opinion than their own."[76] Yuri Orlov explained in 1978: "We do not have the means by which to reach our government. My [1973 Open] appeal to Brezhnev probably got as far as the regional KGB office. . . . The crucial question is what means are there for a Soviet citizen to approach his own government, other than indirectly through the governments of other countries. This is why we want the documents of the Helsinki Group to be discussed at the Belgrade Conference."[77] This sensitivity to inter-

---

[75] Ibid., 57–61.

[76] Marshall Goldman, *Spoils of Progress: Environmental Pollution in the Soviet Union* (Cambridge: MIT Press, 1972), 290.

[77] Walter Parchomenko, *Soviet Images of Dissidents and Nonconformists* (New York: Praeger, 1986), 156.

national opinion in the post-Helsinki era was driven by the same factors that led the Soviets and their allies to participate in the Helsinki negotiations in the first place: access to the political, economic, and strategic benefits accorded to "normal" members of the European and international community. With the signing of the Final Act, though, these benefits were linked to human rights. Accordingly, opposition activists in the East bloc recognized that the best time to press their claims would be just before and during the CSCE Follow-On Meetings scheduled to begin officially in Belgrade in October 1977.

Independent groups all across Eastern Europe and the Soviet Union, many focused on human rights, issued appeals to the participants in the Belgrade meeting. In addition to its original declaration, Charter 77 issued three documents about the Belgrade meeting: a letter to President Husak in October 1977, an appeal to Belgrade delegates in January 1978, and an evaluation of the results of the Belgrade meeting in March 1978.[78] In June 1977, just as the preparatory talks were about to convene in Belgrade, KOR issued a statement that the Helsinki provisions were not being implemented in Poland, citing repression of its own activities as an example. KOR directed a second statement to Belgrade one month later, describing the group's activities and arguing that they contributed to the objectives of the Final Act.[79] In November, the Moscow Helsinki Group and several of its affiliates issued their own appeal for greater attention to human rights at Belgrade. As discussed extensively in Chapter 4, these appeals had a direct influence on the Western agenda.

Across Eastern Europe, the authorities' commitment to maintaining at least the appearance of Helsinki compliance seems to have produced a greater political tolerance in advance of the Belgrade CSCE meeting. In Poland, the pattern of tolerance/repression corresponds closely with the preparations and course of the meeting. In 1976, many activists were arrested and charged with such offenses as "dissemination of false literature" and "associating with hostile foreign organizations." In

[78] For the text of all three documents, see Skilling, *Charter 77*, 270–77.
[79] Lipski, *KOR*, 166–67.

1977, as the CSCE review approached, no Polish citizens were charged with such offenses, despite a notable escalation in opposition and independent activity; beatings of KOR members and coworkers stopped in May 1977. Arrests and harassment of dissidents resumed, however, in early 1978, just as the prospects for détente were being overwhelmed by the ideological battles at Belgrade.[80] Although the authorities in Czechoslovakia were less tolerant than those in Poland, their cautious approach to Charter 77 also reflects concern about Helsinki norms and the Belgrade meeting.

Even the Soviet Union, which had less to lose than its East European allies from a rupture in relations with the West, seems to have moderated its response to the budding Helsinki movement in order to maintain the appearance of compliance with the Final Act, at least at first. The Moscow Helsinki Group constituted an unprecedented violation of the prohibition on independent organizations, yet the authorities responded with uncharacteristic caution to its creation in May 1976. The KGB warned Orlov that the group was "illegal and unconstitutional," but allowed it to function virtually unimpeded over the following eight months, during which time group members conducted several independent investigations and issued eighteen documents on human rights abuses.[81] Only in February 1977, following Jimmy Carter's correspondence with Andrei Sakharov and his White House meeting with exiled dissident Vladimir Bukovsky, were Helsinki group members Aleksandr Ginzburg and Yuri Orlov arrested. Over the next few months, Anatoly Shcharansky was arrested, and Ludmilla Alexeyeva, Petr Grigorenko, Malva Landa, and Vladimir Slepak were exiled.[82] And then, just as the CSCE preparatory negotiations

[80] *Amnesty International Report 1978*, 223–25; Helsinki Committee in Poland, "The Helsinki Accords, the Human Rights Conventions and Poland," March 1986, in *Uncensored Poland News Bulletin* (London: Information Centre for Polish Affairs, August 1986).

[81] U.S. Commission, *Documents of the Helsinki Monitoring Groups in the U.S.S.R. and Lithuania*.

[82] U.S. Commission on Security and Cooperation in Europe, "Fact Sheet: Update on the Soviet Helsinki Movement," mimeographed, December 10, 1979.

were getting under way in Belgrade, the spurt of arrests and exiles came to a sudden end.

Helsinki Watch Groups in Moscow, the Ukraine, Lithuania, Georgia, and Armenia continued to monitor Soviet compliance with the Helsinki Accords. Western delegations used their reports repeatedly at Belgrade to document Soviet violations. Yet despite this mounting challenge to Soviet authority, and its damaging consequences for the friendly East-West relations valued by the Soviets, the Kremlin was remarkably tolerant of dissent throughout the Belgrade meeting: only one member of the Soviet Helsinki watch movement was exiled or imprisoned from August 1977 through early March 1978, when the meeting ended in a political and ideological stalemate.[83] Given the Kremlin's long-standing intolerance of independent organizations, and its proven willingness to repress dissent at the peak of détente in the early 1970s, the only explanation for this restraint is a desire to be seen as acting within the spirit of the Helsinki Accords.

The threat of controversy at Belgrade seems to have been least effective in the Czechoslovak case. Although the beginning of preparatory talks in July 1977 may have contributed to the easing of the anti-Charter campaign three months earlier, a series of arrests, beatings, and trials during the summer and fall demonstrate that the Husak regime valued domestic order over its international reputation. The most blatant example of the regime's willingness to disregard Belgrade was the trial and conviction in October 1977 of four Chartists who had been arrested the previous winter.[84]

CONCLUSION

Across Eastern Europe and the Soviet Union, the Communist Party's monopoly on political space was definitively broken by the mid to late 1970s. In addition, as the Belgrade meeting had

---

[83] Ibid.
[84] Skilling, *Charter* 77, 139–41.

demonstrated, the dissidents' appeals to the West had blocked the material fruits of détente so badly needed by East bloc regimes. Instead of settling outstanding issues and opening the door for trade and investment, the Helsinki process had become a justification for independent or dissident activity incompatible with the "leading role" of the Communist Party. As this chapter has shown, the introduction of human rights norms into East-West relations at Helsinki and their public endorsement by Communist authorities played a significant role in catalyzing and enabling these momentous developments.

This conclusion does not mean, however, that Helsinki norms were alone responsible for this historic change in state-society relations. Another critical factor was the Communist party-state's increasing inability to satisfy consumer demand with existing capital, or to regain legitimacy through more symbolic means, such as nationalism.[85] Moreover, as discussed in Chapter 4, the Helsinki process itself was substantially transformed after 1975 by East European activists' transnational campaign to reorient Western policy toward the CSCE, and then by the inauguration of Jimmy Carter as president of the United States, which encouraged East Europeans in their hope that Helsinki norms could be used to promote and protect independent society. Helsinki norms are thus a necessary but not sufficient explanation for the expansion and organization of opposition in the Communist bloc in the mid to late 1970s.

Helsinki norms encouraged veteran and potential activists to believe that the Communist regimes that they faced would be more tolerant of independent activity linked to the Helsinki process than they been toward earlier dissent. In fact, Communist elites did prove to be more tolerant of Helsinki-oriented opposition. An independent movement in the Communist bloc

[85] See Valerie Bunce, "The Political Economy of the Brezhnev Era: The Rise and Fall of Corporatism," *British Journal of Political Science* 13 (January 1983):129–58; Alex Pravda, "East-West Interdependence and the Social Compact in Eastern Europe," in Morris Bornstein et al., *East-West Relations and the Future of Eastern Europe* (London: Allen and Unwin, 1981), 162–87; and Stephen White, "Economic Performance and Communist Legitimacy," *World Politics* 38 (April 1986):462–82.

that appeared to support Jimmy Carter's foreign policy would not have been tolerated; a movement dedicated to the implementation of the same Helsinki principles that these authorities had continuously praised was far harder to dismiss or crush. Moreover, the political salience of human rights norms occasioned by Helsinki also provided a basis for alliances between domestic societal forces previously divided along class, religious, or ideological lines.

As a result, although some regimes proved more tolerant of independent activity than others over the next few years, the Communist party-state had forever lost its claim (vital for both domestic and international legitimacy) to enjoy the quiet support of a satisfied population. The activists' focus on the Helsinki process, and the authorities' tolerance of dissent, waxed and waned in the following years, but the party-state's monopoly on social and political space was never restored. Instead, the Communist regimes were faced in the 1980s with a difficult choice between political reforms that threatened their hold on power and direct repression of this newly organized and vocal opposition—all in an international normative environment increasingly inhospitable to repression and therefore unlikely to deliver the economic goods needed to rescue the East bloc.

CHAPTER SIX

Backlash: Communism's Response to Human Rights

> As a result of measures taken by the KGB, implemented in strict accordance with the law and under the leadership of Party organs, the anti-social elements, despite the West's considerable material and moral support, did not succeed in achieving organized cohesion on the platform of anti-Sovietism.
> —*S. Tsvigun, KGB First Deputy Chairman, 1981*[1]

> These activities of Charter 77 . . . enjoy international recognition as expressed particularly in the Final Act of the Conference on Security and Cooperation in Europe, signed in Helsinki, and in the interpretation given to this document by participants in the Madrid session of this Conference.
> —*Charter 77 document, 1984*[2]

THE POST-HELSINKI expansion of independent initiatives, including human rights monitoring, nascent trade unions, quasi-political parties, and underground publishing in most countries across the Communist bloc posed a critical challenge to the party-state's monopoly on information and political space. In short, the party-state was faced with losing both its rhetorical claim to represent popular interests and its practical ability to suppress challengers without recourse to the terror tactics of the Stalinist era, which had already been largely (albeit un-

[1] *A Chronicle of Human Rights in the USSR* (New York), no. 44 (October-December 1981):30–34.

[2] Charter 77 document no. 4/84: Letter to the U.N. Secretary General, 21 February 1984, in U.S. Commission on Security and Cooperation in Europe, *Human Rights in Czechoslovakia: The Documents of Charter 77, 1982–1987* (Washington, D.C.: Government Printing Office, 1988), 88.

evenly) repudiated across the bloc. However, the unexpected domestic and transnational reaction to Helsinki norms presented the Communist regimes with a difficult choice: they could pursue the political and economic benefits that were supposed to flow from the CSCE and the improvement of East-West relations, or they could increase repression in an attempt to reestablish the social and political hegemony of the party-state, but they could not do both.

This chapter shows both the continued role of Helsinki norms as the language of opposition in several East European countries in the years 1979 to 1984, and their limitations as a constraint on state repressiveness during this period. Identifying the factors that undermined the constraining effect of Helsinki norms will improve our understanding of both the potential and the limitations of international human rights norms as constraints on state behavior. Likewise, tracing the activists' continued identification with Helsinki norms despite repression sheds further light on the role of international norms in social mobilization.

FROM BELGRADE TO MADRID

Because of the intense disputes at the Belgrade CSCE conference described in Chapters 4 and 5, the participating states managed only to review past compliance and to agree to hold another meeting two and a half years later in Madrid. Although it was widely portrayed as a failure, this outcome ensured that the norms of the Helsinki Final Act would remain the standard by which CSCE participating states would be judged at Madrid, and guaranteed that they would remain on the political agenda in the intervening years. In May 1979, for example, NATO's foreign ministers "re-emphasized that progress in implementation is essential for the continuation of the CSCE process," and expressed particular concern about human rights.[3] As the

---

[3] North Atlantic Council, *Texts of Final Communiqués*, Vol. 3 (Brussels: NATO Information Service, 1985), 112.

Madrid conference drew nearer, they repeated their "concern that in certain countries the situation remained unsatisfactory or had even deteriorated as regards respect for human rights and fundamental freedoms," and warned about linkage to progress on other issues.[4] Helsinki norms were thus as present in the Soviet and East European political environment after 1978 as they had been after 1975.

Besides the survival of the Helsinki Final Act as the normative structure of East-West relations, two other factors were conducive to an improved human rights situation in Eastern Europe: the continued deterioration of centrally planned economies, and the consolidation of the transnational Helsinki network linking activists in the East to supporters in the West. By the late 1970s, signs of impending economic crisis, including declining productivity, technological stagnation, and escalating foreign debt were increasingly evident across Eastern Europe and the Soviet Union. Continued reliance on economic autarchy and centralized economic management appeared less and less likely to reverse these negative trends.[5] Yet increased trade and investment from the West could not be achieved without good diplomatic relations. These trends raised the potential economic costs of political repression.

This effect was reinforced by the consolidation of the transnational network of Helsinki-focused NGOs and governmental agencies that dated back to 1975. As discussed in Chapter 4, the private U.S. Helsinki Watch Committee began operation in early 1979; in September 1980, the committee established an office in Madrid to coordinate its lobbying and media activities at the CSCE preparatory talks. Meanwhile, the increasingly influential U.S. Helsinki Commission ensured that private groups would have an ally within the U.S. delegation.

Once the preparatory talks began in Madrid, Western, neutral, and nonaligned delegations were besieged by Helsinki activists and representatives of groups in the East, as well as re-

[4] Ibid., 125–26.
[5] Author interview with Pavel Bozyk (economic advisor to Polish Premier Edward Gierek), Warsaw, July 7, 1992.

ports on human rights conditions smuggled in from the Moscow, Warsaw, Prague, and elsewhere in the bloc.[6] An Associated Press correspondent reported an "army of dissenters, encamped in the hallways, doing battle on the diplomatic cocktail party circuit and firing salvos of press releases on the flanks of the Madrid security conference."[7] According to *Le Monde*, the Spanish capital had become a "city of dissidence."[8] In the eyes of the *Wall Street Journal*, which five years earlier had urged Gerald Ford not to sign the Helsinki Final Act, the CSCE had become "the least ambiguous human rights forum in international diplomacy."[9]

These facts notwithstanding, several other developments in the broader strategic and political context of East-West relations were not conducive to East bloc compliance with the human rights norms of the Helsinki process. The Soviet Union had continued to grow stronger militarily, while the United States recovered from its post-Vietnam shock and began to reassert itself internationally. Differences between Moscow's view of détente as a reflection of superpower parity, and thus a license for Soviet involvement around the world, and Washington's perceptions of it as an agreement that neither side would challenge the strategic status quo, were revealed in a series of East-West confrontations over civil wars in Angola, Mozambique, and Nicaragua; the Soviet military presence in Cuba; and the actual Soviet invasion of Afghanistan in 1979. The high stakes and ideological tensions of this "second cold war" were hardly conducive to East-bloc restraint on human rights at home, particularly in the face of domestic movements that every month posed a greater challenge to the hegemony of the Communist party-state.

As we see below, this does not mean that Helsinki norms ceased to matter for state or societal actors in the East, but it

---

[6] See Freedom House's *Freedom Appeals* 6 (September-October, 1980), "Special Madrid Issue."
[7] AP newswire item, November 21, 1980.
[8] *Le Monde* (Paris), November 12, 1980.
[9] *Wall Street Journal* (New York), October 14, 1980.

does mean that counterincentives in favor of repression were gaining strength. We start with Poland because, although it was somewhat anomalous during this period, rapid and unprecedented developments there set the political context in which other regimes made their decisions.

POLAND

The evolution of state-society relations in Poland from the late 1970s through the early 1980s seriously weakened the political and ideological foundations of Communist rule throughout Eastern Europe and even the Soviet Union. Popular discontent and unrest in Poland during this period cannot be explained without reference to the Gierek government's policy of financing the country's international debt by increasing the price of consumer goods. The story of Solidarity is far more complex, though, than workers reacting to a decline in their standard of living. By this point it was clear to all that the violent industrial strikes of 1970 and 1976 had produced no more than temporary gains. KOR and other activists recognized that a new strategy was needed to pressure the state while bringing together various social constituencies unsatisfied with the status quo.

Meanwhile, the transnational "Helsinki network" discussed in Chapter 4 was slowly succeeding in its campaign to raise the salience of human rights in East-West relations. Beyond the Belgrade conference, this included increasing pressure by the United States on the Gierek regime to fulfill its Helsinki commitments by giving greater latitude to independent groups. When President Jimmy Carter visited Warsaw in December 1977, he defended the new U.S. activism on human rights and specifically endorsed the Helsinki-monitoring movement: "détente must involve not only governments but must also be supported and encouraged by non-official individuals and groups," he said in written answers to questions provided by Wojciech Ziembinski, a cofounder of KOR and active member of ROP.[10]

---

[10] Robert Zuzowski, *Political Dissent and Opposition in Poland: The Workers' Defense Committee "KOR"* (Westport, Conn.: Praeger, 1992), 104. For the full

Both the Polish government and the opposition took note of Carter's position, and its potential connection to Poland's mounting dependence on Western loans and foodstuffs. The evidence does not, however, suggest any direct relationship between indebtedness and social mobilization: Poland's international debt, measured on a per capita basis, was significantly less than that of Hungary or East Germany, where mobilization was relatively low.[11]

Beginning in 1978, the same KOR and ROPCiO activists who had built alliances with the Church under the banner of human rights in 1975–1976 introduced the concept of human rights into their dialogue with workers. Having experienced the brutal response of the state to illegal protests, these workers were greatly encouraged when they learned that international pacts recently recognized and signed by the government actually guaranteed basic human rights, including the right to free association and specifically the right to form independent trade unions.[12] As Lech Walesa himself remembers, "One of the central freedoms at stake was freedom of expression (a direct corollary of the Helsinki Agreement). Without this basic freedom, human life becomes meaningless; and once the truth of this hit me, it became part of my whole way of thinking. . . . We began to recognize an international dimension to our problems and learned of the existence of human rights groups abroad to whom we could appeal."[13] Walesa's further statement that it was groups of intellectuals such as KOR and ROPCiO who "gave rise to the idea of an independent trade union . . . to defend the rights of workers" reflects

---

text of Ziembinski's letter and Carter's reply, see Peter Raina, *Political Opposition in Poland 1954–1977* (London: Poets' and Painters' Press, 1978), 542–44.

[11] Zuzowski, *Political Dissent and Opposition in Poland*, 83.

[12] Author interviews with Henryk and Luwika Wujec, Warsaw, June 17 and 18, 1991.

[13] Lech Walesa, *A Way of Hope* (New York: Henry Holt and Company, 1987), 97.

the central role played by the human rights movement in the birth of Solidarity.[14]

In fact, the first independent trade union cell was established in Radom in November 1977 by a dismissed worker with close ties to KOR. Five months later, Walesa and other KOR-affiliated workers from Gdansk formed the Committee for Free Trade Unions of the Baltic Seacoast. Before long, they launched their own edition of the KOR newspaper, *Robotnik Wybrzeza* (The Coastal Worker). Other independent industrial and farmers' organizations created the same year included the Katowice Committee for Free Trade Unions (February 1978); the Lublin Region Farmers' Self-Defense Committee (July 1978); the Grojec Region Farmers' Self-Defense Committee (September 1978); Pomorze Region Committee for Free Trade Unions (October 1978); and the Rzeszow Region Farmers' Self-Defense Committee (November 1978).

The election of Cardinal Karol Wojtyla as Pope John Paul II in October 1978 and his repeated references to human rights during his visit to Poland the following year accelerated the awakening of Polish society. As the new pope celebrated mass in Victory Square in Warsaw on June 2, 1979, some among the 250,000 onlookers unfurled a banner reading "freedom, independence, protection of human rights."[15] Such slogans were never officially endorsed by the Church, but they accurately reflected its deepening dialogue and expanded cooperation with the human rights movement. Four months later, the Roman Catholic Church primate of Poland, Cardinal Stefan Wyszynski, received a KOR delegation and assured them of his support.[16]

Meanwhile, independent groups across the ideological spectrum began to discard the earlier, self-imposed taboo against explicitly linking human rights protection to political change. In May 1979, the independent National Committee of Polish Socialists declared that the "most concrete and urgent task" in

[14] Ibid.
[15] "The Cold War," episode 19, CNN broadcast, February 29, 1999.
[16] Zuzowski, *Political Dissent and Opposition in Poland*, 134.

any campaign for political change in Poland was "the struggle to carry into effect the political and economic rights of the citizen, guaranteed by the Polish People's Republic, in the Final Act of the Helsinki Conference and the International Conventions on Human Rights."[17] Leszek Moczulski, once a member of the conspiratorial group "Convent," established the Confederation for an Independent Poland (KPN) on September 1, 1979, to pursue a nationalist agenda not beholden to the gradual civil-society strategy predominant in the Polish opposition.[18] According to Moczulski, the maximalist scenario advocated by KPN—Soviet withdrawal and overthrow of the Polish United Workers' Party—was feasible only because of the constraints imposed on the authorities in Warsaw and Moscow by Helsinki norms and the détente process.[19]

The Polish economy continued to deteriorate during this period. The government had turned to the West in the early 1970s for investment and loans to reverse the technological obsolescence of Polish industry. The government's failure to simultaneously decentralize the economy deterred most foreign investors, however, while public pressure for improvements in the quality of life caused the government to divert most of its hard currency loans from capital improvements to present consumption. The result, not surprisingly, was a steady decline in industrial productivity and increase in foreign debt through the late 1970s. The Polish government was thus trapped between an inefficient economy, an increasingly well-organized and demanding society, and growing pressure from the West for the protection of human rights.

In September 1979, *Robotnik Wybrzeza* published a Charter of Workers' Rights, signed by sixty-five workers, technicians, engineers, and intellectuals from the KOR and ROPCiO-affiliated free trade union cells; they demanded better wages,

---

[17] *Labour Focus on Eastern Europe*, 3:5 (November 1979-January 1980):9–11.

[18] Radio Free Europe/Radio Liberty, "Polish Situation Report," 20 (13 September 1979):1–4.

[19] Leszek Moczulski,"O Co Chodzi Z Tym Belgradem," *Opinia* (Warsaw), no. 2 (1977):32–36 (translated for the author by Eva Busza); repeated in interview with author, Warsaw, June 24, 1991.

shorter working hours, improved safety precautions, promotions by merit, abolition of special privileges, and above all, independent trade unions: "Only independent trades unions, which have the backing of the workers whom they represent, have a chance of challenging the authorities; only they can represent a power the authorities will have to take into account and with whom they will have deal on equal terms."[20] The charter buttressed these claims with relevant clauses from the Convention of the International Labour Organization and the International Covenant on Economic, Social, and Cultural Rights.

By late 1979, then, Polish society was far more assertive and the opposition far more organized than it had been only a few years earlier. By framing its challenge to the status quo in terms of internationally recognized human rights, the opposition had restrained the repressive capacities of the regime. Moreover, the workers' growing insistence on the creation of independent, self-governing unions represented a significant advance on their 1970 platforms, which in most cases had only demanded elections within the official trade unions. The regime's post-Helsinki strategy of consolidation through tactical concessions had reached its limits, yet organized opposition continued to mount.

Workers and intellectuals from these same KOR and ROPCiO circles, free trade unions, and self-defense committees were among the leaders of the strikes that erupted in Gdansk and Szczecin in August 1980 and then spread nationwide. KOR members were particularly influential at this stage in convincing the striking workers to remain within the factory and shipyard walls, rather than spilling out into the streets, where police provocateurs could more easily infiltrate the demonstrations, spark violence, and thus justify a crackdown by the authorities.[21] Fearful of the costs of reversing their earlier concessions, both domestically and internationally, the regime agreed to recognize the independent trade union Solidarity.

[20] Timothy Garton Ash, *The Polish Revolution: Solidarity* (New York: Vintage Books, 1983), 24.
[21] Zuzowski, *Political Dissent and Opposition in Poland*, 222.

Before long, ten million industrial, agricultural, and professional workers (nearly a third of Poland's population) had joined Solidarity, making it the East bloc's first significant mass organization outside the Communist party structure. In the process, Solidarity assumed a leading role in Polish society, including dialogue with the regime on the country's economic and social problems. As Solidarity established itself, the Communist Party lost ground: between 1980 and 1982, membership in the party declined by a third, with even deeper losses among students and the technical intelligentsia.[22] This was far more than a tactical concession by the regime: the unprecedented freedom of expression and independent social organization evident in Poland by late 1980 suggest that human rights norms were finally being incorporated into the institutions that actually determine relations between state and society.

Looking back on this period, Lech Walesa concluded that the emergence of the human rights movement after Helsinki had been a "turning point on the road to Gdansk," the symbolic birthplace of Solidarity.[23] This is not to say that the Helsinki-focused human rights movement was alone responsible for the emergence of Solidarity, but the Helsinki process and the human rights activists who focused on it clearly contributed substantially to the creation and strategy of the national alliance of workers, intellectuals, and the Church that became Solidarity.[24] As Timothy Garton Ash points out, "It is naturally difficult to separate the workers' own autonomous political learning process from the direct influence of KOR [and the other human rights activists]. But certainly these tiny free trade union cells, *Robotnik*'s translation of KOR's general strategy into specific tactics (how to organise an occupation-strike, what to demand) and the nationwide opposition network played a major role in helping discontented workers to generalise their grievances,

---

[22] Ibid., 225–26.

[23] Walesa, *A Way of Hope*, 97.

[24] For a more detailed study of Solidarity as a national coalition, see Jan Kubik, *The Power of Symbols against the Symbols of Power: The Rise of Solidarity and the Fall of State Socialism in Poland* (University Park: Pennsylvania State University Press, 1994).

formulate remedies, and co-ordinate their activities."[25] As if to confirm this connection, one of the ten demands of the Szczecin strikers in August 1980 was that the government publish and distribute fifty thousand copies of the international human rights covenants and the Helsinki Final Act.[26]

In November 1980, three months after the creation of Solidarity, the KOR-affiliated Polish Helsinki Commission (PKH) sent a report on human rights violations in Poland since 1976 to the CSCE review meeting in Madrid.[27] When KOR announced its dissolution at the first Solidarity congress, the PKH then became part of the burgeoning Solidarity network, investigating human rights abuses through Solidarity's Intervention Offices operating in several major cities. The importance of the Helsinki process for the Polish opposition nonetheless diminished considerably with the birth of Solidarity as a nationwide organization with ten million members, internally generated resources, and multiple sources of political leverage.

Both ideologically and politically, the Polish government's decision to legalize Solidarity, and thus concede that it itself did not represent the interests of workers or the society as a whole, was a major defeat for Communist rule. In fact, it sent shock waves throughout the Communist bloc, delegitimizing the political monopoly of the Communist Party, legitimizing independent grassroots initiatives, and causing many elites throughout Eastern Europe and the Soviet Union to question whether the political and economic status quo could be sustained. According to top-secret reports approved by the Secretariat of the Soviet Communist Party, "undesirable materials" were streaming into the Soviet Union from Poland, "work stoppages and other negative incidents" were increasing in frequency and size

[25] Ash, *The Polish Revolution*, 24–25.

[26] David S. Mason, *Public Opinion and Political Change in Poland, 1980–1982* (Cambridge: Cambridge University Press, 1985), 99.

[27] Polish Helsinki Watch Committee, *Prologue to Gdansk: A Report on Human Rights* (New York: U.S. Helsinki Watch Committee, 1980). For more on the Polish Helsinki Commission (PKH) and its successor, the Helsinki Committee in Poland (KHP), see Radio Free Europe Research, *Polish Situation Report* 6 (April 4, 1985), and *Polish Situation Report* 13 (August 16, 1985).

at factories across the Soviet Union, and public protests in support of Solidarity were evident in the Baltic states and Ukraine.[28] In the short term, though, conservative elites still had a firm grip on power, and international norms could not prevent them from taking whatever action they deemed necessary to maintain control.

As the Polish economy continued to deteriorate through 1981, Solidarity pressed the regime to institute fundamental economic reforms. Meanwhile, Warsaw's Soviet and East European allies demanded that the union be eliminated, and the Soviet General Staff prepared detailed plans for a full-scale invasion involving Soviet, Czechoslovak, and East German forces.[29] Within Poland, the first signs of a hard-line response to these pressures came in October, when Minister of Defense General Wojciech Jaruzelski was appointed both prime minister and secretary general of the party. Finally, on December 12, 1981, Jaruzelski declared martial law, outlawed Solidarity, arrested most of its leaders, and drove the rest underground.

Notwithstanding the seriousness of martial law, the Helsinki connection does appear to have contributed to Soviet restraint throughout the Solidarity period. From its very opening in September 1980, one of the most pressing issues at the CSCE meeting in Madrid was how the Soviet Union and its allies would react to the rise of Solidarity in Poland. As Warsaw Pact troops massed on the Polish border during maneuvers in December 1980, Western delegations at Madrid indicated that an invasion would constitute an unacceptable breach of the Helsinki Final Act.[30] In May 1981, as the CSCE considered proposals for a new disarmament forum much desired by Moscow, the North Atlantic Council resolved: "In Europe, efforts to restore East-West co-operation and exchanges on the basis of the Hel-

[28] Mark Kramer, "Soviet Policy during the Polish Crisis," Cold War International History Project, Woodrow Wilson International Center for Scholars, undated, accessed 11/30/98 at http://www.cwihp.si.edu.

[29] Ibid.

[30] U.S. Commission on Security and Cooperation in Europe, "The Madrid CSCE Review Meeting: An Interim Report," unpublished paper, January 6, 1981, 13.

sinki Final Act cannot but be severely undermined by the use or threat of force for intervention in the affairs of other countries. Poland must be left free to resolve its own problems."[31] That same month, the foreign ministers of the European Community, meeting in the Netherlands, instructed their delegations at Madrid to prolong negotiations in the belief that the delay would help deter a Soviet invasion.[32] When Soviet forces again maneuvered near the Polish border in September 1981, U.S. ambassador to the CSCE Max Kampelman threatened in Madrid that the West would not tolerate an invasion.[33]

Notwithstanding its earlier conclusion that the West was unwilling to impose serious sanctions to protect individual dissidents, the Kremlin concluded from these signals that a Soviet invasion of Poland to eliminate Solidarity would spark unacceptably costly economic sanctions. In November 1980, Brezhnev rejected an appeal from East German leader Erich Honecker for a Warsaw Pact invasion of Poland, expressing fear that such action would upset moves toward better relations with the West.[34] One year later, despite the mounting crisis in Poland, and renewed calls for an invasion, KGB chief Yuri Andropov told the Soviet Politburo: "We don't intend to introduce troops into Poland. That is the proper position, and we must adhere to it until the end. . . . [E]ven if Poland falls under the control of Solidarity, that's the way it will be. And if the capitalist countries pounce upon the Soviet Union, and you know they have already reached agreement on a variety of economic and political sanctions, that will be very burdensome for us. We must be concerned above all with our own country and about the strengthening of the Soviet Union."[35]

---

[31] North Atlantic Council, *Texts of Final Communiqués*, Vol. 3, 26.

[32] U.S. Commission on Security and Cooperation in Europe, "The Madrid CSCE Review Meeting: Phase II Interim Report," unpublished paper, August 1981, 2.

[33] U.S. Commission on Security and Cooperation in Europe, *CSCE Digest*, November 6, 1981, 2.

[34] *New York Times*, January 12, 1993.

[35] Translation of the official transcript of the December 10, 1981, meeting of the CPSU Politburo, from "Declassified Soviet Documents on the Polish

The imposition of martial law was a severe blow to Solidarity and to Polish society, but far less disastrous at the time and over the following years than a Soviet invasion would have been. Seeking to limit the new repressiveness, underground activists in Poland turned again to Helsinki norms: in early 1982, they announced the creation of a Polish Helsinki Committee to monitor human rights abuses during martial law. After a five-month campaign of arrests and purges intended to destroy Solidarity as a viable opposition, Jaruzelski made a series of tactical concessions, both real and symbolic, designed to rebuild domestic support while regaining the confidence of the West. Rather than retreat, though, the Helsinki movement took advantage of this opportunity to escalate its pressure on the government.

As soon as the regime lifted the initial crackdown, a renamed Helsinki Committee in Poland emerged publically to investigate reports of human rights abuses and convey such information to international organizations, including the CSCE, the United Nations, and the International Labour Organization. In a preface to one of these reports, issued in 1983, Solidarity's underground Temporary Coordinating Committee declared, "We consider it our civic duty to monitor our country's compliance with the Helsinki agreements and international covenants on human rights."[36] Given Jaruzelski's desire to rebuild contacts with the West ruptured by martial law, one can surmise that such monitoring helped restrain the more reactionary elements within the regime.[37]

Crisis," translated and annotated by Mark Kramer, Cold War International History Project, Woodrow Wilson International Center for Scholars, undated, accessed 11/30/98 at http://www.cwihp.si.edu.

[36] Polish Helsinki Watch Committee, *Poland under Martial Law: A Report on Human Rights*, English edition by the U.S. Helsinki Watch Committee (New York: Helsinki Watch, 1983), ix.

[37] The 1984 disappearance and murder of activist priest Father Jerzy Popieluszko, apparently by a rogue faction of the secret police, is notable politically both for its uniqueness and for the resulting trial and conviction of four police officers. See Gale Stokes, *The Walls Came Tumbling Down: The Collapse of Communism in Eastern Europe* (New York: Oxford University Press, 1993), 112–15.

THE SOVIET UNION

As discussed in Chapter 5, the creation of the Moscow Helsinki Group in 1976 was one of the forces that led Polish activists to launch their own Helsinki movement several months later. Two years later, the Kremlin looked at the blossoming Polish opposition and began to question how long they could tolerate the human rights movement then taking root in the Soviet Union. As soon as the Belgrade meeting was over, the Kremlin escalated its assault on the budding opposition in the Soviet Union. Beginning in the spring of 1978, key members and affiliates of the Helsinki movement in Moscow, Ukraine, Lithuania, and Georgia were sentenced to prison and/or internal exile. Yuri Orlov was sentenced to seven years' imprisonment, and Anatoly Shcharansky received a thirteen-year sentence.

Despite the escalating repression, though, the Helsinki movement sustained its challenge to the Soviet party-state for several more years. Not only did the Moscow Helsinki Group remain active after Belgrade, but new human rights organizations emerged in its shadow. Most of these groups referred explicitly to Helsinki in their work, and cooperated with the Helsinki monitors, reporting on violations in their areas of expertise and educating Soviet citizens about the Final Act. For example, the creation of the Initiative Group for the Defense of the Rights of Invalids was announced at a press conference of the Moscow Helsinki Group on October 25, 1978.[38] More important, the high-profile Jewish refusnik movement, which had always resisted affiliation with political dissidents, began to cooperate with the Helsinki movement during this period, as did constituencies well beyond the familiar urban intellectual circles.

As living and working conditions deteriorated in the late 1970s, Soviet workers began to voice their dissatisfaction and

[38] Ludmilla Alexeyeva, *Soviet Dissent: Contemporary Movements for National, Religious and Human Rights* (Middletown, Conn.: Wesleyan University Press, 1987), 411.

form links with human rights activists. Two aspiring independent unions, the Free Trade Union, established in February 1978, and the Free Interprofessional Association of Working People (SMOT), established eight months later, worked closely with the Helsinki movement, referred to international human rights norms in their founding declarations, and called on the Soviet government to observe its Helsinki obligations.[39] The Moscow Helsinki group also made several declarations on behalf of SMOT, including one which affirmed that "the aims and tasks of this Association derive from the Universal Declaration of Human Rights and from those pacts to which the Helsinki Final Act refers."[40] In addition to their efforts to organize and educate Soviet workers, members of these union cells supplied the Moscow Helsinki group with information about labor conditions and workers' rights throughout the Soviet Union.

Activists Pyotr Abovin-Egides and Pinkhos Podrabinek acknowledged this convergence around Helsinki norms when they called in late 1979 for the Moscow group to take the lead in forming a new, more explicitly political opposition front: "[i]t is the Helsinki Group which has turned out to be the centre for the defence of human rights in the last ten years. . . . Precisely because of the internal and external conditions of the democratic movement, and of the activity of the Moscow-based group itself, this group has become the nucleus around which both the Helsinki groups from various republics and a few working commissions have been gathering."[41] Not surprisingly, Soviet authorities were threatened by the fact that suddenly, as one observer put it, "nationalists in different republics, religious believers, Zionists, and Moscow dissidents

---

[39] Stokes, *The Walls Came Tumbling Down*, 144–46; Alexeyeva, *Soviet Dissent*, 401–13.

[40] U.S. Commission on Security and Cooperation in Europe,, *Documents of the Helsinki Monitoring Groups in the U.S.S.R and Lithuania* (1976–1986), Vol. 1 (Washington, D.C.: Government Printing Office, 1986), 161–62.

[41] Pyotr Abovin-Egides and Pinkhos Podrabinek, "The Democratic Movement in Perspective," Part One, *Labour Focus on Eastern Europe* 3:5 (November 1979-January 1980):18.

could use a common vocabulary and recognize their common antagonist."[42]

Unfortunately for the dissidents, this mounting challenge to the Soviet party-state coincided with two other Helsinki-related developments: increasing tensions in East-West relations and the emergence of Solidarity in Poland. The Helsinki compliance incentives created by the approaching CSCE conference in Madrid were bit by bit overwhelmed by Solidarity's proof of the fragility of Communist hegemony, including its spillover effects throughout the bloc, and by the conclusion that a hard line on dissent could not make East-West relations any worse than they already were after the Afghanistan invasion. With each passing month, Politburo conservatives chipped away at Brezhnev's argument that Soviet interests required the maintenance of détente, and thus at least the appearance of compliance with Helsinki norms.

Between the opening of the Madrid conference in September 1980 and its close three years later, more than five hundred Soviet citizens were arrested for activities on behalf of Helsinki-related goals.[43] In 1981, the first deputy chairman of the KGB declared victory over the Helsinki movement: "As a result of measures taken by the KGB, implemented in strict accordance with the law and under the leadership of Party organs, the anti-social elements, despite the West's considerable material and moral support, did not succeed in achieving organized cohesion on the platform of anti-Sovietism."[44] Although most of its original members were in either prison or exile by 1981, the Moscow Helsinki Group continued to report on human rights abuses until September 8, 1982, when Elena Bonner announced the dissolution of the group. Affiliated groups in Ukraine, Georgia, Lithuania, and Armenia survived, but in this environment they

---

[42] Joshua Rubenstein, *Soviet Dissidents: Their Struggle for Human Rights* (Boston: Beacon, 1980), 228.

[43] U.S. Commission on Security and Cooperation in Europe, *The Madrid CSCE Review Meeting* (Washington, D.C.: Government Printing Office, November 1983), 3.

[44] *A Chronicle of Human Rights in the USSR* 44 (October–December 1981):30–34.

could do little more than smuggle information to sympathizers in the West. In the Soviet case, then, the pull of Helsinki norms during this period could not compete with the reactionary instincts of a conservative regime that felt besieged at home and abroad.

CZECHOSLOVAKIA

Relations between state and opposition in Czechoslovakia between the late 1970s and early 1980s fell somewhere between the Polish and Soviet extremes. As previewed in Chapter 5, preparations for the Belgrade CSCE review conference did create some political space for dissent that enabled the Charter 77 movement to blossom through the spring and summer of 1977. Nonetheless, several leading Chartists arrested earlier in the year were put on trial in October, provoking a huge outcry from the West, both in the halls of the Belgrade conference and through other diplomatic and transnational channels. By the time the conference ended in February 1978, the regime had settled on a new strategy of selective repression designed to undermine the domestic opposition while minimizing the damage to Czechoslovakia's relations with the West. Instead of imprisoning Charter 77's leaders, the regime would isolate the movement from the broader society by arresting, harassing, and often brutalizing its lesser-known supporters and all those who tried to join. In other words, the informal pluralism that began to take hold in Poland in early 1978 would not be permitted in Czechoslovakia.

Charter 77 continued its dual strategy of criticizing the government's human rights practices while appealing for dialogue, but a number of leading members concluded that the government's policy of selective repression required a new approach. In April 1978, they created an additional organization—the Committee for the Defense of the Unjustly Prosecuted (VONS)—to supplement the work of the Charter. VONS would respond directly to arbitrary exercises of state power by monitoring and publicizing all arrests and imprisonments that violated Czechoslovakia's legal code and constitution, as well as the International Covenant on Civil and Political Rights, which had been legally binding since March 1976.[45] Although VONS communiqués referred only to the state's legal obligations, rather than to non-binding Helsinki norms, its members hoped that Charter 77's connections to the Helsinki process would offer them some protection from repression.[46]

For about a year, the well-known members of VONS seemed to benefit from the same selectivity in repression that protected Charter 77. Nonetheless, the Czechoslovak regime (and perhaps its allies in the Kremlin) eventually concluded that more drastic action was necessary to combat the still-growing opposition, especially VONS's direct challenge to the legal and political system. In May 1979, the authorities arrested five leading members of VONS; four months later, they were tried and sentenced to prison.[47] It is nonetheless significant that the five activists were charged for their involvement in VONS, not Charter 77, to which they still belonged. VONS was less identified with the Helsinki process than Charter 77, and as an unregistered formal organization, it was in clear violation of the law, unlike Charter 77, whose informal structure kept it technically within the law. In other words, even during its renewed assault on the opposition, the regime remained selective in its exercise of repression—Helsinki compliance still mattered.

The two groups also provided regular documentation of human rights violations in Czechoslovakia to interested parties in the West, including private Helsinki watch groups, the U.S. Helsinki Commission, and the second major CSCE review conference, held in Madrid from 1980–1983. For example, less than a year after being imprisoned, Charter 77 members Vaclav Benda, Jiri Dienstbier, and Vaclav Havel smuggled a letter to the delegates at the CSCE meeting in Madrid: "Our participa-

[45] See H. Gordon Skilling, *Charter 77 and Human Rights Czechoslovakia* (London: Allen & Unwin, 1981), 145–48; Vaclav Havel, *Open Letters: Selected Writings, 1965–1990* (New York: Knopf, 1991), 109–16.

[46] Author interviews with Jiri Dienstbier, New Haven, Conn., April 14, 1991, and Vaclav Maly, Prague, August 5, 1992.

[47] Skilling *Charter 77*, 145–49, 321.

tion in the movement Charter 77 . . . was and is entirely in harmony with the Final Act of the Helsinki Conference, and, as is evident from the text of Charter 77, the creation of this movement concerning human rights was actually motivated by the Final Act."[48]

When word spread in 1983 that the Final Document of the Madrid CSCE meeting had affirmed the rights of independent monitoring groups, Charter 77 sent another letter to President Husak calling on him to reconsider Charter 77's proposals, and to release imprisoned activists.[49] When Secretary General Javier Perez de Cuellar of the United Nations announced that he would visit Czechoslovakia in February 1984, the Charter expressed its desire for a meeting with him, referring again to its source of legitimacy: "These activities of Charter 77 . . . enjoy international recognition as expressed particularly in the Final Act of the Conference on Security and Cooperation in Europe, signed in Helsinki, and in the interpretation given to this document by participants in the Madrid session of this Conference."[50] Neither Husak nor Perez de Cuellar responded to these and similar appeals, but the continued Helsinki connection does appear to have prevented the regime from entirely eliminating the Charter and its budding affiliates, as it had done to independent initiatives in the early 1970s. Arrests were limited, and those who were sent to prison were generally released before the end of their terms.

The regime's apparent concern for good relations with the West allowed Charter 77 and VONS to survive—as marginalized though persistent moral and legal critics of the regime—

---

[48] "Text of the Letter Sent to the Delegates of the Madrid Conference," in U.S. Commission on Security and Cooperation in Europe, *Human Rights in Czechoslovakia: The Documents of Charter 77, 1977–1982* (Washington, D.C.: Government Printing Office, 1982), 14–15.

[49] Charter 77 letter to Dr. Gustav Husak, president of the CSSR, November 14, 1983, in U.S. Commission on Security and Cooperation in Europe, *Human Rights in Czechoslovakia: The Documents of Charter 77, 1982–1987* (Washington, D.C.: Government Printing Office, 1988), 58.

[50] Charter 77 letter to the UN Secretary General, February 21, 1984, ibid., 88.

both at home and abroad. Whenever a spokesperson was jailed, someone else took his or her place. Their communiqués were distributed clandestinely among those willing to risk being caught with dissident materials, and were regularly broadcast back into Czechoslovakia by Radio Free Europe, giving millions access to frank criticisms of their government. Few dared act on this information, but given the state's total monopoly of other media, it did provide people with some critical perspective on the status quo.

The relationship between state and opposition in Czechoslovakia was thus fairly stable through the early to mid 1980s. In the absence of popular legitimacy, the regime's hold on power rested on three pillars: support from Moscow, an economy capable of providing consumer goods, and repression of all challenges to the Communist party-state. As the economy weakened, the Prague leadership did become more sensitive to relations with the West, which by this period could not be separated from the human rights issue.[51] Nonetheless, the Polish regime's recent experience with Solidarity had convinced Prague of the danger of political liberalization. Meanwhile, knowing that it lacked the broad social network that Polish human rights groups were able to create, Charter 77 continued to rely on international normative pressure in its campaign to highlight and criticize human rights violations by the regime.

The regime in Prague was thus selective in its political repression, granting greater leniency to activists known in the West while intimidating the broader society by targeting lesser-known individuals. Charter 77's continued identification with international norms and monitoring activities may not have enabled it to mount a direct challenge to the regime in the early 1980s, but it did shield the movement from total elimination. As shown in the following chapter, the survival of Charter 77 proved very significant when reformist winds began to blow from Moscow later in the decade.

---

[51] See David Binder, "Czechoslovakia, the East's New Economic Disaster," *New York Times*, November 8, 1981; and Vladimir V. Kusin, "Husak's Czecho-

HUNGARY

In October 1979, the stiff sentence passed by a Prague court against five members of VONS and Charter 77 provoked another protest from the still amorphous Hungarian opposition. Within a week, 243 Hungarian writers, artists, and former politicians signed one of three open letters to Hungarian president Pal Losonczi and Communist Party secretary Janos Kadar describing the imprisonment of the Czech activists as a violation of the Helsinki Accords and urging them to pressure Prague for their release. In addition, three leading oppositionists issued an open letter to Charter 77, saying "We cannot remain indifferent to the persecution of those who struggle for human rights in any East European country."[52]

The following month, a group of young sociologists inspired by the success of Poland's KOR movement decided to organize more formally. The Foundation to Assist the Poor (SZETA) that they established was the first voluntary and autonomous organization in Hungary for almost a quarter century. At about the same time, a circle of critical intellectuals began to coalesce around the samizdat journal *Beszelo*, which was publishing uncensored analyses of social, economic, and political problems in Hungary. Yet unlike their role models in KOR and Charter 77, Hungary's budding "Democratic Opposition" was slow to challenge or engage the state directly.

CONCLUSION

Just as the first few years after Helsinki had demonstrated the unforeseen power of international norms, the wave of repres-

---

slovakia and Economic Stagnation," *Problems of Communism* 31 (May–June 1982):24–37.

[52] "Hungarians Reportedly Protest Prague Trial," CND/AFP newswire item, Paris, October 30, 1979; "Open Letter of Three Hungarian Intellectuals," AFP newswire item, Paris, October 31, 1979; "Hungarians Protest over Jailings in Prague," *Times* (London), December 11, 1979.

sion after 1978, including the declaration of martial law in Poland in December 1981, demonstrated the limitations of norms as catalysts for political change. This reversal reminds us that although norms can expand political opportunities for certain actors, they can also be overwhelmed by competing political interests. Yet as this chapter makes clear, the years between the CSCE conferences in Belgrade and Madrid were actually characterized by two contradictory trends: the dissidents' continued mobilization around Helsinki human rights norms, and the Communist authorities' increased willingness to violate Helsinki norms in defense of their hold on power. The first observation is explained by two facts: first, many of the activists who focused on Helsinki norms truly believed in human rights as the basis for political life, so their identification with the norms was not subject to instrumental calculations; second, international norms were one of the few instruments available to societal forces in confrontation with far more powerful states, so evidence of their limited effectiveness was less important than the lack of alternatives.

A possible explanation for the Communist regimes' increasing willingness to repress dissent is that they determined that Western countries were unwilling to reinforce their rhetorical commitment to Helsinki norms with serious sanctions when those norms were violated. An important test of the Western commitment came when Soviet authorities imprisoned leading members of the Helsinki Watch movement in Moscow and the republics in July 1978, soon after the stalemated CSCE review conference in Belgrade. President Carter initially responded by canceling the sale of an advanced computer to the Soviet news agency Tass and by requiring validated licenses for all exports of oil technology to the Soviet Union.[53] The West Europeans failed to implement comparable sanctions, however, and the U.S. failed actually to deny any licenses for oil technology exports. By April 1979, the U.S. had shifted the justification for the sanction from human rights to national security, and then

---

[53] Lisa L. Martin, *Coercive Cooperation: Explaining Multilateral Economic Sanctions* (Princeton: Princeton University Press, 1992), 198–201.

dropped it altogether. The Soviet leadership might thus have reasoned that if the imprisonment of famous dissidents like Orlov, Ginzburg, and Shcharansky elicited such a weak response, a wider crackdown was unlikely to bring more drastic consequences.

The Soviet leadership's weak identification with Europe and the wider international community during this period suggests, however, that even strong sanctions would not have significantly moderated the behavior of the party-state. The Kremlin and most of its allies in Eastern Europe remained devoted to the Marxist-Leninist strategy for political development, and focused on consolidating or expanding the "socialist community." This nonidentification with a wider international society dominated by liberal values was evident, for example, in disputes regarding the détente system within which Helsinki's human rights norms were nested. For the West, détente was a policy to be pursued or rejected according to Soviet compliance with international norms. In contrast, the Soviets viewed détente as Western accommodation to long-term changes in the international "correlation of forces" benefiting the socialist bloc: now that the Soviet Union had achieved military parity, they considered it natural that the United States should cease to challenge core Soviet interests. As a result, the West grew frustrated by Moscow's continued support for revolution abroad and practice of repression at home, while the Soviets grew frustrated by Western reluctance to treat them as political equals, or to refrain from "interfering" in domestic affairs.[54]

As discussed above, the independent human rights groups that emerged across the bloc after Helsinki had evolved from isolated dissident cells to increasingly well organized movements with broad national and international connections. For example, the Moscow Helsinki Watch Group "provoked the

---

[54] Coit D. Blacker, "The Kremlin and Détente: Soviet Conceptions, Hopes, and Expectations," in Alexander L. George, ed., *Managing U.S.-Soviet Rivalry* (Boulder, Colo.: Westview Press, 1983), 119–37; George W. Breslauer, "Why Détente Failed: An Interpretation," ibid., 319–40; Robert G. Kaiser, "U.S.-Soviet Relations: Goodbye to Détente," *Foreign Affairs* 59 (1980):500–21.

special anger of the authorities by successfully unifying the various hitherto disparate movements into a single campaign."[55] In such circumstances, sustained compliance with Helsinki norms would have seriously endangered the political hegemony of the Communist party-state. The Soviets and their allies may have valued legitimation by trans-European institutions enough to make serious concessions in the negotiation of CSCE norms, but they were not willing endanger the Communist party-state in order to be accepted by a group of states that they still considered fundamentally antagonistic to their values and purposes.

[55] Helen Jamieson, "No Let-Up in Drive against Helsinki Groups," *Labour Focus on Eastern Europe* 1:6 (January-February 1978):18.

CHAPTER SEVEN

Socialization: Human Rights and the Dismantling of Communist Rule

How can one be against human rights nowadays?
It's the same as to be against motherhood.
—*Georgi Arbotov, 1983*[1]

Europe is our common home.
—*Mikhail Gorbachev, in Paris, 1985*[2]

[T]he social impact of so-called independent activities
in totalitarian conditions is never entirely determined, nor
entirely measurable, in terms of the numbers of people
directly participating in these activities.
—*Vaclav Havel, 1988*[3]

CRACKDOWNS on dissent across Eastern Europe and the Soviet Union in the early 1980s seemed to suggest that the human rights norms of the Helsinki process had not affected the fundamental practices and institutions of Communist rule. When Mikhail Gorbachev took power in the Soviet Union in March 1985, Communist parties throughout the bloc retained a legal monopoly over political space, and most showed little evidence of having internalized human rights norms into their conception of legitimacy or self-interest. Within just five years, though, Communism had collapsed as a viable political ideology, and the states of the region were making real (albeit un-

---

[1] Georgi A. Arbatov and William Oltmans, *Cold War or Détente? The Soviet Viewpoint* (London: Zed Books, 1983), 144.

[2] Mikhail Gorbachev, *Memoirs* (New York: Doubleday, 1996), 428.

[3] Quoted in Vaclav Benda et al., "Parallel Polis, or An Independent Society in Central and Eastern Europe," *Social Research* 55 (Spring/Summer 1988): 235–36.

even) progress toward the protection and institutionalization of human rights. This outcome per se does not tell us whether "1989" was part of a "Helsinki effect" in any meaningful sense, or merely consistent with Helsinki norms but determined by other factors. On the surface, it seems to suggest that Mikhail Gorbachev succeeded where Helsinki had failed.

Yet as this chapter demonstrates, the Helsinki Final Act's establishment of human rights as a fundamental norm of East-West relations contributed in multiple and important ways to the relatively peaceful and largely democratic course of change in Eastern Europe and the Soviet Union that ended the Cold War. Both the top-down reforms and the bottom-up protests that led to the dismantling of Communist rule in 1989–1990 can be traced, at least in part, to two dynamics set in motion at Helsinki fifteen years earlier: the transformation of the diplomatic agenda for East-West relations and the mobilization of human rights movements across Eastern Europe and the Soviet Union. The expansion of civil society under the banner of human rights, the corrosive effects of dissent on the legitimacy and self-confidence of the party-state, and Western governments' insistence on linking diplomatic relations to implementation of human rights norms convinced a growing number of Communist elites of the necessity of political (rather than purely economic) reform. These reforms, combined with continued diplomatic linkage from Western states, expanded domestic opportunities for social mobilization and organized opposition that pushed political change well beyond the intentions or expectations of Gorbachev and his advisors, and ultimately overwhelmed the weakened party-state's hold on power in the Soviet Union and across Eastern Europe.

Although none of these effects can be reduced to the economic inefficiencies of central planning or the strategic pressures of geopolitics, the process of normative socialization highlighted in this chapter should not be misunderstood as a monocausal explanation for the demise of one-party Communist rule. Generational changes in the leadership of the Soviet party-state, declining economic productivity and technological competitiveness, an intellectual reorientation toward Europe, and the structural fragility of monopolistic one-party rule greatly facilitated the process of normative socialization. Without attention to the direct and indirect effects of Helsinki norms, though, none of these factors can explain the implementation and escalation of political reforms that fatally undermined the Communist party-state's grip on power throughout the bloc.

The chapter begins with a discussion of the sources of reformism within the party-state, showing how the policy preferences of the "Gorbachev generation" were shaped by the post-Helsinki transformation of state-society relations and by recognition that the Communist countries' relations with the West could not be normalized without fundamental improvements in their compliance with human rights norms. It then demonstrates how the Gorbachev cadre's attempts to satisfy international pressures while overcoming the conservative elite's resistance to reform unleashed an escalation of social mobilization that further weakened the party-state. Finally, it examines Communism's "end game" in Eastern Europe, showing the critical role played by international norms and by human rights activists in achieving a relatively peaceful transition to democratic and rights-protective rule.

MOTIVES FOR SOVIET REFORM

To understand the dynamics of Soviet reform, one must remember that when Mikhail Gorbachev and his advisors began taking steps to liberalize Soviet society and politics, the Soviet state still controlled a powerful army, a vast network of secret police, and the levers of economic policy. In other words, the weakening of the coercive powers of the Soviet state was not a cause but a result of the leadership's policy on democratization. It thus follows that any analysis of the demise of one-party Communist rule in Eastern Europe and the Soviet Union must account for the extraordinary initiatives of Mikhail Gorbachev, without whom the decade (and the century) would have ended quite differently.[4] Beyond personalities, though, Gorbachev and his supporters were motivated by four pressures for political change: economic decline, dissident critiques of repression, the lure of European rapprochement, and the international normative environment. As shown below, all but the first of these pressures were related, directly or indirectly, to the Helsinki Final Act.

Economic Modernization

Trends in the Soviet and global economy apparent by the mid-1980s were critical to the emergence of a reform coalition within the Soviet leadership. In contrast to the expansion of the 1950s and 1960s, the late 1970s and early 1980s were marked by a steady decline in economic productivity. With each passing year, the inability of Brezhnev-style Communism to deliver the consumer goods demanded by an increasingly urban population became more apparent to the party leadership.[5] The increasing globalization of production in the 1980s also exacerbated their concerns about the competitiveness of a highly centralized command economy.[6]

Economic pressures are not sufficient, however, to explain the consistent pursuit of social and political reforms that weakened the party-state, enabled revolutions in Eastern Europe, and contributed to the ultimate break-up of the Soviet Union. One need only reflect on China's Tiananmen Square massacre and its aftermath to doubt claims that any reform of a centrally planned economy must be accompanied by a parallel program of political liberalization. Large comparative studies have also

---

[4] See Archie Brown, *The Gorbachev Factor* (Oxford: Oxford University Press, 1996).

[5] See Moshe Lewin, *The Gorbachev Phenomenon*, expanded edition (Berkeley and Los Angeles: University of California Press, 1991).

[6] See Stephen G. Brooks and William C. Wohlforth, "Power, Globalization and the End of the Cold War: Reevaluating a Landmark Case for Ideas," *International Security* 25 (Winter 2000/01): 5–53.

confirmed that economic liberalization does not require or necessarily promote greater political freedom.[7]

These data are consistent with the fact that when Mikhail Gorbachev took power, relatively few members of the Communist elite questioned the social or political monopoly of the party-state upon which the entire system depended. In fact, when the members of the Central Committee elected Gorbachev as general secretary on March 11, 1985, they expected him to revitalize the Soviet system through a program of economic restructuring guided by a reformed party-state, not to oversee its dismantling. As the radical nature of Gorbachev's policies became evident, many of his initial supporters expressed concern about undermining the party-state's hold on power.[8] Why, then, did Gorbachev and his closest advisors reject the conservatives' version of reform, which would have liberalized the economy while maintaining a politically repressive party-state?

Gorbachev's social and political agenda is best explained as a consequence of the lessons that some members of the party elite learned from the human rights campaigns of the late 1970s and the early 1980s, and of their quest for rapprochement with Europe at a time when a state's "European identity" could not be divorced from its respect for human rights. Once implemented, this agenda created space for the mobilization of independent media and political movements that overwhelmed the Kremlin's reformist intentions.

The Dissidents' Message

Among the supporters of reform who elected Mikhail Gorbachev as general secretary, a relatively small group of party leaders and "institutniks" had been affected by the message and persistence of human rights campaigners across the bloc, and were thus inclined to restructure the Soviet Union's social and politi-

[7] See Adam Przeworski and Fernando Limongi, "Modernization: Theories and Facts," *World Politics* 49 (January 1997):155–83.

[8] Yegor Ligachev, *Inside Gorbachev's Kremlin*, translated by Catherine A. Fitzpatrick (New York: Pantheon, 1993), chapter 1.

cal order as well as its economy. This openness to dissident thinking resulted partly from the fact that Gorbachev's generation emerged politically during the tumultuous period between Khrushchev's denunciation of Stalin's crimes in 1956 and the crackdown on independent voices following the invasion of Czechoslovakia in 1968.[9] Although few members of the "thaw generation" rejected the party to become dissidents or human rights campaigners, even after 1968, official repression of independent initiatives did not shield party elites from the dissidents' message. Through seizures and informers, the secret police kept the party leadership abreast of samizdat publishing and aware of the ease with which such publications circulated through their societies. Most officials cared only about advancing within the party, but some were affected by the dissidents' message and/or by their own participation in the repression of dissent.

Mikhail Gorbachev's attentiveness to the dissidents was linked to his exposure to reformist thinking within Communist circles. While rising through the ranks of the Soviet Communist party in the 1960s, Gorbachev remained in close contact with his law school friend Zdenek Mlynar, who had joined reformist circles within the Czechoslovak Communist Party. During a visit to the Soviet Union in the summer of 1967, Mlynar stayed with the Gorbachevs in Stavropol and the two men discussed reformist ideas then circulating in Prague. When the Soviet invasion of Czechoslovakia the following year provoked protests at home, Gorbachev was troubled by the Kremlin's crackdown on dissent: "I had qualms of conscience about the cruel and undeserved punishment meted out" to critics of the regime, and began to question "the underlying causes of many grievous phenomena in our domestic and foreign policies."[10] Gorbachev's questioning of political repression throughout the bloc could only have been reinforced when he learned that Mlynar had signed Charter 77 and openly criticized the denial of human rights in Czechoslovakia.

[9] See Ludmilla Alexeyeva and Paul Goldberg, *The Thaw Generation: Coming of Age in the Post-Stalin Era* (Boston: Little, Brown, 1990).

[10] Gorbachev, *Memoirs*, 83.

As a member of the party's Central Committee in the early 1980s, Gorbachev sought out contacts with an informal circle of intellectuals whose thinking had also had been shaped by exposure to dissidents and the human rights movement. Among these was Aleksandr Yakovlev, who had been exposed to a great deal of independent and samizdat materials on human rights conditions in the Soviet Union during his long tenure as ambassador to Canada before Gorbachev brought him back to Moscow to direct the Institute on World Economy and International Relations.[11] In fact, dissident materials, including those of the Helsinki network, were read and discussed quite openly at several of the top research institutes in Moscow. As a result, says Georgi Arbatov, director of the Institute for Study of the United States and Canada, many "institutniks" began to see the Communist system through "dissident" eyes.[12] The same can be said for some members of the party's International Department, such as Anatoly Chernyaev, who recalls that dissident literature seized him "by the throat."[13]

Once Gorbachev was elected general secretary in 1985, he appointed many of these individuals to influential positions in government and the media. He also rehabilitated "half-dissidents" Len Karpinsky and Roy Medvedev, who had developed extensive contacts with independent activists after being expelled from the party for their unconventional thinking during the early Brezhnev era.[14] What was significant about all these

[11] For Yakovlev's evolving views on Communism, see Steven F. Cohen and Katrina Vanden Heuvel, *Voices of Glasnost: Interviews with Gorbachev's Reformers* (New York: W. W. Norton, 1989), 33–75, Alexander Yakovlev, *The Fate of Marxism in Russia*, translated by Catherine A. Fitzpatrick (New Haven: Yale University Press, 1993), and Yakovlev, *Striving for Law in a Lawless Land: Memoirs of a Russian Reformer* (Armonk, N.Y.: M.E. Sharpe, 1996).

[12] Georgi Arbatov, *The System: An Insider's Life in Soviet Politics* (New York: Times Books, 1992), 237.

[13] Robert D. English, "Introduction," in Anatoly S. Chernyaev, *My Six Years with Gorbachev*, translated and edited by Robert D. English and Elizabeth Tucker (University Park: Pennsylvania State University Press, 2000), xxi.

[14] Cohen and Heuvel, *Voices of Glasnost*, 294. See also Roy Medvedev and Giulietto Chiesa, *Time of Change: An Insider's View of Russia's Transformation* (New York: Pantheon Books, 1989).

moves was not Gorbachev's attempt to establish his own power base within the regime, but that he did so by empowering or rehabilitating individuals with such heterodox ideas.

For other state and party officials, the experience of direct participation in the repression of dissent caused them to rethink the status quo. For example, a KGB agent assigned to eavesdrop on Soviet human rights groups concluded privately that the dissidents were telling the truth: "The chaos and filth; the fact that we put people in jail who only want good for this country—it was all true!"[15] Before he was arrested himself, the agent warned activists Yuri Orlov, Alexander Podrabinek, and Anatoly Shcharansky of many forthcoming searches and arrests, including at least a dozen targeted just at Podrabinek and his family. Nonetheless, says Karpinsky, most of those who "wanted a more efficient and humane system . . . knew they had to wait until their time came, remain in the apparatus, develop their ideas, seek out like-minded people, and be ready when their hour struck."[16]

One of the most important of these was Eduard Shevardnadze, whose experiences as party boss and interior minister in his native republic of Georgia prompted him to question the Soviet Union's social and political order. "I knew many of the people in the dissident movement in Georgia quite well" and "spoke with them a number of times," he says. Though admittedly not yet prepared "either inwardly—psychologically—or politically" to protest the system's treatment of dissent, Shevardnadze recalls that his role in each of these encounters provoked a "difficult internal struggle."[17] Over time, such experiences transformed his outlook: "This struggle, along with my knowledge of the true state of affairs in our country, has led me to conclude that the root of existing evils is not the individual people, but in the system. And if some people seethe with ha-

---

[15] Quoted in Yevgenia Albats, *The State within a State: The KGB and Its Hold on Russia—Past, Present, and Future*, translated by Catherine A. Fitzpatrick (New York: Farrar, Straus, Giroux, 1994), 213–17.

[16] Cohen and Vanden Heuvel, *Voices of Glasnost*, 299.

[17] Eduard Shevardnadze, *The Future Belongs to Freedom*, translated by Catherine A. Fitzpatrick (New York: Free Press, 1991), 37.

tred for the system, that is only because the system is ruthless toward the individual," he concluded.[18]

For others, the simple fact of having remained within the Brezhnev regime despite its repression of dissent was a strong motivation to work for reform in the late 1980s. As Yuri Afanasyev explained: "Even those of us who did not personally persecute or harm anyone, and who sincerely wanted changes in the country, bear a heavy responsibility for having been silent. Unlike people like Andrei Sakharov, Alexandr Solzhenitsyn and Roy Medvedev, we did not openly or actively fight against what was happening in our country. Therefore, we—and I include myself—must repent for our responsibility."[19] So although many of Gorbachev's initial supporters just wanted economic reform, some were determined to act on what they had long been hearing from the dissidents—that "the country's economic malaise was intrinsically linked to a deeper moral, social and cultural crisis."[20] As Shevardnadze told Gorbachev in the winter of 1984, a full year before the latter's elevation to general secretary: "Everything's rotten. It has to be changed."[21] For the first time since the Bolshevik Revolution, a significant portion of the Soviet leadership thus viewed political repression as an ineffective *and* unacceptable form of rule.

Even those within the party leadership who were not sympathetic to the human rights critique of Communist rule could not deny the abundant evidence of popular sympathy for human rights movements across the Communist bloc. On May Day 1985, six weeks after Gorbachev's election but three and a half years after Poland's declaration of martial law, fifteen thousand pro-Solidarity demonstrators filled the streets of Warsaw.[22] In Czechoslovakia, the Interior Ministry had long ago estimated that some two million people might have signed the

[18] Ibid.

[19] Cohen and Vanden Heuvel, *Voices of Glasnost*, 100.

[20] John M. Battle, "Uskorenie, Glasnost and Perestroika: The Pattern of Reform under Gorbachev," *Soviet Studies* 40 (July 1988): 370.

[21] Shevardnadze, *The Future Belongs to Freedom*, 37.

[22] Peter Schweizer, *Victory* (New York: Atlantic Monthly Press, 1994), 225.

Charter 77 human rights manifesto, had they not been afraid.[23] Within the Soviet Union, the persistence of independent initiatives for human rights and national self-determination despite the KGB's massive efforts at repression were testament to the party's illegitimacy. Politburo members who were otherwise not inclined to support Gorbachev's initiatives thus understood the significance of his argument that political reforms were necessary because had they been initiated earlier in Poland, "there would have been no 1980."[24]

The Soviet Union as a "European" State

The Gorbachev cadre's thinking on Soviet relations with Europe was far less instrumental in nature than that of the Brezhnev generation that had launched the CSCE. As Gorbachev and his advisors considered alternatives to the centralization and repressiveness of the status quo, they saw in Europe not only the resources necessary to modernize the Soviet economy but also inspiration for the type of democratic socialism that they hoped to achieve within the Soviet Union. Above all, they saw a shared cultural heritage that had long been denied by conservative Russophiles and Communists alike.[25] As one of Gorbachev's closest advisors put it, "Europe for Gorbachev was

[23] Vladimir V. Kusin, "Challenge to Normalcy: Political Opposition in Czechoslovakia, 1968–77," in Rudolf L. Tökes, ed., *Opposition in Eastern Europe* (Baltimore: Johns Hopkins University Press, 1979), 52.

[24] Anatoly Chernyaev's notes from the Politburo session, July 11, 1986; in Vladislav Zubok et al., eds., "Understanding the End of the Cold War: Reagan/ Gorbachev Years," a compendium of declassified documents and chronology of events, prepared for an oral history conference, May 7–10, 1998, Brown University, by the National Security Archive, Washington, D.C. and the Cold War International History Project, Washington, D.C., pages unnumbered. (Hereafter cited as Zubok, "A Compendium of Declassified Documents.") See also Gorbachev, *Memoirs*, 478.

[25] See Robert D. English, *Russia and the Idea of the West: Gorbachev, Intellectuals, and the End of the Cold War* (New York: Columbia University Press, 2000).

something that had a meaning of its own."²⁶ Although this fundamental identification with Europe was not shared by Politburo conservatives, they did agree on the importance of expanded economic ties with Western Europe, and this interest became a powerful motive to protect human rights within the Soviet Union.

Though inchoate at first, and impeded by divisions within the Kremlin, Gorbachev's rethinking of the Soviet Union as a "European" state began early in his rule: "Reflecting on the goals to set for our new foreign policy, I found it increasingly difficult to see the multicoloured patchwork of Europe's political map as I used to see it before. I was thinking about the common roots of this multiform and yet fundamentally indivisible European civilization."²⁷ Before long, says Shevardnadze, this reflection resulted in a "sober recognition" that the existing political and geostrategic division of Europe "could not continue."²⁸ The new Soviet leadership thus set out to strengthen the CSCE, the one institution that already transcended the continental divide. As Gorbachev explains, he was attracted to "the potential opportunities for a pan-European policy which lay in the 'spirit of Helsinki,' a unique achievement in itself."²⁹

Eduard Shevardnadze's first international conference as Soviet foreign minister was the July 1985 CSCE meeting to commemorate the tenth anniversary of the Helsinki Accords. Although too new on the job to launch any initiatives, Shevardnadze listened to the litany of reciprocal criticisms and grew concerned that the Helsinki process was "running down." Back in Moscow, he and Gorbachev deliberated on how to "breathe life" into the CSCE, and thus advance the Soviet Union's rapprochement with the rest of Europe.³⁰ In October, at a Paris press conference during his first official foreign visit

²⁶ Chernyaev comment, in Nina Tannenwald, ed., "Understanding the End of the Cold War, 1980–87," transcript of an oral history conference, Watson Institute for International Studies, Brown University, May 7–10, 1998, 235.
²⁷ Gorbachev, *Memoirs*, 428.
²⁸ Shevardnadze, *The Future Belongs to Freedom*, 112.
²⁹ Gorbachev, *Memoirs*, 429.
³⁰ Shevardnadze, *The Future Belongs to Freedom*, 112.

as general secretary, Gorbachev tried "to drive home to the French—and to others as well—that compliance with the Final Act would improve the climate in Europe and dispel the clouds." In response to a question, he repeated a view that he had first expressed to the British Parliament less than a year earlier: "Europe is our common home."[31]

The International Normative Environment

By this time, though, the international normative environment had made it virtually impossible for the Soviet Union to normalize relations with the West without first improving its human rights record. The European Community's commitment to linking trans-European rapprochement to respect for human rights had not weakened since the negotiation of the Helsinki Final Act in the early 1970s, while the U.S. government's commitment was now far stronger than it had been in those years, thanks to the lobbying successes of "Helsinki network" activists in New York and Washington (see Chapters 1–2 and 4, respectively). Human rights activists across the Communist bloc were also skilled at exploiting the CSCE's busy schedule of diplomatic meetings, as well as other international forums, to ensure that any attempt to create a "Potemkin village" of superficial reforms would be exposed at home and abroad. Respect for human rights was thus a legitimate and irrevocable part of the diplomatic agenda among CSCE states by the mid-1980s.

As CSCE diplomats gathered to observe the Final Act's tenth anniversary, the Solidarity-affiliated Helsinki Committee in Poland declared: "The Helsinki Final Act and the Final Document of the Madrid Conference continue to be a valuable foundation for the aspirations of Eastern European peoples. The Accords broaden the number of activists engaged in the struggle for human rights. They bring an awareness of citizens'

---

[31] Gorbachev, *Memoirs*, 428.

rights to the everyday confrontations with the government."[32] Czechoslovakia's Charter 77 announced: "We must keep fighting, we must continually point to the Helsinki Accords and say 'You signed this, you must honour this.' "[33] Likewise, Hungarian dissidents used the occasion of the CSCE Cultural Forum, held in Budapest in October 1985, to organize a parallel meeting in private apartments of writers, artists, and intellectuals from across Europe.[34]

As a result, Western media and governmental attention remained focused on political repression in the East. At a special CSCE meeting of human rights "experts" held in Ottawa just two months after Gorbachev took office, Western governments pushed hard (but ultimately unsuccessfully) for stronger measures to protect non-governmental monitoring of compliance with Helsinki norms.[35] At the tenth anniversary meeting in Helsinki, Secretary of State George Schultz challenged the new government in Moscow, "My country and most other countries represented . . . believe that the truest tests of political intentions are actual steps to improve co-operation among States, to enhance contacts among people and to strengthen respect for individual rights."[36] Similar calls for expanded protections of human rights were heard at the Budapest Cultural Forum and at the CSCE Meeting on Human Contacts, held in Bern the following spring.[37] Meanwhile, editorial writers in Western

[32] U.S. Commission on Security and Cooperation in Europe, "Human Rights and the Helsinki Process in Eastern Europe; Human Rights and the CSCE Process in the Soviet Union," Hearings, February 25 and 27, 1986 (Washington, D.C.: Government Printing Office, 1986), 101.

[33] Reuter newswire item, Vienna, 26 July 1985.

[34] *Report on the Cultural Symposium: Budapest, October 1985* (Vienna: International Helsinki Federation for Human Rights, 1986).

[35] U.S. Commission on Security and Cooperation in Europe, "The Ottowa Human Rights Experts Meeting and the Future of the Helsinki Process," Hearing, June 25, 1985 (Washington, D.C.: U.S. Government Printing Office, 1985).

[36] Conference on Security and Cooperation in Europe, Tenth Anniversary Meeting, Helsinki, Verbatim Record, 30 July–1 August 1985, CSCE/TAM/ VR.2, p. 41.

[37] See Michael Novak, *Taking Glasnost Seriously* (Washington, D.C.: AEI Press, 1988).

newspapers continued to insist on linkage between implementation of the CSCE's human rights norms and improved East-West relations in other issue-areas.[38] Police interference with the dissident symposium in Budapest also attracted widespread criticism in the international press.[39]

For the reasons discussed earlier, Gorbachev was personally sympathetic to some of these critiques of the Soviet record. Just weeks after his Paris declaration that "Europe is our common home," he told George Schultz that he was willing to discuss human rights at the upcoming Soviet-American summit in Geneva.[40] At that meeting, he recalls, "I myself spent time trying to fend off accusations of human rights abuses, even though I was not always convinced that these were not justified."[41] Five months later, he met with the co-chair of the U.S. Congress' Helsinki Commission, Representative Dante Fascell, who repeated that East-West relations could not improve without human rights reforms in the Soviet Union, including freedom of emigration and the release of Andrei Sakharov from internal exile. Senior foreign policy advisor Anatoly Chernyaev recalls that this meeting with Fascell "hardened [Gorbachev's] already existing resolve to end 'the Sakharov affair.' "[42]

Whatever Gorbachev's preferences, though, the international normative environment ensured that the "common European home" valued by some in the Kremlin as a means to secure economic resources and by others as an alternative to cultural isolation could only be built upon concrete steps to comply with the Helsinki Final Act. The reformers' conclusion that the continued denial of basic human rights was both morally unacceptable and politically unsustainable thus coincided with a broader recognition among party leaders that rapproche-

---

[38] "Helsinki: The Second Act," *The Times* (London), editorial, August 3, 1985; F. Stephen Larrabee, "The West Is Hardly the Loser," *International Herald Tribune*, August 3, 1985.

[39] See articles reprinted in *Report on the Cultural Symposium: Budapest, October 1985.*

[40] George P. Schultz, *Turmoil and Triumph: My Years as Secretary of State* (New York: Charles Scribner and Sons, 1993), 589–94.

[41] Gorbachev, *Memoirs*, 406.

[42] Chernyaev, *My Six Years with Gorbachev*, 58.

ment with Western Europe required greater respect for human rights and self-determination in Eastern Europe.

THE ESCALATION OF SOVIET REFORM

Some contemporary scholars have suggested that the Soviet party-state was structurally incapable of surviving reform. According to this logic, drawn from the earlier "totalitarian model," Communist rule was based upon coercion and social atomization, so any reduction of repression or expansion of independent initiative was bound to unleash social forces capable of bringing down the whole system.[43] Yet although it is true that repressive political systems of all types are difficult to reform without unintended consequences, this simple fact cannot explain why the Gorbachev reforms had far more revolutionary consequences than earlier efforts, such as Khrushchev's "thaw." The answer lies in Gorbachev's ability to advance his goals within a divided party leadership by exploiting domestic and international pressures for Soviet compliance with international human rights norms that had not existed in Khrushchev's time.

As discussed above, the selection of Mikhail Gorbachev as general secretary in February 1985 reflected strong but not unanimous support in the Central Committee for reforms in central planning to revitalize the Soviet economy. This shaky proreform consensus did not extend, however, to transforming the social and political order of the Soviet Union or its East European neighbors. Even among those in the leadership who believed that the party-state should allow greater space for independent voices and interests, many did not favor the type of political liberalization that many in the West equate with "human rights."[44] In addition, the status quo was well institutionalized in the coercive apparatus of the state. In this context, even the strong and convergent motives for political reform

[43] Rasma Karklins, "Explaining Regime Change in the Soviet Union," *Europe-Asia Studies* 46 (January 1994):29–45.
[44] Chernyaev, *My Six Years with Gorbachev*, 71.

discussed above would not necessarily translate into revolutionary change.

Before Gorbachev and his inner circle could implement even limited political reforms, they first had to overcome broadly based and well-entrenched opposition from Communist Party conservatives.[45] It is thus hardly surprising that during Gorbachev's first year in office, independent organizations remained illegal and dissidents were still arrested, applications for emigration denied, and religious believers harassed. During the winter of 1986, party conservatives strongly contested ideological reformulations that Gorbachev and his allies had proposed for the Twenty-Seventh Party Congress. As a result of this infighting, perestroika was stalled at home and abroad by the middle of Gorbachev's second year in office.

During Gorbachev's travels around the country that summer, Soviet citizens complained loudly that perestroika had failed to affect their daily lives, yet conservative resistance within the party and state bureaucracy blocked attempts to increase economic efficiency. And notwithstanding the Twenty-Seventh Party Congress decision to replace the Soviet Union's ideological commitment to class struggle, which had long been used to justify repression at home and in allied states, with a new doctrine emphasizing the priority of "universal human values," including human rights and self-determination, Western governments were unwilling to provide significant assistance without real evidence of political reform. It was thus clear to Gorbachev and his allies that they could neither win the confidence of the West nor overcome conservative forces at home without an acceleration of social and political reform.

Their answer was to take steps to democratize Soviet society and alleviate popular fear of the party-state: "That's when Gorbachev started to talk about the inclusion of the human factor in perestroika."[46] Though limited at first to greater tolerance

---

[45] For a sample of such infighting, see Ligachev, *Inside Gorbachev's Kremlin*, 105–7, and Shevardnadze, *The Future Belongs to Freedom*, 47.

[46] Chernyaev comment, in Tannenwald, "Understanding the End of the Cold War," 195.

of "nonthreatening group activity," such steps represented a radical step into the political unknown hardly imaginable if Gorbachev and his close allies had not already been affected by the dissident and human rights movement.[47] As shown below in more detail, they used the idea of a "common European home" and Western pressures for Helsinki compliance to justify the partial lifting of repression that they favored but that conservatives opposed. "It was clear to me that both the changes in Eastern Europe and the prospects for building a united continent without blocs . . . would directly reverberate in domestic walls and cause cracks," says Shevardnadze.[48]

However, the dissidents and human rights campaigners who emerged and regrouped during this period did far more than provide a convenient lobby for Gorbachev's reforms. By linking their cause to the trans-European CSCE that Gorbachev and Shevardnadze valued so highly, and refusing to accept limited reforms, they greatly extended the bounds of political debate and social mobilization within the Soviet Union and Eastern Europe.

The Vienna CSCE Meeting

The Vienna meeting of the CSCE that opened in the autumn of 1986 reiterated the international normative preconditions for improved East-West relations, empowering reformers within the Kremlin and encouraging local movements for political change across the Communist bloc. By the time it ended in early 1989, the Vienna CSCE had "shaken the iron curtain," admits Eduard Shevardnadze.[49] At the preparatory talks, held September 23–October 6, Western and neutral delegations made clear that any normalization of relations would require

---

[47] See Jerry F. Hough, *Democratization and Revolution in the USSR, 1985–1991* (Washington, D.C.: Brookings Institution, 1997), chapter 5.

[48] Shevardnadze, *The Future Belongs to Freedom*, 118.

[49] Vojtech Mastny, ed., *The Helsinki Process and the Reintegration of Europe, 1986–1991* (London: Pinter, 1992), 18.

concrete improvements on human rights from the East. Mean-while, nationalist and human rights activists in the non-Russian republics of the Soviet Union—many of whom had been active in the Helsinki-focused movements of the late 1970s—began to reassert their claims. In Latvia, activists created the group Helsinki '86 to organize protests against Soviet occupation and human rights violations.[50] Zviad Gamsakhurdia, cofounder of the Georgian Helsinki Watch Group in 1977, launched a new movement for the independence of Georgia.

Such pressure from below and abroad could not have failed to impress those within Gorbachev's governing coalition who viewed the Helsinki process in terms of its potential impact on domestic economic reform. For Shevardnadze and other Kremlin reformers, though, the Vienna meeting offered a cru-cial opportunity to advance their political agenda: "I was con-vinced that the conference was essential to show the country and the world how far we intended to go and, beyond that, to provide an impetus for democratization and the perestroika of legislation in everything related to human affairs."[51] Within the Politburo, they began to discuss releasing large numbers of po-litical prisoners—far more than the small numbers proposed that autumn by George Schultz before the Reykjavik summit.[52]

These proposals provoked a stormy reaction from conserva-tives, who preferred to continue divorcing rhetoric from action: "It was one thing to make declarations, but let Andrei Sakharov and other prisoners of conscience serve out their sentences," they argued.[53] Gorbachev disagreed, and told the Politburo: "We need to work out a conception on human rights, both at home and abroad. And to put an end to the routine. It only produces dissidents."[54] At another Politburo meeting that au-

[50] "Documents: Helsinki '86 Group," *Voice of Solidarity* (London), no. 131–132 (July-August 1987):31–33.

[51] Shevardnadze, *The Future Belongs to Freedom*, 86.

[52] Pavel Palazchenko, *My Years with Gorbachev and Shevardnadze* (University Park: Pennsylvania State University Press, 1997), 53.

[53] Shevardnadze, *The Future Belongs to Freedom*, 86.

[54] Chernyaev's Notes from the Politburo Session, November 13, 1986; in Zubok, "A Compendium of Declassified Documents."

tumn, he declared: "On human rights. Let us see what we can do. We need to open a way back to the Soviet Union to the thousands of emigrants, to move this current in the opposite direction."[55] Although informed by the KGB that Soviet dissidents were beginning to "connect their statements" to the political changes of perestroika, Gorbachev decided to release one-third of the 240 political prisoners then being held, and one-half at a later date.[56] In so doing, he both prepared to answer Western demands on human rights and expanded the domestic constituency that was pressuring for further reforms.

Just over a month later, Shevardnadze surprised the diplomats assembled for the opening session in Vienna by proposing that a special CSCE conference on humanitarian concerns be held in Moscow. However carefully prepared within the Politburo, this initiative was truly radical within the CSCE context, where Soviet delegations had always been reluctant to discuss human rights. The Vienna newspaper *Die Presse* likened Shevardnadze's proposal to holding a meeting of chickens in a fox den.[57] So while Gorbachev and Shevardnadze praised the CSCE as a means to create a "common European home" where shared norms would replace mutual hostility, Western governments and human rights groups insisted on more concrete evidence of political reform.

Andrei Sakharov and the "Nyeformaly"

With conservative opposition to reform consolidating in advance of the January 1987 party plenum, and significant Western assistance still not forthcoming, even more radical measures were necessary. On December 1, Gorbachev informed the Politburo of his intention to release physicist Andrei Sakharov, the Soviet Union's most famous political prisoner, from internal

[55] Chernyaev's Notes from the Politburo Session, October 8, 1986; ibid.
[56] Transcript, Meeting of Politburo of CPSU, 25 September 1986; ibid.
[57] Mastny, *The Helsinki Process and the Reintegration of Europe*, 11.

exile in Gorky.[58] Two weeks later, in a widely publicized move, Gorbachev personally telephoned Sakharov and invited him to return to Moscow. As Gorbachev must have expected, Sakharov began to campaign publicly for the release of more dissidents as soon as he returned to Moscow, and openly criticized the insufficiency of Gorbachev's domestic reforms. Official media soon conceded that many of the dissidents' long-standing critiques were correct.[59]

Over the following couple of years, the organizational and philosophical descendants of the Helsinki movement re-emerged in Moscow, Leningrad, and elsewhere as independent associations and quasi-political parties. Veteran human rights activists also played a leading role in the establishment of samizdat newspapers and weekly discussion groups that agitated for more fundamental reforms. Alexander Podrabinek established *Express Chronicle*, which quickly gained influence as a source of independent reporting through which dissidents and radical reformers could express their views. Meanwhile, thousands of new activists joined or created informal groups—*nyeformaly*—whose numbers increased from approximately one hundred at the time of Sakharov's release to a few thousand by September 1987.[60]

The Soviet Union's first opposition political party, the Democratic Union, was created in May 1988 by the merger of two such groups, Perestroika '88 and the Democracy and Humanism Seminar. Reflecting the influence of members once active in the human rights movements of the 1970s, the Democratic Union called for a multiparty parliamentary system, free trade unions, full civil liberties, a free press, and a national right to self-determination.[61] Although still illegal, and often harassed

---

[58] Chernyaev's Notes from the Politburo Session, December 1, 1986, in Zubok, "A Compendium of Declassified Documents"; and Chernyaev comment, in Tannenwald, "Understanding the End of the Cold War," 196–97.

[59] Medvedev and Chiesa, *Time of Change*, 170.

[60] Ibid, 169. "Nyeformaly" is the Russian word for the informal discussion and activist groups that emerged in the USSR during the late 1980s.

[61] Richard Sowka, *Gorbachev and His Reforms 1985–1990* (Oxford: Oxford University Press, 1990), 207–8.

by the KGB, the new party organized public demonstrations in Moscow on August 21 to mark the twentieth anniversary of the invasion of Czechoslovakia, and on December 10 to celebrate International Human Rights Day.[62] The political significance of these initiatives should not be underestimated: "Stepping beyond the bounds of perestroika, both ideologically and tactically, the Democratic Union was shunned by Russia's liberal intelligentsia still hoping for reform from above. But the shock value of the DU's open defiance of the Soviet regime reverberated throughout the other informal discussion groups."[63] Human rights activists in the *nyeformaly* and the Democratic Union thus helped push the mobilization for reform beyond what many in the party elite considered desirable.[64]

The social mobilization and open debate that emerged in 1986–1988, and the conservative reaction that ensued, also appear to have pushed some of Gorbachev's closest advisors from a reformist to a revolutionary vision of change. As Aleksandr Yakovlev explains, "At some point in 1987, I personally realized that a society based on violence and fear could not be reformed and that we faced a momentous historical task of dismantling the entire social and political system with all its ideological, economic and political roots."[65] Although Gorbachev's own record is more mixed, he too appears to have rethought the limited commitment to "democratization" he first enunciated

[62] Vera Tolz, *The USSR's Emerging Multiparty System* (New York: Praeger, 1990); Michael McFaul and Sergei Markov, *The Troubled Birth of Russian Democracy: Parties, Personalities and Programs* (Stanford: Hoover Institution Press, 1993), chapters 1–2.

[63] McFaul and Markov, *The Troubled Birth of Russian Democracy*, 4.

[64] For more discussion of these "informal" groups and proto-parties, see Vladimir Brovkin, "Revolution from Below: Informal Political Associations in Russia, 1988–89," *Soviet Studies* 42 (April 1990):233–58; U.S. Helsinki Watch Committee, *Nyeformaly: Civil Society in the USSR*, (New York, 1990); Judith B. Sedaitis and Jim Butterfield, eds., *Perestroika from Below: Social Movements in the Soviet Union* (Boulder, Colo.: Westview Press, 1991); and Nicolai N. Petro, "Perestroika from Below: Voluntary Sociopolitical Associations in the RSFSR," in Alfred J. Rieber and Alvin Z. Rubinstein, eds., *Perestroika at the Crossroads* (Armonk, N.Y.: M.E. Sharpe, 1991): 102–35.

[65] Yakovlev, *The Fate of Marxism in Russia*, 227.

in 1986. "Gorbachev was talking about it first in terms of the democratization of socialism, but over time the socialism part actually got smaller and smaller," says close advisor Anatoly Chernyaev.[66] In the end, whatever the nature of Gorbachev's commitment to expanding social autonomy and democratizing the Soviet state, the *nyeformaly* and new media unleashed by his policies significantly radicalized the political debate in Moscow, Leningrad, and the outlying republics.[67] At the same time, Soviet diplomats at the Vienna CSCE conference made ever-more significant concessions in their attempt to gain Western confidence and support.

Dismantling the Coercive State

As discussed above, Western governments and human rights groups within the transnational Helsinki network had responded skeptically to Shevardnadze's 1986 proposal that Moscow host a special CSCE meeting on humanitarian affairs. To win their support and achieve Gorbachev's goal of closer relations with Europe and the West, Soviet diplomats began to show unprecedented flexibility with respect to international monitoring of compliance with human rights norms. First, the Kremlin agreed to accept visits by foreign judges, prosecutors, and psychiatrists focused on human rights.[68] In mid-1987, the Soviet delegation at Vienna agreed that the CSCE should establish a new "human dimension mechanism" by which participating states could request information and bilateral consultations on apparent violations of human rights; as a last resort,

[66] Chernyaev comment in Tannenwald, "Understanding the End of the Cold War," 196.

[67] See M. Steven Fish, *Democracy from Scratch: Opposition and Regime in the New Russian Revolution* (Princeton: Princeton University Press, 1995); and Timothy J. Colton, *Moscow: Governing the Socialist Metropolis* (Cambridge: Harvard University Press, 1996).

[68] David K. Shipler, "Dateline USSR: On the Human Rights Track," *Foreign Policy* 75 (Summer 1989):164.

states could convene a special CSCE meeting to address their concerns.[69]

In September, Soviet ambassador Yuri Kashlev announced that the Kremlin had accepted a request from the non-governmental International Helsinki Federation for Human Rights (IHFHR) to visit the Soviet Union.[70] This organization, which linked Helsinki monitoring groups in the East and West, had long been criticized by the Kremlin for what it considered interference in internal affairs. During its week-long visit in January 1988, the IHFHR delegation met with dozens of human rights and opposition activists, and also with senior Soviet officials to press for even greater openness.[71] Soon thereafter, the Kremlin announced the creation of a new official Commission on Humanitarian Affairs and International Cooperation to oversee Soviet implementation of CSCE norms.

Western governments also pressed at the Vienna conference and in bilateral forums for the Kremlin to comply with Helsinki norms by releasing all its political prisoners. Fyodor Burlatsky, chairman of the new Commission on Humanitarian Affairs, echoed their call. During 1987–1988, more than six hundred political prisoners were freed. Although conditional on signing a pledge not to participate in political activity, these releases and the simple admission that Soviet jails actually held "political prisoners," further undermined the party-state. Most of the released prisoners quickly resumed their political activities, and the publication of samizdat increased still further. Attempts by Soviet conservatives to curtail democratization in the spring of 1988, including the furor surrounding Nina Andreeva's sharply critical letter to *Sovetskaia Rossia* that criticized perestroika, simply resulted in the dismissal of Ygor Ligachev from the number two position in the Politburo. By late 1988, the number of political prisoners had fallen to unprecedentedly low levels: be-

[69] Mastny, *The Helsinki Process and the Reintegration of Europe*, 14–15.

[70] *Financial Times* (London), September 23, 1987.

[71] International Helsinki Federation for Human Rights, *On Speaking Terms: An Unprecedented Human Rights Mission to the Soviet Union, January 25–31, 1988* (Vienna, 1988).

tween 11 and 52, according to Soviet officials, and 140, according to Amnesty International.[72]

That summer, Soviet diplomats in Vienna resumed their effort to gain Western acceptance of Shevardnadze's earlier offer to host a CSCE conference in Moscow, arguing that the prospect of such conference was needed to support the advocates of democratization within the Soviet Union. Once again, Western diplomats held out, leveraging this issue and progress on conventional arms reductions to win further human rights reforms from the Kremlin, including greater freedom of travel and information and the establishment of joint U.S.-Soviet working groups to address Soviet human rights abuses.[73] In October, the Moscow Television Service broadcast excerpts from a speech Ronald Reagan had delivered to Soviet dissidents during the May summit in Moscow, followed by an unprecedented commentary that acknowledged human rights problems in the Soviet Union and implicitly accepted an American president's legitimate interest in such issues.[74] Bit by bit, the party-state was losing both the means and the justification for maintaining its power.

As independent voices grew louder and more forceful, an article in *Pravda* expressed concern that "The slogans of democratisation, *glasnost* and increased human rights and freedoms are increasingly being manipulated by various groups of people who while passing themselves off as advocates of *perestroika* are in fact its vicious opponents." In a June 1989 speech to the Supreme Soviet of the new USSR Congress of People's Deputies, Gorbachev himself attacked the Democratic Union and other independent forces for being "hostile to the socialist system."[75] Whether such public comments reflected continued belief in the guiding role of the Communist Party, a tactical attempt to satisfy party ideologues, or both, the party-state was

[72] Sowka, *Gorbachev and His Reforms 1985–1990*, 218, 226.
[73] Mastny, *The Helsinki Process and the Reintegration of Europe*, 15–16.
[74] Shipler, "Dateline USSR," 165.
[75] Sowka, *Gorbachev and His Reforms 1985–1990*, 213, 228.

badly weakened by this point, both in the Soviet Union and within the allied states of Eastern Europe.

COMMUNISM'S END GAME IN EASTERN EUROPE

The interaction of external pressure, top-down reforms, and bottom-up mobilization within the Soviet Union fatally undermined the cohesion and stability of the Communist party-state throughout the Warsaw Pact countries. The social uprisings and revolutions that swept across Eastern Europe in 1989 are therefore partly explicable as the product of interdependent and cascading "assurance games" set in motion by the Soviet reforms discussed above.[76] According to this logic, the risk-benefit calculations of individuals are shaped by the behaviors of others, so small but visible challenges to state authority can unleash a cascade of challenges by assuring others that the risks are small, or at least distributed among a growing number of challengers. Meanwhile, state actors' calculations regarding the feasibility and acceptability of using force to resist a social challenge are shaped by the behavior of other state actors and by the scale of social unrest, so that minor concessions to social challengers increasingly undermine the state's sense of both its legitimacy and its capacity to coerce social compliance.

Yet however much it tells us about the escalation of protest, the assurance game explanation of Communism's collapse greatly exaggerates the spontaneity of social mobilization in mid to late 1989, while greatly underplaying the extent to which incentives then in place were actually the result of earlier normative disputes. As demonstrated in earlier chapters, independent groups and movements persisted in their challenge to the

[76] Timur Kuran, "Now Out of Never: The Element of Surprise in the East European Revolution of 1989," *World Politics* 44 (October 1991):7–48; Rasma Karklins and Roger Petersen, "Decision Calculus of Protesters and Regimes: Eastern Europe 1989," *Journal of Politics* 55 (August 1993):588–614; Susanne Lohmann, "Dynamics of Informational Cascades: The Monday Demonstrations in Leipzig, East Germany, 1989–1991," *World Politics* 47 (October 1994):42–101.

repressiveness of the Communist party-state during the decade that followed the Helsinki Final Act, despite limits on political change set by Soviet hegemony. Every sign of greater tolerance from Moscow thus encouraged East European activists to press their governments for even more far-reaching changes at home, while Helsinki norms remained a key point of reference for state and nonstate actors alike.

In Hungary, where the ruling party had long been the most liberal in Eastern Europe, opposition activity had centered for several years around three issue-focused groups: the Democratic Opposition focused on civil rights and cultural freedoms; the Danube Circle focused on environmental protection; and nationalist forces focused on the rights of Hungarian minorities in neighboring states. In 1987, intellectuals from all these groups, as well as reformist members of the ruling party, formed the Hungarian Democratic Forum to press for greater pluralism and dialogue between state and society. In May 1988, a new reform-oriented government under Prime Minister Miklos Nemeth accelerated reforms and expanded the space available to independent political groups.

In the relatively hard-line political climate of Czechoslovakia, opposition forces were greatly encouraged by news of reforms in the Soviet Union, and particularly by Gorbachev's May 1987 renunciation of the 1968 invasion during his visit to Prague. In 1988, with the internationally known Charter 77 shielding them somewhat from the regime, young people in Prague launched new independent associations dedicated to peace, the environment, alternative music, and other issues. A new generation of underground publishers disseminated countless unofficial periodicals. About half a million Catholics signed a petition for greater religious freedom and human rights. Charter 77 also organized a series of public demonstrations to protest the continued repressiveness of the regime and to accustom the wider population to asserting its rights. Each demonstration attracted a larger crowd, while the authorities' heavy-handed responses further alienated the population.

Besieged by protests, yet unwilling to entertain proposals for reform, the Czechoslovak government attempted to maintain its grip on power without isolating itself any further internationally. In December 1988, the government agreed to permit a demonstration in commemoration of the fortieth anniversary of the Universal Declaration of Human Rights, and then, in response to Moscow's example and CSCE pressure on freedom of information, lifted jamming of Radio Free Europe. Several weeks later, in January 1989, opposition activists chose the closing day of the CSCE meeting in Vienna, when the diplomats and media were gathered for the signing of the latest agreement in the Helsinki process, to organize another human rights demonstration in Prague. Notwithstanding its own diplomats' participation in the signing ceremony, the Czechoslovak government instructed the police to beat the demonstrators. This event publicized the superficiality and hypocrisy of the government's concessions and racheted pressures for reform still higher. Further concessions during early 1989 included the release of Vaclav Havel from prison, unprecedented official responses to inquiries from other states under the CSCE's new "human dimension mechanism," and loosened restrictions on travel and the press. By this point, though, the activity of independent groups had outpaced "even the most radical reformists" within the Czechoslovak Communist Party.[77]

An even more fundamental challenge to the party-state emerged simultaneously in Poland, where several years of martial law had failed to stifle opposition. "[C]onstant pressure applied by the opposition since the days of KOR, coupled with Jaruzelski's willingness to respond to that pressure, had produced a real opening of the public space."[78] In fact, Poland's Helsinki movement had played an active role in monitoring abuses by the Jaruzelski regime during the martial law period, and contributed, by its influence on Western policy, to the further lifting of repression as the country's economic crisis

---

[77] Borek Hnizdo, "Czechoslovak-Soviet Relations," in Alex Pravda, ed., *The End of the Outer Empire: Soviet-East European Relations in Transition, 1985–90* (London: Sage Publications/Royal Institute of International Affairs, 1992), 176.

[78] Gale Stokes, *The Walls Came Tumbling Down: The Collapse of Communism in Eastern Europe* (New York: Oxford University Press, 1993), 121.

worsened. Fearful of renewed industrial strikes, and encouraged by Soviet reforms, the Polish government reestablished formal contacts with Solidarity in late 1988.

In keeping with its long-standing commitment to political reform, the union immediately insisted that the country's crisis could not be resolved without a power-sharing arrangement. In February 1989, the government launched roundtable negotiations among the ruling party and its allies, Solidarity, and the Catholic Church. Nine weeks later, they reached agreement: Solidarity would be relegalized and permitted to field candidates in partly free parliamentary elections; economic reforms would be implemented, and civil liberties would be expanded. In other words, fundamental principles of human rights were accepted as the basis for political and social reconstruction in Poland. Unlike the situation in 1980, though, the threat of Soviet invasion had been removed, greasing the slope to revolutionary change.

When the Polish elections were held in June, voters turned out overwhelmingly in favor of Solidarity. Many members of the ruling party crossed out candidates from the "national" list; even in closed military districts, approximately 40 percent of soldiers voted for Solidarity. As a result, Solidarity candidates won every freely contested seat, whereas 33 of the 35 ruling party candidates failed to secure the required majority of votes cast for seats that had otherwise been shielded from real competition. Nobody had expected such an landslide victory for Solidarity, but both domestically and internationally it was impossible to turn back. The Polish party leadership was demoralized and confused: in secret discussions, some Central Committee members confessed that they did not understand the election result, while others concluded that the party had "outlived itself."[79]

Heads of state and communist parties at a Warsaw Pact meeting in Moscow several weeks later stated their commitment to

[79] Transcript of the Central Committee secretariat meeting of the Polish United Workers Party, Warsaw, June 5, 1989, accessed April 17, 2000 at http://www.gwu.edu/~nsarchive/news/19991105/index.html.

"the application, in every country, of the entire gamut of free-doms and fundamental human rights, as they were formulated in the Universal Declaration of Human Rights and the last act of Helsinki."[80] Although several East European governments remained hard-line in practice, this statement essentially elimi-nated major rhetorical differences between the ruling Commu-nist authorities and the human rights movements that opposed them. As word of Solidarity's electoral victory spread across the border from Poland, followed by the Moscow communiqué, tens of thousands of Czechoslovak citizens signed "A Few Sen-tences," a new petition for political liberalization and dialogue drafted by Charter 77 veterans.[81] A Solidarity-dominated gov-ernment led by Tadeusz Mazowiecki took power in late August, making Poland the first country in Eastern Europe to end the Communist Party's formal monopoly on political power and moving the country irrevocably toward a new political system constitutionally and ideologically committed to the protection of human rights.

Meanwhile, Hungary's increasingly well-organized opposi-tion increased the pressure for change in Budapest. On June 13, the government and ruling party opened roundtable talks with the opposition. One opposition figure proposed that all sides "refrain from questioning the legitimacy of each other, since the legitimacy of all of us is debatable. It is a question which belongs to the future—who will be given credit by his-tory and who will be forgotten."[82] Public support for reform was nonetheless abundantly clear three days later, when 200,000 people turned out for an opposition-organized public reburial of Imre Nagy, the former prime minister executed thirty-one years earlier for his role during the Hungarian upris-

---

[80] *Pravda* 9 July 1989, as cited in Jacques Lévesque, *The Enigma of 1989: The USSR and the Liberation of Eastern Europe*, translated by Keith Martin (Berkeley and Los Angeles: University of California Press, 1997), 8

[81] U.S. Helsinki Watch, *Toward Civil Society: Independent Initiatives in Czecho-slovakia* (New York, 1989).

[82] Transcript of the Opening Full Session of the National Roundtable Nego-tiations, June 13, 1989, accessed April 17, 2000 at http:/www.gwu.edu/~nsarchive/news/19991105/index.html.

ing of 1956. In the late summer, the roundtable talks produced an agreement to hold free and direct presidential elections in late November, and parliamentary elections ninety days later. In neighboring East Germany, though, the party-state continued to resist reform. Since 1985, when a group of East Berlin activists founded the Initiative for Peace and Human Rights, independent groups had begun building opposition networks and organizing public appeals for greater freedoms throughout the GDR.[83] In June 1989, as part of a campaign to deter further social mobilization, the parliament publicly applauded the Chinese government's violent reprisal against demonstrators in Tiananmen Square. Two months later, the secret police nonetheless warned party leaders that membership in dissident groups was growing.[84] As the summer ended, tens of thousands of East Germans vacationing in neighboring Hungary decided not to return home; by September 1, approximately six thousand of them had crossed illegally into Austria and requested asylum at the West German embassy in Vienna. On September 10, invoking its obligations under the Helsinki process, as well as the UN Convention on Refugees, the Hungarian government legalized this emigration by opening its borders to Austria.

Hungary's open-border policy created an instant political crisis in the GDR. The following day, members of the Initiative for Peace and Human Rights created New Forum and began to organize regular demonstrations for political change in Dresden, East Berlin, and especially Leipzig. With each passing demonstration, the social-psychological legacy of decades of intimidation by the most repressive regime in Eastern Europe was replaced by a growing sense of popular efficacy.[85] Mean-

[83] John C. Torpey, *Intellectuals, Socialism, and Dissent: The East German Opposition and Its Legacy* (Minneapolis: University of Minnesota Press, 1995), chapter 3.

[84] Philip Zelikow and Condoleeza Rice, *Germany Unified and Europe Transformed: A Study in Statecraft* (Cambridge: Harvard University Press, 1995), 37.

[85] See Dirk Philipsen, *We Were the People: Voices from East Germany's Revolutionary Autumn of 1989* (Durham: Duke University Press, 1993); Karl-Dieter Opp, Peter Voss, and Christiane Gern, *Origins of a Spontaneous Revolution: East Germany, 1989* (Ann Arbor: University of Michigan Press, 1995).

while, demonstrations continued to escalate in East Germany, and thousands of refugees continued to flow into Hungary.

The (Relative) Non-use of Force

Erich Honecker's resignation one month later as party leader in the GDR raises the critical question of why the Kremlin and its allies did not instead seek to intimidate the opposition through an overwhelming use of force during the autumn of 1989, as they had years before. The killing of a small number of demonstrators in T'blisi, Georgia, demonstrated that at least some senior officials in the Soviet party-state apparatus were not opposed to maintaining the status quo by force.[86] And yet, despite massive crowds calling for revolutionary change across Eastern Europe, the Red Army remained in its barracks, and Gorbachev urged his counterparts in Budapest, East Berlin, Prague, and Sofia to refrain from using force. The explanation for this puzzle involves both instrumental learning and a more profound transformation of the leadership's definition of state interests.

To start, the Soviet military was still reeling from its defeat and withdrawal from Afghanistan. More important, though, the experience of martial law in Poland had long since taught Gorbachev and many of his advisors that force could not suppress popular ferment. As Shevardnadze recalls, "The 'window to Europe' opened for me long before my 'discovery of America.' . . . It was a window to the countries of Eastern Europe or, as we put it, the countries of the socialist community. Everything that I saw through that window . . . strongly influenced the formation of my views and attitudes toward the events of 1989–90." And given the scale of demonstrations across Eastern Europe, Gorbachev knew that any massive use of force would have resulted in the deaths of hundreds of people, and thereby de-

---

[86] Gorbachev's role in this incident remains unclear.

stroyed the environment necessary for glasnost and perestroika within the Soviet Union.[87]

In addition to such evidence of instrumental thinking, Gorbachev and some members of his inner circle appear to have been motivated, as well, by a normative rethinking of state interests. "[W]e could not sacrifice our own principles regarding the right of peoples to freedom of choice, noninterference in internal affairs, and the common European home," says Shevardnadze.[88] At the Malta summit in December 1989, Gorbachev went to great lengths to convince Bush and Baker to portray the democratic transitions then underway in Eastern Europe as being consistent with the Helsinki Final Act and "universal human values," rather than the "Western values" formula that they had first proposed.[89] Given that Gorbachev's domestic opponents (Ligachev and other conservatives) had already rejected the priority of international norms and universal human values, this persistence is strong evidence of the fundamental nature of Gorbachev's reconceptualization of Soviet interests.

The norms and oversight of the Helsinki process also contributed to the non-use of lethal force in Bulgaria, where the government had never been very tolerant of dissent. In the slightly eased political atmosphere of early 1989, a number of Bulgarian activists established the independent group Ecoglasnost to link human rights and environmental problems in a critique of Communist rule. In mid-October, with Communist regimes under siege throughout the bloc, thirty-four foreign delegations arrived in Sofia for a CSCE Meeting on the Protection of the Environment. On October 26, Ecoglasnost demonstrators were beaten by police while protesting a recent prohibition against their collecting signatures on a petition in a public park. The CSCE meeting was immediately halted, and most delegations demanded an official explanation for the

---

[87] Shevardnadze, *The Future Belongs to Freedom*, 112, 118.
[88] Ibid, 120.
[89] Zelikow and Rice, *Germany Unified*, 128–30.

crackdown. Bulgaria's environment minister apologized, and promised greater tolerance for independent activities.

One week later, seeking to benefit from the last day of the CSCE meeting, Ecoglasnost attracted five thousand supporters for another demonstration, and they succeeded despite police resistance in presenting their petition to the parliament.[90] Looking around the bloc, at the growing demonstrations at home, and at the international attention focused on Bulgaria via the CSCE, the Communist Party elite concluded that the status quo could not be maintained. Their last-ditch attempt to forestall radical change by replacing Todor Zhivkov with a reform Communist as president and general secretary of the party failed to put an end to demonstrations for free elections.

In another desperate attempt to stem the tide of unrest, Honecker's successor in the GDR, Egon Krenz, announced on November 9 that East Germans would henceforth be allowed to travel freely to the West. The Berlin Wall, which for twenty-eight years had been a physical barrier between the two Germanies and a symbolic barrier between the two halves of Europe, was soon breached by surging crowds of East Berliners. Within a few weeks, West German Chancellor Helmut Kohl began the process that culminated in the unification of the two Germanies eleven months later.[91]

After the Wall

In Czechoslovakia, the party-state again exhibited its stubborn resistance to reform by ordering the Prague police to beat demonstrators gathered in the capital on November 17. Student

---

[90] U.S. Commission on Seccurity and Cooperation in Europe, "The Sofia CSCE Meeting on the Protection of the Environment, October 16-November 3, 1989," *Implementation of the Helsinki Accords* (Washington, D.C.: Government Printing Office, 1990), 123, 132–33.

[91] In addition to Zelikow and Rice, *Germany Unified*, see Peter H. Merkl, *German Unification in the European Context* (University Park: Pennsylvania State University Press, 1993); and Richard A. Leiby, *The Unification of Germany, 1989–1990* (Westport, Conn: Greenwood Press, 1999).

leaders responded by fanning out around the country to organize a public strike. Yet even now, eight days after the fall of the Berlin Wall, there was no guarantee of peaceful change in Czechoslovakia. Unlike some its neighbors, the Communist regime in Prague had no experience with gradual liberalization or roundtable talks. Many of its leaders, placed in power by Soviet tanks twenty years earlier, believed that Gorbachev's reforms had gone too far, and feared that concessions to student demonstrators would result in anarchy, if not in their eventual lynching. (This is precisely what happened in Romania, where an equally conservative Communist regime collapsed into chaos and violence in late December, and its leaders were summarily executed by their captors.)

In this critical moment, the international normative environment again proved crucial. Rather than issue a written protest that would soon be bypassed by events, opposition veterans of the Charter 77 generation formed a new organization, Civic Forum, to coordinate protest activities and attempt to negotiate with the regime. Demonstrators now numbering in the hundreds of thousands cheered the appearance of Vaclav Havel, Vaclav Maly, and other Charter 77 leaders known previously only by name and reputation. Just four days after the beating of the students, Havel reappeared on a balcony overlooking Prague's Wenceslas Square and announced to the crowds assembled below that the Communist authorities had begun negotiations with the opposition.

The party leadership nonetheless continued to debate internally whether to use even greater force against the protesters. At a critical November 24 meeting of the party's Central Committee, Premier Ladislav Adamec considered the possible use of force, but stressed two reasons for favoring a political solution. First, he said, previous crackdowns had only provoked greater resistance and further delegitimated the party. Second, "It would also be a mistake to underestimate the international risks of a broad application of force. We mustn't labor under the illusion that various democratization, environmental and other movements end at our borders. Also signed international treaties dealing with human rights cannot be taken lightly."

Only after discussing these domestic and transnational dimensions did he briefly mention that "the international support of the socialist countries can no longer be counted on" and that "capitalist states" were likely to impose a "political and economic boycott."[92]

In secret discussions that same week, members of Civic Forum worked to reassure the regime that peaceful abdication would not be followed by criminal prosecution or vendettas.[93] On December 10, the Communist government of Czechoslovakia handed power peacefully to a transition coalition dominated by Civic Forum. By the end of the year, the Federal Assembly elected veteran human rights activist Vaclav Havel as the country's new president. Without the international legitimacy and domestic credibility that Charter 77 had gained through years of peaceful protest for human rights, Civic Forum would undoubtedly have had a far more difficult task negotiating a peaceful transition to democratic rule.

Faced with continued protests, the Bulgarian Communist Party renounced its "leading role" on January 15, 1990, and agreed to hold free elections six months later. Free elections in East Germany on March 18 brought a non-Communist government to power, followed by the same outcome one week later in Hungary. Elections in Poland on May 27 swept all remaining Communist authorities from government there. Finally, on June 9, the Civic Forum coalition won parliamentary elections in Czechoslovakia and began to fill the ranks of the new government and diplomatic service, as well as educational, cultural, and media institutions with former human rights activists from Charter 77. As multiparty democracies and rights-protective states were established across Eastern Europe, the Cold War between East and West slowly evaporated.

This process accelerated with the deepening crisis of the Soviet Union. One hundred thousand people gathered in the

[92] Speech by Premier Ladislav Adamec at the extraordinary session of the Czechoslovak Communist Party Central Committee, November 24, 1989, accessed April 17, 2000 at http://www.gwu.edu/~nsarchive/news/19991105/index.html.

[93] Jan Urban, interview by author, Prague, July 25, 1992.

streets of Moscow on February 4, 1990 to demonstrate against the Communist Party; three days later, the party renounced its "leading role" in society. In mid-March, opposition parties won semifree elections in Moscow and Leningrad. Meanwhile, protests against Soviet occupation and human rights violations begun in Latvia by the Helsinki '86 movement spread across Lithuania and Estonia, as well.[94] Conservative forces counterattacked with an attempted coup in August 1991, but their failure simply hastened the banning of the Communist Party and final break-up of the Soviet Union.

CONCLUSIONS

As this chapter shows, the salience of international human rights norms and the mobilization of domestic and transnational human rights movements were critical to the demise of Communist rule in Eastern Europe and the Soviet Union. Neither the structural contradictions of the party-state and centralized planning nor generational changes in the Soviet leadership would have brought about the largely peaceful and rights-protective political transitions of 1989 without the changes in international norms and state-society relations connected to the Helsinki Final Act. Over time, the human rights norms established at Helsinki affected both the behavior of state actors and the fundamental constructions of self-interest and identity that shape behavioral choices. In particular, they changed the beliefs and the strategies of Communist Party elites, the outlook and the organization of independent activists who refused to settle for cosmetic reforms, and the political conditions for normalized relations with the West. Helsinki norms thus contributed substantially to ending one-party Communist rule, as well as the Cold War division of Europe and the world into two armed

---

[94] See Rasma Karklins, *Ethnopolitics and Transition to Democracy: The Collapse of the USSR and Latvia* (Washington, D.C.: Woodrow Wilson Center Press, 1994); Anatol Lieven, *The Baltic Revolution: Estonia, Latvia and Lithuania and the Path to Independence*, 2nd ed. (New Haven: Yale University Press, 1994).

camps. This was no small accomplishment for a set of norms originally dismissed by skeptics as an unacceptable concession to totalitarianism and Soviet hegemony.

The implications of these findings for international relations theory and for our understanding of Communism and the Cold War are discussed in the following chapter.

The Helsinki Effect

The existence of a formal, written document, to which the
Eastern regimes gave their public consent and their formal
stamp of legitimacy, has made a difference. The words matter
and are beginning to move human minds. . . . Perhaps we
in the West, who pay such frequent tribute to the worth
of ideas, should be a little embarrassed that at the time of
Helsinki we entertained such a low opinion of their power.
—U.S. Ambassador Leonard Garment, 1976[1]

The Soviets desperately wanted the CSCE, they got it and it
laid the foundations for the end of their empire. We resisted
it for years, went grudgingly, Ford paid a terrible price for
going—perhaps reelection itself—only to discover years
later that CSCE had yielded benefits beyond our wildest
imagination. Go figure.
—former CIA director Robert Gates, 1997[2]

THE HUMAN RIGHTS norms of the CSCE had consequences that
were entirely unforeseen by those who signed the Helsinki
Final Act in 1975. To understand their implications for our
broader understanding of the politics of international norms
and the socialization of states, though, we must do more than
conclude that "norms matter." This chapter assesses the explan-

---

[1] U.S. Commission on Security and Cooperation in Europe, *The Belgrade
CSCE Follow-Up Meeting: A Report and Appraisal*, Hearings, March 21, 1978
(Washington, D.C.: Government Printing Office, 1978), Appendix B.

[2] Robert Gates, *From the Shadows: The Ultimate Insider's Story of Five Presidents and How They Helped Win the Cold War* (New York: Simon & Schuster,
1996), 89.

atory power of Liberal and Constructivist theories of human rights norms, comparing their expectations regarding the origins, framing, and effects of norms to critical aspects of the Helsinki process. It then explores the implications of these findings for our understanding of the demise of Communist rule and the end of the Cold War, and for broader issues in international relations and comparative politics.

THE ORIGINS OF INTERNATIONAL NORMS

During the early decades of the Cold War, relations between Eastern and Western Europe were not governed by a norm that states should respect the human rights of their citizens. The 1948 Universal Declaration of Human Rights imposed no obligations on states and did not address the role of human rights in international relations. The 1966 covenants on human rights did impose obligations on states, but were still unratified by most of the Warsaw Pact countries a decade later. There was, in other words, no shared expectation that the issue of human rights belonged on the East-West or trans-European agenda. Some governments were frustrated by this fact, and others relieved, but their diplomatic behavior clearly reveals a shared understanding that human rights had *not* been established as an international norm for all the states of Europe.

"Respect for human rights" was established as a formal norm for relations among European states in 1975 by the Conference on Security and Cooperation in Europe. This outcome resulted from the collective initiative of the member states of the European Community, who convinced all the other states participating in the CSCE, including the two superpowers, to include human rights as one of the Helsinki Final Act's ten basic principles. The record also shows that most governments participating in the CSCE planned carefully for the conference, and supervised their diplomats very closely during the negotiations to ensure an outcome consistent with their understanding of state interests. When the negotiations appeared likely to establish human rights as a trans-European norm but unlikely to realize many of the Eastern bloc's original geopolitical and economic goals, the Soviet Union threatened to block the conclusion of the conference, which was already in its second year. And yet, they returned to the table and signed the Final Act.

These observations, documented in Chapters 1 and 2, highlight two puzzles that need to be explained if we are to understand the evolution of international norms in Europe culminating in the Helsinki Final Act. The first puzzle is the EC states' persistent effort to establish a strong human rights norm to govern the behavior of states in the CSCE. The second puzzle is the willingness of the Soviet Union and its allies to establish such a norm, which so clearly contradicted the ideology, structure and practices of the Communist party-state. Both Liberal and Constructivist theories of the origins of international norms can engage these puzzles, but as shown below, the latter proves more powerful.

EC Preferences

The American government's resistance to the idea of establishing a human rights norm within the CSCE that is documented in Chapters 1 and 2 fatally undermines any suggestion that the EC member states were acting on behalf of their superpower ally's interest in weakening its global competitor. In fact, Henry Kissinger's principal argument against pushing for human rights within the CSCE was that it would destabilize the East-West relationship in a manner that he and President Nixon considered contrary to America's strategic interests.

Liberal theory would explain the EC states' interest in placing human rights issues on the trans-European agenda as rational multilateralism in the pursuit of national policy preferences. By this logic, the EC states' concern about the impact of Communism in Eastern Europe on democratic stability in Western Europe would motivate them to promote democratization in the East. At the same time, their desire to benefit from improved bilateral relations with Eastern Europe—as seen in the Bonn government's *ostpolitik* agenda—would limit their willingness to push unilaterally on politically sensitive issues.[3] The EC states might thus have concluded that promoting human rights in a multilateral forum like the CSCE would advance their interest in political change in the East while shielding their bilateral relations from retaliation. In contrast, the United States government was less threatened by totalitarianism in Eastern Europe, and would thus be less interested in building human rights norms into the East-West agenda.

Liberal theory thus offers a parsimonious explanation of EC preferences that accords with their opening position within the CSCE. The problem with the Liberal explanation, though, is its weakness on process: it cannot explain critical aspects of EC diplomacy regarding the content of the Helsinki Final Act. Contrary to the implications of Liberal theory, West European diplomats and foreign ministers involved in CSCE planning did not expect that the human rights norm that they were advocating would have any significant impact within Eastern Europe or the Soviet Union. Why, then, did the EC persist in its demands for a strong human rights norm when the issue provoked threats from the Soviets in mid-1974 to abandon the CSCE if the proposed norm was not substantially weakened?

Liberal theory might expect that EC governments would continue to push human rights as a symbolic gesture to parliamentary or public opinion, but this explanation is inconsistent with the low levels of public and media attention to the CSCE. In the end, Liberal theory's assumptions that interests are determined at the national level and that multilateral outcomes reflect states' bargaining leverage imply that the EC would bow to French and German interest in a speedy conclusion to the talks, even if this meant accepting a weak norm on human rights. And yet, as described in Chapter 2, the EC maintained its collective insistence on creating a strong human rights norm within the CSCE.

In contrast, Constructivist theory would explain the EC governments' sustained interest in establishing a human rights

[3] See Timothy Garton Ash, *In Europe's Name: Germany and the Divided Continent* (New York: Random House, 1993).

norm for East-West relations as a reflection of behavioral norms embedded in their collective understanding of themselves as a political community. Several years before the CSCE talks began in Geneva, the EC heads of states chose the European security conference as a first venue for the common foreign policy that they hoped to develop, but did not specify what goals the EC should pursue. Instead, the task of developing an EC position for the CSCE was given to senior foreign ministry officials of the member states meeting under the new mechanisms of "European political cooperation." As shown in Chapter 1, their definition of EC goals for the East-West conference was made not by merging national expressions of interest in human rights but by importing expressions of human rights as a defining value of the EC that had been articulated during the 1960s as the basis for sanctions against authoritarian regimes in the non-member states of Greece and Spain and then formalized in the 1973 Copenhagen Declaration on the European Identity.

In response to the East bloc's initial proposals for a trans-European security conference, EC policymakers decided that any agreement on trans-European relations must reflect the commitment to human rights with which they had repeatedly identified European integration. As the conference approached, they concluded that the human rights norm that they had established within Western Europe must be matched by a definitive commitment to human rights as a basic norm of East-West relations. And finally, when Moscow and Washington tried to pressure the EC into moderating its demands during the negotiating stalemate of 1974, the smaller member states used these early definitions of the European Community's political identity to maintain a tough position. Constructivist theory's hypothesized linkage between collective identity and behavior thus explains both the EC's original preference for institutionalizing human rights within the CSCE and the reinforcement of this commitment despite stiff resistance during the three years of negotiation.

Soviet Agreement

The second critical puzzle in the origins of the Helsinki Final Act is why the Soviet Union and its allies agreed to establish a norm—"respect for human rights and fundamental freedoms"—that so directly contradicted the ideology, structure, and practices of the Communist party-state. The arguments and repressive practices of these states during the mid-1970s that are documented in Chapters 2 and 3 render implausible any suggestion that Brezhnev and his allies signed the Final Act because they actually wanted to expand protections of human rights in their countries. Liberal theory offers a powerful explanation for the East bloc's intense bargaining over human rights, but fails to explain why Moscow ultimately acquiesced. Constructivist theory explains both the Communist states' resistance to including a human rights norm within the CSCE and their ultimate decision to sign the Final Act.

Liberal theory suggests that states which systematically violate human rights will seek to prevent the establishment or dilute the content of international human rights norms. It also suggests, at least implicitly, that they will agree to be bound by human rights norms only if they receive valued material goods in return (such as access to foreign markets, technology, or investment) and if they believe that the norms will not fundamentally undermine their hold on power. In other words, dictators will make normative commitments with which they have no intention of complying if doing so appears economically lucrative and politically safe.

As discussed in Chapter 1, the Warsaw Pact's early calls for a multi-issue European security conference were motivated in large part by their desire to gain the West's acceptance of the postwar boundaries in Eastern Europe, including the German Democratic Republic, and to decouple the United States from its West European allies. As their centrally planned economies began to deteriorate, though, the governments of the East bloc came to see the conference as a means to gain Western technology and financial credits. When the conference began in late

1972, the Soviets and their allies presumably calculated that the potential economic and political gains from such a conference outweighed the risks posed by an agenda that included vague references to human rights. During the actual negotiations, they worked hard to ensure that the resulting agreement would not establish clear or enforceable obligations to respect human rights.

By early 1975, though, many of the Warsaw Pact's initial goals for the CSCE had either been satisfied elsewhere or shown to be unrealistic. From a narrowly legal perspective, Western recognition of postwar borders had already been achieved through the bilateral treaties between West Germany and Poland, and between West Germany and the Soviet Union. Continued close cooperation among NATO member states had contradicted any hopes that the CSCE might promote decoupling of the Western alliance. Likewise, the East bloc quest for concrete Western commitments to increase lending or technological assistance had produced only indefinite reference to expanded cooperation in economic and scientific affairs. On the other hand, the European Community's resolve to establish human rights as a CSCE norm had only strengthened as the talks continued, resulting in proposals to legitimate independent human rights monitors and to link human rights to other issues on the diplomatic agenda.

The EC position essentially asked the Soviet Union and its allies to place themselves within a human rights regime that was stronger, and thus more politically dangerous, than the two UN covenants on human rights that they had refused to ratify, in exchange for vague references to economic and technical cooperation that might never materialize. Given such incentives, Liberal theory would expect the Kremlin to prefer quitting the CSCE over accepting the EC's proposals. And yet, as an American journalist observed, "Moscow's interest in getting a European security document signed at a mammoth meeting never seemed to flag."[4] To understand why the Communist governments would accept an agreement that promised so few mate-

---

[4] *New York Times*, July 1, 1975.

rial rewards in exchange for establishing a human rights norm that was far stronger than others that they had long considered incompatible with their interests, we must look beyond Liberal theory.

Constructivist theory maintains that the interests that shape states' international preferences are shaped by the interaction of their internal and external identities. Governments that identify with a domestic ideology or a structure of state-society relations that is incompatible with the protection of human rights will therefore be strongly motivated to resist the establishment of effective international norms in this area. Constructivist theory also emphasizes, however, the intrinsic value that states place on recognition and legitimation by international society. This dual motive explains both the Soviet Union's attempts to weaken all references to human rights in the CSCE and its ultimate decision to sign the Final Act.

As Chapter 2 shows, the Communist states participating in the CSCE tried hard to prevent the establishment of human rights as a trans-European norm, and when that failed, they worked to undermine the norm with indeterminate language and escape clauses. Before and during the negotiations, though, the Soviet Union and its allies also acted on the assumption that the geopolitical status quo in Eastern Europe was only secure if ratified (and thus legitimated) by an international society whose membership extended well beyond the Warsaw Treaty Organization. In the words of an American diplomat at Geneva, "it is one thing for Moscow to have a treaty signed by Mr. Brandt and another to have the inviolability of frontiers endorsed by 35 heads of state, including the United States."[5] This quest for legitimation committed the Communist governments to the extended and multilateral process of CSCE diplomacy, even as it produced human rights norms that threatened to undermine the patterns of state-society relations upon which their rule depended.

To start, the procedural rules of the CSCE systematically disempowered otherwise powerful states. As a confidential report

[5] Ibid.

prepared for British Foreign Secretary Douglas-Home at the end of the preparatory talks explains,

> The Russians have pressed for the Conference for their own purposes. . . . The preparatory talks suggest that they did not judge the situation very accurately. From the first they found themselves in a forum where they could expect the regular support of only six out of thirty-four delegations; and where the neutral countries, because of the consensus rule, had much more incentive to express, and persist in expressing, their individual points of view than is the case in international meetings operating under majority voting procedures. . . . [T]hey remained in a defensive position; and one where their only hope of making their point was by rational argument rather than by the exercise of pressure.

Only in such a context, the British report continues, would one "find the Russians, in the hearing of representatives of all their satellites, obliged to give a detailed defence of their domestic policies on, for example, the increase of human and cultural contacts, in order to answer criticism by Liechtenstein."[6] The self-entrapping character of multilateralism was even evident one year later, when another British diplomat observed, "It is as if the 35 participants had invented, wound up and set in motion a machine which has now got a life and pace of its own that is very hard to control."[7]

This dynamic was also due to the fact that the first multi-issue, all-European conference since the Second World War had brought starkly into question the political meaning of "Europe." A subsequent memo to Foreign Secretary Douglas-Home explained: "No one who has sat through the apparently interminable debates of the last eight months in Helsinki would deny that there was a great deal of cynicism around the table. But no one could fail to notice, either, that there was a vague but genuine sentiment, not only on the part of Western delegates, that the barriers between European countries ought ultimately to become less significant than the links of their com-

[6] FCO, *The Conference*, 144.
[7] Ibid., 318 n. 3.

mon civilisation."[8] This sense of a common European endeavor carried over to the official negotiations in Geneva, where Romanian envoy Valentin Lipatti declared to his fellow diplomats: "Europe is here in this Conference; this is Europe!"[9]

The Soviets could "bring the process of discussion to a halt by denying final consensus," the British diplomat concluded, but they could "hardly do so without putting themselves in the position of obstructing the development of the European idea."[10] And given that the East bloc's overriding goal for the CSCE was to achieve diplomatic recognition from the rest of Europe, walking out on the conference was unacceptable. The process that Kissinger later described as "multilateral diplomacy run amok" and compared to "cloistered medieval monks elaborating sacred texts" was thus essential to gaining Soviet acquiescence to the establishment of human rights as a formal norm of East-West relations.[11]

Implications

Negotiations on the creation of human rights norms engage the identities of participating states as members of international society, and thus tend to entrap governments in commitments that exceed their original intentions or contradict their ideological claims. The evolution of European norms culminating in the 1975 Helsinki Final Act suggests that while Liberal theory may be powerful with respect to the sources of human rights norms created within groups of democratic or democratizing states, it is weaker as an explanation for why a state that relies on systematic violations of human rights would agree to cooperate in the establishment of norms that are so evidently antithetical to its political survival. In contrast, Constructivism's

---

[8] Ibid., 167.

[9] John J. Maresca, *To Helsinki: The Conference on Security and Cooperation in Europe, 1973–1975* (Durham: Duke University Press, 1987), 137.

[10] FCO, *The Conference*, 167.

[11] Henry Kissinger, *Years of Renewal* (New York: Simon & Schuster, 1999), 642.

emphasis on state identity as the basis for interests, including its emphasis on the lure of international legitimation, explains both the preference of democratic states to establish international human rights norms and the frequently observed willingness of repressive governments formally to accept these norms. Strong evidence of this connection between identity and behavior in the CSCE addresses what has heretofore been called Constructivism's "missing link."[12]

More generally, the origin of international norms is best understood as a negotiated process through which states seek to confirm their status as members of international society while developing collective standards of appropriate behavior that serve their particular preferences. The value that states place on recognition and legitimation by international society reduces their willingness to defect from negotiations in the face of indications that they are unlikely to achieve other goals. Even where this value is not itself sufficient to motivate actual compliance with the dictates of international norms, it may motivate them to go through the motions—to behave, in other words, *as if* they intended to fulfill the expectations of international society. It thus produces preferences that cannot be reduced to instrumental calculations of material gain or political power, and negotiating behavior that cannot be explained by traditional cost-benefit analysis. In particular, it may motivate them to participate in the establishment of new norms with which they have little or no intention of complying.

The quest for international legitimation is not felt equally by all states, however. A state's (or political community's) understanding of what it has or does not have in common with others affects how it defines its interests, and thus its preferences in particular negotiations. States that doubt their legitimacy in international society (like the Soviet Union and its allies) will seek recognition and legitimation from other states, even if this means endangering other interests. In contrast, states that are confident of their international legitimacy (like the EC member

[12] Ted Hopf, "The Promise of Constructivism in International Relations Theory," *International Security* 22 (Summer 1998):171–200.

states) are more likely to pursue interests defined by what makes them distinctive. The irony of international legitimacy is thus that states whose international status is unquestioned are more sensitive to domestic than international pressures.

On the other hand, the definition of self-interest that determines a state's position on the creation of new norms is not necessarily determined by whatever international norms that state has lived with or formally accepted in the past. In this sense, states are more autonomous in their definition of self-interest with respect to new international norms than some Constructivist theorists would expect. In particular, the intensity of East-West bargaining prior to the signing of the Helsinki Final Act supports the argument that international norms are shaped more by the deliberate choices of state actors than by "cascades" set in motion by the persuasion and agenda-setting efforts of transnational norm-entrepreneurs.[13]

THE FRAMING OF INTERNATIONAL NORMS

By the time CSCE diplomats wrapped up their work in Geneva and sent the Final Act off to be signed in Helsinki on August 1, 1975, by thirty-five heads of state and government, they had struggled over the text for almost three years, and achieved compromise on every controversial point. Almost immediately, though, the Final Act became the focus of an intense argument about which interpretation of its norms would prevail thereafter in domestic and international politics. Not surprisingly, the Communist authorities of Eastern Europe and the Soviet Union argued that the Helsinki agreement had recognized and legitimated the status quo, while independent activists argued that it had established "respect for human rights" as a standard to which all CSCE states should be held accountable. The U.S. government had never valued the CSCE, and therefore in-

---

[13] See Martha Finnemore and Kathryn Sikkink, "International Norm Dynamics and Political Change," *International Organization* 52 (Fall 1998):887–917.

structed its diplomats to ignore the Final Act after it was signed in Helsinki. As shown in Chapters 3 and 4, though, the interpretation of the Helsinki Final Act as an agreement to respect human rights triumphed over the status quo frame in just over a year, both within the countries of the Communist bloc and in East-West relations.

Framing "Helsinki"

How then can we explain the outcome of this framing debate? The Communist authorities' preference for the "status quo" frame could be explained with equal plausibility by the Liberal argument that state actors' preferences are determined by their interest in maintaining power, or by the Constructivist argument that preferences are determined by actors' identities—in this case, by their understanding of themselves as the protectors of "real existing socialism." However, Liberal theory's emphasis on bargaining leverage cannot explain the ability of individual activists or even loosely networked social movements to overcome powerful states in determining the framing or interpretation on an international agreement like the Final Act. The nonstate actors had not participated in drafting the document and did not control any material resources valued by the Communist states.

Instead, the activists' success at framing the Helsinki norms is better explained by the Constructivist expectation that states seek legitimation by domestic and international audiences, and thus prefer to avoid glaring inconsistencies between their rhetoric and their formal normative commitments. Relatively small numbers of activists across Eastern Europe and the Soviet Union refused to accept their governments' interpretation of the Helsinki agreement, and worked to spread public awareness of Principle 7 and Basket III as widely as possible. To ensure that the human rights content of the Helsinki Final Act not be overlooked internationally, they also created a transnational network with journalists, activists, and other sympathetic elites in the West who linked "Helsinki" to the constitutional principles of liberal democracy . Given such public attention to Helsinki's human rights norms, neither the Kremlin nor the White House could sustain their claims that the Final Act had ratified the status quo in East-West relations. They were trapped within their own commitments by the mobilization and arguments of non-state actors.

The resulting framing of the normative agreement made at Helsinki did not ensure compliance, but it did shift the terms of debate in a manner disadvantageous to continued repression. For dissidents and party bureaucrats alike, the word "Helsinki" came to signify acceptance of the principle that states should protect the human rights of people within their borders and that the CSCE would monitor human rights conditions in all participating states, including those of the Communist bloc. Henceforth, states that had signed the Final Act could expect that their behavior would be scrutinized at home and abroad, and that any attempts to deny the human rights commitments undertaken at Helsinki would lack credibility. As a senior figure in the Hungarian ruling party told his colleagues, it would be counterproductive to argue otherwise. Communist authorities switched from denying that the Final Act imposed any new obligations related to human rights to insisting that they were complying with their Helsinki obligations.

Implications

Both Liberal and Constructivist theories of international norms should devote greater attention to the intersubjective framing of formal international norms. Norm framing is a politically contested but socially structured process in which state and non-state actors seek to raise or lower the salience of particular norms and to persuade other actors to accept particular interpretations of the duties and obligations that flow from them. Its outcome determines the expectations that political actors have regarding their relationship to formally established standards of appropriate behavior.

Norm framing is politically contested because of its possible consequences for the legitimacy and behavioral autonomy of various actors. First, the response of state and non-state actors to international norms and other ideational structures (just like material structures) is often based less on their discursive content than on their social or political significance. Norms that are salient in particular social or institutional settings will thus have a greater impact on behavior and identities than a less salient norm that is equally clear or binding.

Norm framing is also politically contested because its outcomes limits the ability of actors to shop around for norms in pursuit of their goals. There are many international norms, and the duties and obligations that they create are not necessarily mutually consistent. (The Helsinki Final Act's simultaneous establishment of human rights and non-intervention as basic norms for relations among European states is typical.) As a result, actors who find one norm disadvantageous or unappealing will often seek to identify themselves or their demands with a more advantageous or appealing norm. The viability of norm shopping is greatly curtailed, however, once a particular issue-area or relationship is framed with a particular norm or interpretation thereof.

Notwithstanding its intensely political or contested character, the process of norm framing is also structured by pre-existing ideas and institutions. The effectiveness of an actor's arguments that a particular norm should be interpreted in a particular way depends first upon the elasticity of its formal prescriptions and proscriptions: interpretations that stick closer to the common-sense reading of a norm have a distinct advantage in the "court" of public opinion. The viability of a particular interpretation also depends upon cultural and institutional resonance: interpretations are more likely to prevail if they can be linked to how members of the intended audience understand themselves and the society to which they belong.[14]

---

[14] Notwithstanding these points, the concept of norm-framing does not refer to the courtroom process by which advocates seek to persuade judges or juries to issue legally binding rulings in their favor.

THE EFFECTS OF INTERNATIONAL NORMS

As documented in Chapters 5 through 7, the human rights norms established by the Helsinki Final Act gradually transformed state-society relations across Eastern Europe and the Soviet Union, and consequently the agenda of East-West relations, to an extent not intended by any of the Communist leaders who signed the original agreement. These norms contributed significantly to the demise of Communist rule in 1989–1990. Answers to three empirical puzzles provide, however, greater insight into why, how, and under what conditions international human rights norms affect political change. Both Liberal and Constructivist theories explain pieces of these puzzles, but as shown below, the ultimate explanatory power of Liberal theory depends upon variations in state identity that only Constructivist theory can explain. Explanations for these outcomes that are unrelated to international norms were presented and critiqued in the relevant empirical chapters.

The first puzzle is the sudden mobilization of independent activists under the "Helsinki" banner in the immediate aftermath of the 1975 agreement, despite a harsh crackdown on dissent during the CSCE talks. The second is the unprecedented leniency of the Communist authorities in their initial response to this mobilization, followed by their resort to a campaign of repression aimed at protecting the hegemony of the party-state. The third puzzle is the Soviet leadership's move toward Helsinki compliance and political liberalization in the late 1980s, and its relationship to the revolutionary changes that ensued.

Social Mobilization

When word of the Helsinki agreement spread in 1975, veteran dissidents and other individuals long intimidated by the threat of repression came together to create independent monitoring groups, letter-writing campaigns, and social movements whose size, persistence, and internal diversity were unprecedented in the region. Although most of these activists focused on the governments under which they lived, some appealed to America and other CSCE states to use their leverage on behalf of compliance with Helsinki norms. The "Helsinki network" that emerged out of these domestic and transnational campaigns played a major role in the subsequent evolution and effects of the Helsinki process.

This post-1975 mobilization was not distributed evenly across the countries of the Warsaw Pact, however. As shown in Chapters 3 and 5, the strongest and most persistent movements for compliance with Helsinki's human rights norms emerged in Czechoslovakia, Poland, and the Soviet Union. Individuals in East Germany and Romania appealed to the authorities to comply with the Helsinki Final Act, but their appeals never coalesced into sustained movements. There was even less mobilization around Helsinki norms in Bulgaria or Hungary. A persuasive explanation for the social mobilization in the immediate aftermath of the Helsinki Final Act must therefore account for the willingness of individuals to challenge repressive regimes in the name of human rights, and for the variation in mobilization evident across the countries of the region. As explained at the end of Chapter 3, explanations for these outcomes based on theories of socioeconomic modernization, developmental crisis, elite fragmentation, and economic interdependence are either unpersuasive or incomplete.

Both Liberal and Constructivist theories offer explanations for the upsurge in social mobilization across Eastern Europe and the Soviet Union in 1975–1976. Liberal theory suggests that the willingness of non-state actors to challenge a repressive state depends upon the relationship between the apparent risks of mobilization and the likelihood of success. This expectation is consistent with the comments of activists who say that they mobilized around Helsinki norms because they expected that the CSCE's review process and their governments' interest in Western "credits" would shelter them from repression. It is also consistent with the apparent diffusion of "Helsinki activism" as a new way to challenge structures of power that had long appeared immune to internal demands for change. As one Polish activist concluded after learning of the new Helsinki movement in Moscow, "if they can do it, so can we."

However, it is not clear that the decisions of activists involved in this wave of mobilization were shaped primarily by an increased sense of security or efficacy. When the protests began in the summer of 1975, the U.S. government had given little reason to believe that it would adjust its foreign policy priorities in response to the appeals of dissidents in the East. Moreover, the Kremlin's conservative rhetoric and recent crackdowns on dissent indicated that any challenge from below would be repressed. In addition, the pattern of mobilization across Eastern Europe does not accord with variations in the states' prior repressiveness or in their potential vulnerability to economic sanctions, as Liberal theory would expect. For example, human rights-focused mobilization increased dramatically in both Poland and Czechoslovakia, despite the fact that the Polish government was generally far more tolerant of independent activity than its Czechoslovak counterpart, and the fact that Poland's hard-currency debt and trade deficit were roughly ten times greater and climbing far faster than those of Czechoslovakia.

The post-Helsinki wave of mobilization is better explained by the Constructivist argument that individuals will mobilize for the implementation of international norms that are consistent with their principled beliefs, even if this means incurring a risk of repression whose consequences for the individual exceed any foreseeable material gain. As explained above, those who mobilized for human rights across the Communist bloc in 1975–1976 did so despite a reasonable expectation that their efforts would be met by police harassment and loss of employment, if not beatings and imprisonment. The fact that many continued their protests during the renewed repression of the late 1970s also defies Liberalism's logic of material opportunities. Instead, the unexpected social mobilization of 1975–1976 appears to have been motivated by a shared belief in the desirability of "human rights" as the basis for political reform, and thus a shared interest in pressing the Communist governments to follow through on formal acceptance of the norms of the Helsinki Final Act.

Variations in the intensity of mobilization from country to country are also explained by this focus on principled beliefs. Significant mobilization occurred in Czechoslovakia, Poland, and the Soviet Union, where intellectuals had long been committed to liberal ideas. Relatively little mobilization occurred in Bulgaria or Romania, where intellectuals tended to be nationalist rather than liberal, and in East Germany, where most intellectuals remained committed to Marxism. The case of Hungary—the only country with a liberal intelligentsia but little sustained Helsinki movement—is explained by the considerable cultural freedom available there by the 1970s. Both the overall increase and the specific pattern of social mobilization are thus more consistent with Constructivism's emphasis on individual interests determined by principled beliefs than with Liberal theory's focus on material incentives.

Limited Compliance

Across Eastern Europe and the Soviet Union, the upsurge in social mobilization and expansion of independent activity that followed the Helsinki agreement was checked by the party-state's return to repression in the years 1978–1981. Communist authorities across the bloc did respond initially to the challenge from below with unprecedented leniency, however, and were generally more tolerant of "Helsinki" activists than of other dissidents who identified themselves with nationalist or explicitly political causes. Their behavioral response to the CSCE's human rights norms prior to the mid-1980s can thus be described as partial or superficial compliance limited in scope and time by a commitment to defending the social and political hegemony of the party-state. A persuasive explanation for this limited compliance must account for both the switch from relative tolerance to repression and the preferential treatment of dissidents identified with the norms.

The Constructivist argument that states are motivated by their domestic as well as international identities offers a plausible explanation for this outcome. The Communist governments of Eastern Europe and the Soviet Union were sufficiently concerned about international legitimation to make significant concessions while negotiating the Helsinki Final Act. Neither the Soviet Politburo nor its East European allies identified with the liberal values and institutions of the West during this period, however; instead, they remained devoted to a Leninist strategy for political development and focused on consolidating or expanding the "socialist community." This combination of identities explains their policy of curtailing compliance with Helsinki norms at the point where compliance threatened to undermine the ideological coherence and institutional stability of "real existing socialism."

An alternative explanation for the East bloc's limited compliance with Helsinki norms during this period is based on Liberal theory's dual argument that international human rights norms are most likely to affect the behavior of otherwise repressive states when access to valued goods is linked to compliance, when other capable actors are committed to enforcing this linkage, and when mechanisms exist to monitor compliance, but that the leaders of repressive states will refuse concessions that appear likely to undermine their hold on power. In fact, the structure of material incentives in East-West relations does appear to have been a crucial determinant of the ups and downs of the "Helsinki effect" in the late 1970s.

The various "baskets" of the Final Act contained no reliable commitments of aid, trade, technical assistance, or NATO arms reductions that East-bloc leaders could be confident of achieving if they complied with the commitment to respect human rights, but Brezhnev and some others remained hopeful that détente and the CSCE would bring material advantages to the Communist countries. In addition, the CSCE's provision for review or follow-on meetings expanded the otherwise limited possibilities for human rights monitoring and issue linkage created by the scarce flows of information, trade, and investment across the East-West frontier. By 1979, though, regional wars and the ongoing nuclear arms race had eliminated any near-term prospect of expanded Western loans or technical assistance to the Communist countries.

The resulting combination of incentives explains the East-bloc governments' tendency to be more tolerant of dissent before and during CSCE review conferences than after, their tendency to be more tolerant of independent activists affiliated with the transnational Helsinki network than they were of those who lacked international recognition, and their crackdown on independent activity when it began to threaten their control. It also explains these outcomes with greater precision than the Constructivist argument outlined earlier. Before we can reach any conclusions about the relative merits of Liberal and Constructivist theories for understanding the effects of human rights norms, though, we must consider their explanations for the fundamental changes of the mid-late 1980s.

Revolutionary Change

Since it was the Soviet Union that set limits on change throughout Eastern Europe, the Communist bloc was relatively unconcerned about compliance with Helsinki norms. Beginning in the mid 1980s, though, their denial of noncompliance with human rights norms and repression of dissent were replaced by an increasing openness to international monitoring and a policy of political liberalization. These changes opened the door to mass protests across Eastern Europe, the collapse of one-party Communist rule, and its replacement by largely democratic and rights-protective institutions from 1989 to 1991. As discussed in Chapter 7, international human rights norms were salient throughout this process, both for state and societal actors. The question is what role they played.

Although Liberal theory assumes that international norms do not affect the interests that drive states' policy choices, it does suggest that repressive states might increase their compliance with international human rights norms if necessary to gain access to material goods that they deem necessary for political survival. A Liberal explanation for the contribution of human rights norms to policy reversals by a repressive regime such as the Soviet Union would thus treat the norms as a constraint on policy choice, but focus on changes in state preferences driven by internal variables such as economic performance.

Given the declining productivity of the Soviet Union's centrally planned economy in the early to mid 1980s, key members of the Politburo and Central Committee concluded that the administrative status quo had to be reformed in order to encourage greater initiative by individuals and economic enterprises. This interest in reform led to the election of Mikhail Gorbachev as general secretary in February 1985. Some of these elites recognized that concessions on human rights were necessary to satisfy the conditions that Western governments had placed on further economic or technical assistance. And once he was elected, Gorbachev repeatedly referred to international normative constraints when trying to convince reluctant conservatives in his Politburo to support deeper political reforms. This much is consistent with the expectations of Liberal theory.

The Liberal theory of human rights politics cannot explain, however, the fundamental redefinition of the interests and goals of the Soviet state evident during Gorbachev's rule. Even if one concludes that Gorbachev did not intend to bring about the dismantling of Communist rule, the Liberal theory of norms as external constraints cannot explain why a party-state that had relied on political repression for decades would implement such extensive reforms that it could be overwhelmed by unarmed demonstrators. The progressive embrace of CSCE norms and systematic dismantling of the repressive apparatus of the Communist party-state discussed in the previous chapter were simply not required by the convergence of economic decline and Western conditionality on human rights. As the Chinese leadership had already begun to demonstrate, economic liberalization can be combined with the denial of civil and political rights.

In contrast, the Constructivist theory of human rights politics argues explicitly that the identities that determine state interests and behavior may be transformed through sustained participation in international society and contacts with international norms. This would explain how the same CSCE norms that had proven too weak to constrain the repressive instincts of the Communist party-state in the late 1970s could eventually transform the leadership's understanding of its purposes in relation to international society, and thereby redefine the state's interests and behavior so fundamentally that losing allies abroad and power at home was deemed preferable to massive repression. As discussed in Chapter 7, this redefinition of the interests driving the Kremlin's policy on human rights was driven by the interaction of two processes, each closely related to the effects of Helsinki norms: social mobilization and international criticism.

The social mobilization for human rights that emerged in the immediate aftermath of the Helsinki Final Act did not disappear with the renewed repression of the late 1970s and early 1980s. Particularly in Poland, but also in the Soviet Union and elsewhere, it left in its wake the nascent attitudes and structures of civil society, including individuals accustomed to demanding protection of their rights and independent organizations with the skills and connections to monitor the behavior of state authorities. At the same time, the salience of human rights norms within East-West relations established by the transnational appeals of activists in the 1970s had not diminished. The governments and political elites of the Communist bloc were reminded at every diplomatic encounter with the West that they would not be fully welcomed into European or international society until they ceased to practice political repression. In other words, they would only be recognized as "normal" states if they complied with the international human rights norms established at Helsinki in 1975.

Although well aware of dissident movements and samizdat publications, most senior figures in the party during the late Brezhnev years viewed their persistent critique of the party-state as nothing more than an obstacle to domestic peace and/or improved relations with the West. A small number, though, including Mikhail Gorbachev, quietly drew a far more radical conclusion from the dissidents' message and the outside world's refusal to embrace or even trust the Soviet Union—that a government's legitimacy at home and abroad depends upon its respect for human rights, including international norms of human rights. When the members of Central Committee elected Gorbachev as general secretary in 1985 with the hope that he would reform the economy, they inadvertently brought to power a group of people with a radically new conception of the Soviet state.

Henceforth, the Kremlin's choices would no longer be guided by the idea of the Soviet Union as the leader of a separate "socialist" international community with its own norms for relations between the individual, society, and the state. Soviet policy would no longer be determined by a state identity that equated the national interest with the continued hegemony of the party-state. Instead, the new leadership identified Soviet interests with "universal human values," international norms, and the wider society of European states. This reconception of Soviet identity did not make Gorbachev and all of his advisors into liberal democrats, but it did motivate them to pursue unprecedented changes at home and abroad. Despite resistance from party conservatives, Gorbachev and his associates began to dismantle the hegemonic ideology and repressive apparatus of the party-state and to embrace international institutions like the CSCE almost as soon as they took power.

In response, individuals and groups that had long been frustrated by one-party Communist rule rushed to take advantage of their new freedoms, filling the newspapers and public squares with appeals for ever more radical change. Meanwhile, international NGOs and Western governments continued to press the Kremlin to fulfill its commitments to respect human rights. At a series of critical moments, Politburo conservatives argued for an end to political reform, and even for a crackdown on nonparty forces. Each time, though, the new occupants of the Kremlin stuck to their conclusion that respect for human rights was more important than the survival of the party-state. The transformation of the identity of the Soviet state set in motion by Helsinki norms thus paved the way for the democratic revolutions that swept across Eastern Europe and the Soviet Union in 1989–1991.

Implications

The evidence of the contribution of Helsinki norms to the demise of Communist rule in Eastern Europe and the Soviet Union presented here and in Chapters 3 through 7 clearly disconfirms the hard-core Realist claim that international norms do not matter.[15] The fact that Helsinki norms mattered despite the United States' initial lack of interest in their implementation even confirms that norms can matter even when the most powerful actors have no intention of promoting or implementing them. It thus disconfirms the modified Realist claim that norms may reinforce but never challenge practices and institutions determined by the distribution of power.[16]

International human rights norms affect the behavior, the interests, and the identity of states by specifying which practices are (or are not) considered appropriate by international society. It is difficult to understand their effects, however, with a state-centric view of international society. Human rights norms empower domestic opposition to repressive states by providing a mobilization frame ("our government must respect its human rights commitments") that is accessible to individuals and political forces with varying ideological preferences, and difficult for governments to discredit. The social mobilization that can result from such opportunities erodes a repressive regime's control of information and public space. Human rights norms also provide an internationally legitimate frame ("international norms must be implemented") that enables domestic social and political forces blocked by a repressive regime to construct transnational networks that engage the interest and influence of

[15] See John J. Mearsheimer, "The False Promise of International Institutions," *International Security* 19 (Winter 1994/95):5–49.

[16] See Stephen D. Krasner, *Sovereignty: Organized Hypocrisy* (Princeton: Princeton University Press, 1999).

state and non-state actors in other countries. Such transnational networking and issue framing can transform an international political environment once hospitable to a repressive regime into one filled with arguments and sanctions on behalf of human rights.

Their impact depends, however, upon the presence of local or domestic social forces committed to monitoring their government's implementation of the norms, and upon the identity of the target state. International human rights norms have a greater domestic impact when sympathetic non-state actors are available to mobilize around the norms and frame them publicly in a manner conducive to change. Helsinki norms mattered not because the Communist regimes were immediately anxious to comply, nor largely because Western governments forced them to comply. They mattered because individuals and non-governmental organizations, first in the East and then in the West, insisted at home and abroad that states must be accountable to their international obligations, and thereby entrapped the signatories in a transnational process of political change structured by formal international norms. As a result of their efforts, the Helsinki Final Act was transformed from a triumph of East-bloc foreign policy into a diplomatic Trojan horse that Communist leaders regretted ever accepting. The Helsinki effect thus gives a new, transnational meaning to Ernst Haas's observation that even in the competitive world of international relations, "words can hurt you."[17]

Furthermore, the ways in which international human rights norms affect the behavior and interests of states depends upon how strongly their leadership identifies with the international society or particular group of states that expects compliance. When state actors identify weakly with international society, as the leaders of the Soviet Union did until the mid-1980s, their response to international human rights norms will be guided by Liberal theory's logic of expected consequences: comply as

[17] Ernst B. Haas, "Words Can Hurt You; or Who Said What to Whom about Regimes," in Stephen D. Krasner, ed., *International Regimes* (Ithaca: Cornell University Press, 1983), 23–59.

much as necessary to achieve other goals without endangering their own hold on power. When they identify strongly, as the leaders of the Soviet Union did in the mid-late 1980s, their response to international human rights norms will be guided by Constructivist theory's logic of appropriateness, institutionalizing human rights protections because that is what "normal" states do, even when doing so could endanger their hold on power.

This evidence suggests that the validity of Liberal hypotheses regarding state behavior depends upon variations in a distinctively Constructivist variable: state identity. The evidence also contradicts Liberal theory's implicit claim that norms do not affect the identity or interests of states. As we have seen, the domestic and international consequences of Helsinki norms exerted a considerable impact on the conception of Soviet identity that informed Mikhail Gorbachev's policy choices, and thus contributed to the total reconstitution of state identity and interests across the entire Communist bloc. Such evidence is critical because one could argue that most states—and particularly those most likely to deny human rights—identify so weakly with international society that international norms will only ever matter through their connection to material incentives. If this were true, and states' interests were unaffected by international and transnational processes, then the modified Constructivist position presented above would be both plausible and irrelevant. As shown above, though, the identity and interests of a once repressive state can be transformed by the new ideas and pressures that result from the norms' initial impact on behavior.

On the other hand, the Helsinki effect contradicts Constructivist arguments that international norms shape the behavior of state actors when their prescriptions are specific (meaningthat they clearly distinguish between compliant and noncompliant behavior), durable (meaning that they have survived challenges to their prescriptions and legitimacy), and concordant (meaning consistent with other relevant norms and diplomatic discourses). As shown in Chapter 1, the human rights norms established by the Final Act did not exist previously in trans-European or East-West relations, so their durability and interpretation had never been tested. As shown in Chapter 2, compromises during the negotiation process made the Helsinki text quite vague on which behaviors would constitute violations of the human rights norm, balancing the human rights norm with the potentially contradictory norm of non-intervention in internal affairs, which itself was supported by numerous other international agreements on the proper conduct of international relations.

IMPLICATIONS FOR THE HISTORICAL RECORD: THE END OF COMMUNISM AND THE COLD WAR

The Cold War that divided both Europe and the international system for five decades ended with the breaching of the Berlin Wall and the demise of Communist rule across Eastern Europe in 1989–1990. These revolutionary changes were set in motion by the Conference on Security and Cooperation in Europe's establishment in 1975 of human rights as a formal norm for relations among European states. At first, the human rights norms of the Helsinki Final Act lacked the support of the United States and were actively resisted by the Soviet Union, whose ideology and political structure were incompatible with individual liberties. Yet despite Communist ideology's intolerance of dissent, and the party-state's near monopoly of political space, the Helsinki norms created a formal standard of behavior against which the regimes of Eastern Europe and the Soviet Union could be judged.

This change in the international normative environment created unprecedented opportunities for individuals across the Communist bloc to challenge the repressiveness of the party-state by organizing human rights "watch groups" and opposition coalitions focused on human rights, and by engaging the influence of otherwise uninterested foreign governments and media. The resulting domestic and transnational alliances, referred to in this book as the "Helsinki network," weakened the institutions, drained the resources, and delegitimated the arguments that sustained repressive, one-party rule. In the end,

Communist rule succumbed to the convergence of popular demands for change and the initiatives of within-system reformers like Mikhail Gorbachev, who were themselves significantly influenced by the arguments of local dissidents and foreign governments that insisted upon compliance with Helsinki norms.

The dissident and human rights groups that emerged immediately after the Helsinki agreement, as well as the new independent associations that they spawned, played central roles in the revolutions of 1989–1990 and the ensuing transition from rights-abusive to rights-protective states. In Czechoslovakia, Poland, and to a lesser extent Hungary, which did have independent human rights movements, Communism was rapidly replaced by liberal democratic, rights-protective states. Given the relative tolerance of opposition in Poland and Hungary, compared to repression in Czechoslovakia, this outcome cannot be attributed to the behavior or structure of the Communist-era states themselves. In contrast, in Bulgaria and Rumania, which never tolerated sustained human rights movements, several more years passed before relatively rights-protective states were established. (East Germany cannot be included in this comparison because of its rapid incorporation into the Federal Republic of Germany.)

As explained in various chapters, the mobilization of these individual dissidents, social movements, and lobby groups, linked together by a transnational network, cannot be explained by standard socioeconomic, political, or geostrategic factors, such as modernization, the decay of a domestic social contract, or America's Cold War struggle with the Warsaw Pact. Neither the timing nor the pattern of social mobilization correlates with levels of literacy, economic development, or foreign indebtedness. American diplomatic influence was only brought to bear on behalf of dissidents struggling for change within the Communist bloc because of a transnational campaign mounted by them and sympathetic human rights activists in the West— against the preferences of the Ford White House and State Department, and before the election of Jimmy Carter.

The study also shows that the Kremlin reforms that dismantled the coercive capacities of the Soviet party-state were driven in large part by domestic and international demands for compliance with human rights norms, not by Ronald Reagan's Strategic Defense Initiative or even by the declining productivity of central planning. Its findings thus challenge arguments that the Gorbachev reforms that precipitated the final collapse of Communism and the end of the Cold War were caused by the Soviet Union's inability to match America's military buildup or to compete in an increasingly globalized economy.[18] In fact, it adds to the growing evidence of the importance of ideational change and transnational networks in bringing about the end of the Cold War.[19] Unlike most other works in this genre, though, it suggests that new norms for state-society relations (and the transnational activism that emerged around them) were at least as important as "new thinking" about the dynamics of the international system.

IMPLICATIONS FOR FUTURE RESEARCH: SOFT LAW AND THE SOCIALIZATION OF STATES

This study highlights the need for further research on the socialization of states by confirming some findings from previous studies of how international human rights norms affect domestic change, and challenging others. As previous studies have indicated, once repressive regimes are caught between their own commitment to respect human rights, a mobilized local constituency, and engaged foreign interests, they are slowly de-

[18] Stephen G. Brooks and William C. Wohlforth, "Power, Globalization, and the End of the Cold War: Reevaluating a Landmark Case for Ideas," *International Security* 25 (Winter 2000/01): 5–53.

[19] See Jeffrey Checkel, *Ideas and International Political Change: Soviet-Russian Behavior and the End of the Cold War* (New Haven: Yale University Press, 1997); Sarah E. Mendelson, *Changing Course: Ideas, Politics, and the Soviet Withdrawal from Afghanistan* (Princeton: Princeton University Press, 1998); Matthew Evangelista, *Unarmed Forces: The Transnational Movement to End the Cold War* (Ithaca: Cornell University Press, 1999); Robert D. English, *Russia and the Idea of the West: Gorbachev, Intellectuals, and the End of the Cold War* (New York: Columbia University Press, 2000).

prived of the popular legitimacy, international recognition, and material resources that they need to survive. Rhetorical concessions simply increase the pressure for compliance. Partial compliance expands opportunities for domestic mobilization and increases the likelihood that the regime will be persuaded to reform or be thrown out of power. Repressive backlashes are possible but difficult to sustain because they deepen the regime's domestic and international isolation. Instead, many elites will begin to identify more strongly with international society, internalizing the motivation for compliance and institutionalizing human rights protections within the state.[20]

However, modeling this process as a "spiral" understates the real contingencies of transnational socialization. As the cross-national variation and temporal stops and starts of the Helsinki effect demonstrate, a state's formal acceptance of international human rights norms does not necessarily guarantee significant changes in its behavior, much less its identity and interests. In fact, this study finds that states which identify weakly with international society will calculate the instrumental value of compliance with international norms, whereas states that identify strongly with international society will comply more routinely out of an inherent sense of obligation.

The study also provides strong evidence that the mobilization and arguments of non-state actors can increase a state's identification with international society. We need to know much more, though, about the conditions under which non-state actors mobilize around international norms, about how the form of institution in which such norms are embedded affects the mobilization of non-state actors, and about whether particular state structures are more or less resistant to such effects. Transnational influences on the identities and interests of states, particularly those involving changes in ideational structures and in the mobilization of non-state actors, thus remain

---

[20] See Thomas Risse, Stephen C. Ropp, and Kathryn Sikkink, eds. *The Power of Human Rights: International Norms and Domestic Change* (Cambridge: Cambridge University Press, 1999).

one of the most promising areas for future research in world politics.[21]

In sum, the significance of the "soft law" that has begun to attract attention among scholars of international relations and international law cannot be fully understood without theorizing its role in a transnational context that involves both state and non-state actors.[22] Given recent developments such as discussions of a second "Helsinki process" to promote political reconstruction in the Balkans after the devastating wars of the 1990s, the ratification of international human rights treaties by China and other countries, and the multilateral "Warsaw Declaration" to support the spread and consolidation of democracy worldwide, such research is sure to remain relevant to policy making for a long time to come.[23]

[21] For a provocative discussion of such issues, see Sidney Tarrow, "Transnational Politics: Contention and Institutions in International Politics," *Annual Review of Political Science* 4, forthcoming 2001.

[22] See various articles in *International Organization* 54 (Autumn 2000).

[23] See, respectively, *Le Monde* (Paris), May 29 1999; *New York Times*, November 21, 2000; *New York Times*, June 28, 2000.

Appendix

Interviews

INTERVIEW subjects are grouped by their country or region of origin. Organizations in parentheses are intended only to identify affiliations relevant to the subject and time period of this study.

United States

Robert Bernstein (U.S. Helsinki Watch Committee), New York, January 12, 1994.

McGeorge Bundy (Ford Foundation), telephone, January 24, 1994.

Guy Coriden (U.S. State Department and U.S. Helsinki Commission), Washington D.C., March 31, 1994.

Lynne Davidson (U.S. Helsinki Commission and U.S. State Department), Washington, D.C., January 19, 1993; March 31, 1994.

John Finnerty (U.S. Helsinki Commission), Washington, D.C., January 21, 1993.

Cathy Fitzpatrick (U.S. Helsinki Watch Committee), New York, January 26, 1993.

Max Kampelman (U.S. State Department), Washington, D.C., January 25, 1993.

William Korey (B'nai B'rith), New York, January 26, 1993; April 12, 1994.

Jeri Laber (U.S. Helsinki Watch Committee), New York, January 11, 1994.

John Maresca (U.S. State Department), Washington, D.C., February 9, 1993.

Spencer Oliver (U.S. Helsinki Commission), Washington, D.C., January 25, 1993.

Susan Osnos (U.S. Helsinki Watch Committee), New York, January 12, 1994.

Richard Schifter (U.S. State Department), Washington, D.C., January 24, 1993.

Erika Schlager (U.S. Helsinki Commission), numerous conversations, Washington, D.C. and Helsinki, 1990–1995.

Martin Sletzinger (U.S. Helsinki Commission), Washington, D.C., April 1, 1994.

Joanna Weschler (U.S. Helsinki Watch Committee), New York, January 27, 1993.

Samuel Wise (U.S. Helsinki Commission), Washington, D.C., January 21, 1993.

Christopher Wren (*New York Times*), telephone, August 22, 1995.

Warren Zimmerman (U.S. State Department), Washington, D.C., January 19, 1993.

Western Europe

Arie Bloed (Netherlands Helsinki Committee), Helsinki, July 6, 1992; Utrecht, March 16, 1994.

Edouard Brunner (Swiss Foreign Ministry), Paris, March 14, 1994.

Etienne Davignon (Belgian Foreign Ministry), Brussels, January 12, 1996.

Jacques Eggermont (Belgian Foreign Ministry), Brussels, September 16, 1994.

Pierre Filatoff (French Foreign Ministry), Paris, March 10, 1994.

Gotz von Groll (West German Foreign Ministry), personal correspondence, May 20, 1999.

Harm Hazelwinkel (Netherlands Foreign Ministry), The Hague, March 18, 1994.

J.L.R. Huydecoper (Netherlands Foreign Ministry), The Hague, March 18, 1994.

Jacques Laurent (Belgian Foreign Ministry), Brussels, September 14, 1994.

Hans Meesman (Netherlands Foreign Ministry), Utrecht, March 17, 1994.

Leif Mevik (Norwegian Foreign Ministry), Brussels, March 15, 1994; June 27, 1994.

Jacques Raeymaekers (Belgian Foreign Ministry), Brussels, January 19, 1996.

Henri Segesser (Belgian Foreign Ministry), Brussels, September 16, 1994.

Max van der Stoel (Netherlands Foreign Ministry), The Hague, March 18, 1994; telephone, September 14, 1994.

J. van der Valk (Netherlands Foreign Ministry), The Hague, March 18, 1994.

Robert Zaagman (Netherlands Foreign Ministry), Helsinki, June 12, 1992; The Hague, March 18, 1994.

Czechoslovakia

Vaclav Benda (Charter 77), Prague, June 5, 1991.
Ivan Busniak (Ministry of Foreign Affairs), Prague, July 27, 1992.
Jiri Dienstbier (Charter 77), New Haven, April 14, 1991.
Jiri Hajek (Charter 77 and Czechoslovak Helsinki Committee), Prague, June 7, 1991; July 27, 1992; August 2, 1992.
Ladislav Hejdanek (Charter 77), Pisek, August 1, 1992.
Jan Kavan (samizdat editor in exile), Boston, June 12, 1990; Prague, June 13, 1991.
Vaclav Maly (Charter 77), Prague, August 5, 1992.
Zdenek Matejka (Ministry of Foreign Affairs), Prague, July 27, 1992.
Jiri Oprsal (Ministry of Foreign Affairs), Prague, July 30, 1992.
Martin Palous (Charter 77), Prague, June 12, 1991; July 31, 1992.
Vilem Precan (samizdat editor in exile), Prague, June 13, 1991.
Pavel Seifter (Charter 77), Prague, July 30, 1992.
Libuce Silhanova (Charter 77 and Czechoslovak Helsinki Committee), Prague, June 11, 1991; July 30, 1992.
Zdena Tominova (Charter 77), Prague, June 11, 1991.
Petr Uhl (Charter 77 and Czechoslovak-Polish Solidarity), Prague, June 14, 1991.
Jan Urban (Charter 77 and Civic Forum), Ithaca, November 27, 1990; Prague, June 12, 1991; July 25, 1992.

Hungary

Ivan Baba (Democratic Opposition and Danube Circle), Budapest, July 16, 1992.
Gyorgy Bence, Budapest, July 15, 1992.
Miklos Haraszti (Democratic Opposition and samizdat editor), Szekesfehervar, July 16, 1992.
Gabor Havas (Democratic Opposition), Budapest, July 13, 1992.
Peter Havas (Institute for Political Science), Budapest, July 14, 1992.
Istvan Hulvely (Kossuth Lajos University), Budapest, July 14, 1992.
Gabor Kardos (Eotvos University), Budapest, July 16, 1992.
Janos Kennedi (samizdat editor), Budapest, July 17, 1992.
Ferenc Koszeg (Democratic Opposition and samizdat editor), Budapest, July 13, 1992.
Gyorgy Markus (Institute for Political Science), Budapest, July 14, 1992.

Poland

Pavel Bozyk (economic advisor to Edward Gierek), Warsaw, July 7, 1992.

Jozef Czyrek (Ministry of Foreign Affairs), Warsaw, June 23, 1992.

Bronislaw Dembowski (Catholic archbishop), Warsaw, June 23, 1992.

Marian Dobrosielski (Ministry of Foreign Affairs), Warsaw, June 26, 1992.

Konstanty Gebert (Solidarity), Ithaca, April 8, 1991; Warsaw, June 20, 1991; June 17, 1992.

Bronislaw Geremek (KOR, Solidarity), Cambridge, England, April 19, 1995.

Wojciech Giertych (Dominican Order), Cracow, June 29, 1992.

Aleksander Gleichgewicht (Solidarity), Warsaw, June 27, 1992.

Janusz Grzelak (Solidarity), Warsaw, June 17, 1992.

Jan Litynski (KOR and Solidarity), Warsaw, June 27, 1992.

Antoni Maciarewicz (KOR and ROPCiO), Warsaw, June 24, 1991.

Leszek Moczulski (Confederation for an Independent Poland), Warsaw, June 24, 1991.

Emil Morgiewicz (Amnesty International and ROPCiO), Warsaw, June 21, 1991.

Adam Michnik (KOR and Solidarity), Warsaw, June 25, 1992.

Marek Nowicki (Solidarity and Helsinki Committee in Poland), Warsaw, June 20, 1991.

Marek A. Nowicki (Helsinki Committee in Poland), Warsaw, June 18, 1991, June 24, 1992.

Janusz Prystrom (Ministry of Foreign Affairs), Warsaw, June 26, 1992.

Janusz Reykowski (Central Committee, Polish United Workers' Party), Warsaw, June 22, 1992.

Barbara Rozycka (KOR and Solidarity), Warsaw, June 22, 1991.

Stefan Starczewski (KOR and samizdat editor), Warsaw, June 24, 1991.

Andrzej Towpik (Ministry of Foreign Affairs), Warsaw, June 26, 1992.

Bronislaw Wildstein (Student Solidarity), Cracow, July 2, 1992.

Stefan Wilkanowicz (Clubs of Catholic Intelligentsia), Cracow, July 2, 1992.

Edmund Wnuk-Lipinski (Institute of Political Studies), Warsaw, June 24, 1992.

Henryk Wujec (Clubs of Catholic Intelligentsia, KOR, and Solidarity), Warsaw, June 22, 1991; with Ludwika Wujecka, June 17 and 18, 1992.

Soviet Union

Ludmilla Alexeyeva (Moscow Helsinki Watch Group), Washington, D.C., January 21, 1993.

Viacheslav Bakhmin (Moscow Helsinki Watch Group), Vienna, July 20, 1992.

Sergei Kovalev (Moscow Helsinki Watch Group), Brooklyn, January 27, 1993.

Yuri Orlov (Moscow Helsinki Watch Group), numerous conversations, Ithaca, 1990–1992.

Tatyana Osipova (Moscow Helsinki Watch Group), Brooklyn, January 27, 1993.

Others

Nils Eliasson (CSCE Secretariat), Prague, July 24, 1992.

Nicolae Gheorghe (International Romani Union), Helsinki, June 11, 1992.

Tanja Petovar (Yugoslav Helsinki Committee), Vienna, July 20, 1992.

Stane Stanic (Slovenian Helsinki Committee), Vienna, August 7, 1992.

Yadja Zeltman (International Helsinki Federation for Human Rights), Vienna, July 22, 1992.

Jack Zetkulic (CSCE Office for Democratic Institutions and Human Rights), Warsaw, June 16, 1992.

Informal conversations with many diplomats and NGO representatives to the CSCE Summit, Helsinki, June-July 1992.

Index